CRUSADE
FOR
DEMOCRACY

By V. M. Newton, Jr.

Managing Editor
The Tampa Tribune

The Iowa State University Press, *Ames,* Iowa

PN
4899
T35
T75

... and the truth
shall make you free

By K. R. MARVIN

Head, Department of Technical Journalism,
Iowa State University

Virgil Miller Newton, Jr., widely known as "Red" Newton, is likewise widely known as a vigorous man with an ever-glowing purpose.

The Newton vigor sparkled early when Red played varsity basketball, served as sports editor of the Gainesville, Florida, *Sun* and as correspondent for eight other papers while earning his B.A. (1926) at the University of Florida. A footnote to his university record adds, "Elected to Blue Key for leadership."

Such a torch of *purpose* illuminated the steps up: sports editor of *The Tampa Times* 1927, of *The Tampa Tribune* 1930, city editor and assistant managing editor 1935, managing editor 1943. A similar climb carried him through numerous offices of the Associated Press Managing Editors Association to its presidency in 1956.

Simultaneously Red Newton and *The Tampa Tribune* were building reputations as crusaders for the people's right to know. Frustrations in gaining access to information about operations of government by the people for the people were not overcome without some well-prompted house cleanings in government. The systematic and persistent crusades started in Tampa spread through north Florida, thence southward to encompass the state, and eventually on to Washington, D.C.

The Tampa-based crusades attracted the attention and support of newspapermen across the land, especially a small group in Washington which was battling secrecy in Federal Government. Newton was elected chairman of the Freedom of Information Committee of Sigma Delta Chi in 1953, and continued to serve in that capacity through 1960. He was chosen vice president of this national professional journalism fraternity in 1959 and president in 1960.

National recognition came from many quarters. As an individual, Newton received the Free Enterprise Award in 1954 from the National Association of Management Corporation; the Freedoms Award in 1957 from the Virginia Press Association; and Wells Memorial Key from Sigma Delta Chi in 1957 for his freedom of information work. He was chosen Editor of the Year in 1958 by the National Press Photographers Association, and the National Editorial Association gave him the Distinguished Service Award in 1960. Also in 1960, a board of 50 leading newspaper editors selected Newton for the John Peter Zenger Award presented by the University of Arizona in recognition of his freedom of information work.

The Tampa Tribune was presented the 1959 Public Service Award of Sigma Delta Chi for the newspaper's crusade in behalf of migrant farmers in Florida. The following year the National Headliners Club of Atlantic City, New Jersey, honored the *Tribune* with its Public Service Award for the exposure of a gambling bribery case which resulted in the conviction of the St. Petersburg, Florida, postmaster, the former county attorney of Pinellas County and two Tampa hoodlums.

Newton himself would be the first to declare that these plaques or certificates have little material value, yet they are highly prized and energetically sought after in the journalistic profession because they epitomize the obligations of a free press to keep the American people informed.

A newspaper winning one of these national awards enjoys a brief period of glory, then the plaque or certificate is hung on the wall of the office of the publisher or editor, and only occasionally remembered. But the cumulative effect is valuable. There can be no doubt that the stimulation to others provided by efforts of winning papers has raised the standards of American journalism in recent years.

Though Newton and his stalwart crusaders found resistance to the people's right to know firmly entrenched in high places, his torch began to illuminate a few dark corners. As more and more absurd secrecy measures were exposed, more people began to ask *why.* Newton realized the importance of public understanding and support for the people's cause. In the immediate period involved he has responded to invitations from civic groups to speak in 60 cities and on the campuses of 21 universities across the country.

At his alma mater, the University of Florida, he delivered a series of lectures detailing the strategy and results of his campaigns in *The Tampa Tribune* against corruption in government. The story these accounts unfold and the objectives of these crusades of Newton and his colleagues are so fundamentally basic to the survival of a democracy that the Iowa State University Press enthusiastically undertakes to makes these experiences, exposures and philosophies available to all who are interested.

That free democracy cannot function satisfactorily without an informed citizenry may be a trite and simple truth. But it is a vital truth that needs everlasting emphasis. Virgil Miller Newton, Jr., presents the case for the people's prosecution in his typically vigorous. colorful detail.

Crusade Route

CRUSADE FOR DEMOCRACY

1.

A Challenge
to Our Free Press

FREEDOM OF THE PRESS was an issue even in Colonial times, as Arthur M. Schlesinger, noted Harvard historian, points out in his book, *Prelude to Independence* (Alfred A. Knopf, Inc., 1958), when he quotes from a letter written January 29, 1776, by John Holt, editor of the *New York Journal,* to Boston patriot Samuel Adams:

> It was by means of newspapers that we received and spread the notice of tyrannical designs formed against America, and kindled a spirit that has been sufficient to repel them.

Thus this courageous Colonial editor jubilantly described in one sentence, the birth pains of crusading newspapering and cut the pattern of free American journalism which has held to this day.

At the start of this fateful year, dedicated to free government and the individual rights of man, there were 38 newspapers in the 13 American colonies and 33 of them devoted full attention to the dangerous business of teeing off on the royal English government and ripping the cover off the iniquities of taxation without representation.

Later in his book Schlesinger makes this observation, based purely on fact:

> The prolonged agitation enormously enhanced the influence of the press, instilling a newspaper-reading habit which has characterized all succeeding generations.

Created also during this period, as an integral part of the character of the free American people, was the acceptance of, and even expectance of and reliance upon, crusading journalism by their newspapers, and particularly against corruptions of government.

There can be no doubt that this was the prevailing sentiment when our founding forefathers, well aware of the key role played by the crusading Colonial press in the fight for freedom, drew the American Bill of Rights, which set forth in plain and vigorous language that government may adopt no law abridging the freedom of the press. Schlesinger concludes his book by describing this great Constitutional principle of freedom of the press:

> Next to Independence itself, it was the Revolutionary generation's greatest legacy to the American people.

To put this in different words, when a free people bestow freedom upon their press, they also bestow the very great obligation upon the press to report *all* facts of government, the bad as well as the good, at the time they are happening and not after the fact when, as history has often proved, it has been disastrous to the people. There is no essential difference between the reporting of the details of the secret Stamp Act by the New London, Connecticut, *Gazette* in 1765, and the 1958 reporting by the New York *Post* of Boston industrialist Bernard Goldfine's gift of a $2,400 oriental rug to Presidential Aide Sherman Adams. Similarly, the New York *Herald Tribune* exposed the "five per centers" and the mink coat and freezer scandals of the Truman Administration which contributed to the defeat of that political party in 1952. All three are good examples of crusading journalism.

An informed public opinion is the very lifeblood of free government, and if the free press does not meet this challenge of informing people of corruption in their government, then free government is certain to die. And that is the challenge that I bring to you — to defend with all your heart and your vigor, the freedom of the American press.

Early American politicians objected to crusading journalism, just as they do today, and in 1798 they put through Congress the Alien and Sedition Act which made it a crime punishable by a jail sentence for any citizen to criticize the government. A dozen American citizens, including a number of editors, did go to jail for the great crime of disseminating news of government actions, and this proved too much for the American people.

In 1800, the people overwhelmingly elected as president Thomas Jefferson, the world's greatest crusader for freedom, and forced the repeal of the Alien and Sedition Act. Thus was written into American history the official precedent of the American people's approval of crusading journalism and their disapproval of penalizing the American editor for his stories against the government.

Since the earliest days of American freedom, newspapers have conducted tens of thousands of crusades. Their graphic portrayals of the inequalities of life have sparked every American advance in the field of welfare, regardless of whether it had to do with the monopoly of big business and child labor or the revelation by the Portland *Oregonian* of Dave Beck's teamster union tie-up with the rackets. Likewise, newspaper disclosures of corruption in government, be it in City Hall or the White House, have sparked every drive for governmental reform.

It was a newspaper editor, William Lloyd Garrison, who led the drive in the North for abolition of American slavery and resulted in the War Between the States. And after this bloody fight between brothers, two newspaper editors, Henry Watterson of the Louisville *Courier-Journal* and Henry Grady of the Atlanta *Constitution,* led the great crusade for understanding between the North and the South.

Every day of every year since 1800, at least 100 American newspapers have been preoccupied with crusades for American people. It may be a little daily's fight in a midwestern community for better street lights or it may be a mammoth drive like that of Horace Greeley for honest government.

It may be the expose of the Orville Hodge scandal in Illinois by the Chicago *Daily News,* wherein this so-called public servant stole $2,500,000 of the people's tax funds; or it may be The Tampa *Tribune*'s revelations of squalid and terrible living conditions of thousands of migrant farm workers left stranded in the Everglades by winter freezes.

It may be the New York *World-Telegram*'s account of how Mayor Wagner tried to hush up a real estate scandal wherein millions of tax funds were poured down the drain; or it may be the Indianapolis newspapers' expose of the million-dollar turnpike scandal in Indiana. It may be the Yonkers, New York, *Herald Statesman* drive for better zoning laws; or it may be the Texas newspapers' expose of state insurance scandals.

It may be revelations by the Cleveland *Press* of payoffs in the police department; or it may be the fight of the Raton, New Mexico, *Daily Range* against the hush up of automobile accident figures. It may be the Kansas City *Star*'s crusade against the Pendergast machine in Missouri; or it may be the campaign of the Danielson,

Connecticut, *Windham County Transcript* against political privilege in the secret manipulation of a new courthouse site in Pompfort.

But all of these, and many more thousands too numerous to list, are living, pulsating testimonials to the very great traditions of American newspapering which were first written for the world to see in bloody footprints at Valley Forge. These newspaper crusades, from lowliest to mightiest, have been solely in the interests of the American people; they have guaranteed an informed public opinion; and they have charted "the American way of life" into the greatest free civilization known to man.

Now let us contrast this, for the moment, with the Russian way of life. In November, 1956, *Pravda,* the big Moscow newspaper, carried the following statement:

> The American press has been waging a furious campaign against the U.S.S.R. and the people's democracies in connection with the events in Hungary. The purpose of this campaign is to divert attention from the failure of the Anglo-French-Israeli aggression in Egypt and to encourage the defeated Fascists in Hungary with promises of U.N. support. Now, more than ever before, the responsibility of the U.S.A. for the counter revolutionary Putsch in Hungary is obvious. Irrefutable facts testify that it was indeed American reactionary circles who incited and activated the Horthyist underground which unleashed the bloody events in Hungary.

Within a week, every one of Russia's 7,246 newspapers printed this hogwash, and they kept hammering away at it for many months. They did this simply because as goes *Pravda,* the official voice of Khrushchev, so go every one of the 7,246 Russian newspapers.

If *Pravda* tells Russian women that they must "pretty up," as was the recent case, then every one of Russia's 7,246 newspapers hustle into print the official beautification "line." If *Pravda* sneers at some Russian poet because one of his poems varied a little from the Khrushchev thinking, then that poor long-haired Russian's name is mud in 7,246 Soviet newspapers. Should a Russian editor stray from the *Pravda* "line," or should he dare crusade on his own for the benefit of the Russian people, he would shortly find himself digging ditches in Siberia.

The Russian government's absolute control of all news and their spoon-feeding it to the Russian people is exactly what Thomas Jefferson warned the American people against 150 years ago when he swore on the altar of God "eternal hostility against every form of tyranny over the mind of man."

Certainly government censorship and bureaucratic propaganda are modern forms of tyranny over the mind of man. And Russia's absolute tyranny over the minds of the Russian people is one reason why American journalism should rededicate itself to the great tradition of crusading newspapering which first flowered in our War for Independence.

America, too, is veering in the direction of government censorship and bureaucratic propaganda, and it will take this rededication to the principles of crusading journalism to avert eventual Washington tyranny over the American public mind. If there is any doubt in your mind as to this very great danger to American freedom, permit me to outline briefly four definite steps taken by the American government in the last 25 years that would increase governmental tyranny over the American public mind.

FIRST: There is a stifling curtain of secrecy draped over virtually all of Federal Executive Government and over much of Federal Legislative and Judicial Government. No records of the annual Federal expenditure of approximately 80 billions of the American citizens' tax dollars are open to inspection of the citizen, and no audited reports of these expenditures are made available to the citizen. Furthermore, most decisions of government relative to these expenditures are made in secret "executive sessions."

As just one small example, our Federal Government never has accounted to tax-paying citizens for one penny of the nearly 75 billions of dollars it has spent on foreign aid since the close of World War II.

This is not to be taken as an attack on foreign aid. Actually, American foreign aid, designed to help our underprivileged neighbors in the free world, is the greatest Christian act in the history of the world's nations, and I am certain that most American citizens approve it. But these same American citizens, who paid for these billions of foreign aid, are entitled to a constant check to ascertain whether or not their hard-earned tax dollars are being spent wisely.

This question moved into Congress in a big way in 1959 and precipitated a titanic battle between the people's representatives and bureaucracy, a battle which probably will rock Federal Government during the next 10 years.

Foreign aid bureaucrats declined to give the General Accounting Office, which is Congress' auditing arm of government, the facts and figures on the program in such countries as Pakistan, India, Brazil, Guatemala and Laos, even though an investigation by the House Foreign Operations Subcommittee uncovered evidence that pointed to widespread waste, mismanagement and bribery.

This caused Representative Porter Hardy, Jr. (Dem., Va.), chairman of this House Subcommittee, to offer an amendment to the 1960 Foreign Aid Bill which would bar funds to the program unless the bureaucrats provided the facts and figures to Congress. The House of Representatives, close to the people, twice adopted this amendment during the summer of 1960, but each time the U. S. Senate, apparently under the influence of bureaucratic charm and intimidated by the bureaucrats' "doctrine of executive privilege," threw the amendment out the congressional window.

The question of which is to prevail in the American people's government — the people's representatives or the appointed bureaucrats — is still to be settled. And as a further example, both the Air Force and the National Aeronautics and Space Administration declined to give facts and figures on the U. S. space programs to Congress, and Dr. T. Keith Glennan, chairman of the latter bureau, gave the "doctrine of executive privilege" as his reason.

This bureaucratic secrecy in our space programs will explain to you the great public confusion in America today over whether or not we are in a position to match missiles with communistic Russia.

The American press is engaged in an equally titanic struggle with the power-happy bureaucrats over the matter of furnishing to the American people information of Federal expenditures of tax funds.

It took weeks and weeks of argument, cajolery and threats of national publicity before *The Tampa Tribune* could extract from the Department of Agriculture the record of soil subsidy payments in Florida and from the Federal Housing Administration the record of FHA projects in Florida. Likewise, it required a series of crusading stories by Clark Mollenhoff, crack Washington correspondent of the Des Moines *Register* and *Tribune,* to pry from the Department of Treasury the record of applications for tax exemptions of nonprofit, nonpolitical organizations and the record of out-of-court settlements in cases involving the refilling of liquor bottles.

The same Department of Treasury — while issuing touching press handouts on the tax plight of Joe Louis, the former heavyweight boxing champion, who was delinquent nearly a million dollars — declined to give the Indianapolis *News* the record of the 20 top tax delinquents of the country.

The Portland *Journal* had to crusade over six months before it could give its readers a report of the Veterans Administration on residential lot values in the Portland metropolitan area. And likewise, the Louisville *Courier-Journal* had to crusade for several weeks before it could flush out of the Department of Defense the facts and figures on a junket of Louisville big shots to Navy maneuvers in Florida.

The U. S. Post Office Department declined to give to the Martinsville, Virginia, *Bulletin,* the terms of a lease of a new post office at Fieldvale, Virginia; and it took the Providence *Journal* and *Bulletin* nearly six months to dig out of the same Post Office Department the fines it had levied against the New Haven Railroad for slow delivery of mail in Rhode Island.

These are but a few of the hundreds of almost daily clashes between American newspapers from coast to coast and Federal bureaucracy in Washington over the censorship of legitimate news of government. And I can truthfully state that, after 10 years concentrated study of this problem, I know not a single case wherein an American newspaper knocked on the door of a Washington bureau and received with even reasonable promptness, any facts and figures of government for the benefit of its readers.

Of all departments of Federal Government, the Pentagon, is by far the worst. If an innocent citizen should wander into this governmental maze, I am afraid he would eventually emerge with "top secret," "secret," "confidential" or "for official use only" stamped on his back.

Representative Daniel J. Flood (Dem., Pa.) found this out in 1957 when he requested pictures of plush furnishings inside military transport planes. The Pentagon not only declined his request but stamped "Secret" upon the Congressman's letter.

"It appears to me," said Flood, "that this classification is designed to protect bureaucrats from embarrassment and not to protect genuine military secrets from potential enemies of the country."

Pentagon censorship often ranges from the sublime to the ridiculous. As an example, it affixed the censorship stamp "For Official Use Only" on all its military weather data. Yet the Soviet Ambassador in Washington could telephone the Department of Defense, ask for Extension 79355, and a recording would give the latest 24-hour weather forecast from nearby Bolling Air Force Base. This automatic recording concluded with the following words: "This information is for military use only and dissemination to the public is not authorized."

Equally farcical was the Pentagon's use of its "Secret"

stamp on news of the use of monkeys in rockets after a Department of Defense press release on the matter already had been printed in the Washington *Post* and *Times Herald,* New York *Times* and Dayton, Ohio, *Daily News* and had been carried nationally by the Associated Press.

As early as July, 1950, Representative John E. Moss (Dem., Calif.), chairman of the House Subcommittee on Government Information, issued a report on his five-year study in which he said that the Pentagon was wielding the secrecy stamps today at a rate which ". . . equals the creation each week of a stack of classified documents higher than the Empire State Building" (1472 feet).

"The power to withhold the facts of government," said Representative Moss, "is the power to destroy that government in a democratic society. Such power is not to be lightly granted nor recklessly used."

Mr. Moss' continued efforts to batter down bureaucratic secrecy won for him the 1960 Sigma Delta Chi Freedom of the Press plaque.

There has been a seemingly incongruous distribution to lesser agencies and bureaus, the privilege of stamping "Top Secret" on their documents. Many of them could have no conceivable need for such classification, and this abuse will be discussed in a later chapter.

SECOND: There is an unhealthy "hostility of attitude" among millions of Federal bureaucrats toward the American press and its obligation to report all the facts of government to the people. This is substantiated in the following four concrete examples that took place in 1957:

1. The Wright Commission on Government Security, appointed by the President, proposed that an editor or publisher be fined $10,000 and sent to prison for five years for the crime of publishing "secret" information of government.

2. The Coolidge Committee on Classified Information proposed that newsmen be summoned in grand jury

investigations and, under the threat of jail, be forced to disclose the source of "leaks" of security information from government to the press.

3. The Civil Rights Bill, which was written in the Attorney General's office and as first passed by Congress, carried a provision that would make it a jail crime for anyone, including newsmen, to reveal information from behind the closed doors of the secret "executive session" of the new Civil Rights Commission.

4. Senate Bill No. 2461, introduced by Senators Henry M. Jackson (Dem., Wash.) and John L. McClellan (Dem., Ark.) would make it a crime punishable by a fine and jail sentence for anyone to reveal information, including statements, actions and even how the board members voted on the people's business, from behind the locked doors of the secret "executive sessions" of the Civil Aeronautics Board, the Interstate Commerce Commission, the Federal Trade Commission, the Securities and Exchange Commission, the Federal Power Commission and the Federal Communications Commission. And this bill, had it become law, would have protected Richard Mack, Florida's member of the Federal Communications Commission, Presidential Aide Sherman Adams and all Federal bureaucrats from future exposure as recipients of political favors and gifts.

This line of thinking still prevails in Washington, and it marks the first time since the Alien and Sedition Act of 1798 that our Federal bureaucrats have seriously entertained the idea of throwing free American citizens, including newspaper editors, into jail for the great crime of dissemination of news of government.

Pressure from the press killed the secrecy provision of the Civil Rights Bill, and the Jackson-McClellan bill died in Senate Committee. But the Wright and Coolidge reports produced immediate public explosions, which are worth exploring here briefly simply to show how the bureaucrat wields his tar brush on the press at every opportunity.

The minute a man dons the toga of the American bureaucrat, he apparently assumes he has a monopoly on patriotism. And the next minute he usually points a finger at the press. Such was the case with the Wright Commission and the Coolidge Committee, both of which based their reports on the general premise that the press was promiscuous in disclosing American security information for the benefit of the enemy.

The Wright Commission was particularly vicious in its criticism of the press. Said its report on June 22, 1957:

> The final responsibility for the difficult decisions of what shall be secret must be confined in those loyal and devoted public servants who are qualified to make the judgment.

It then pronounced that most of the press "had lived up to those limits," but, added the report:

> There are a few exceptional cases which for some reasons have escaped prosecution. The purveyor of information vital to national security, purloined by devious means, gives aid to our enemies as effectively as the foreign agent.

The press promptly called upon Mr. Lloyd Wright, chairman of the commission, to define the standards of "those loyal and devoted public servants who are qualified to make the judgment" and to make public the names of those in the press who had "purloined by devious means" our security information. This he has not done.

On June 30, Mr. Wright replied, stating that he knew of certain "dark chapters of betrayal" but could not talk about them. "An unnamed government official persists in stamping the cases secret," he said, "and has buried them forever in the bureaucratic graveyard of a maze of files."

Under questioning, Wright gave a general indictment of the press without naming names, then he fell back on World War II and said that a story in the Chicago *Tribune* had informed the Japs that we had broken their code.

Three weeks later, J. Russell Wiggins, executive editor of the Washington *Post* and *Times Herald,* rose at the San Francisco meeting of the American Society of Newspaper Editors Convention and gave documentary evidence that the Chicago *Tribune* had in no way informed the Japs of the code breaking.

Whereupon, Mr. Wright, on the ASNE platform at the time, promptly apologized to the Chicago *Tribune*.

In the middle of the controversy, Maj. Gen. Guy S. Meloy, Jr., the Army's public information chief, told the House Subcommittee on Government Information that "he had never heard of any secret information being purloined or stolen from military files by the press." This prompted Chairman John E. Moss to label the Wright charges as ". . . an unsubstantiated indictment of the American Press."

The Coolidge Committee was not so outspoken as the Wright Commission, yet it harped throughout its report and later in the questioning by the House Subcommittee on Government Information on the matter of "leaks" of security information to the press. Furthermore, Chairman Charles A. Coolidge of the Commission named names in the press.

On March 11, 1957, Mr. Coolidge testified that the *Wall Street Journal* had "leaked" the national security secret of the list of Air Force contractors building ballistic missiles. An investigation of this charge showed that the so-called "leak" was a news story of August 3, 1956, which reported accurately the public speech of a top Air Force general to the Air Force Association at New Orleans, in which he listed the names of nearly a score of firms working on the project.

Similarly, Coolidge accused the press of "leaking" national security information in the form of the speed of the flight of the jet X-2. An investigation disclosed the accusation was based on a story in the New York *Times* of August 2, 1956, which reported, again accurately, on a public speech made by Secretary of the Air Force Donald C. Quarles. Previously, the Pentagon had declined to reveal this information and one of its public relations officials gave as the reason: ". . . the ebb and flow of Secretary of Defense Wilson's indigestion."

Again on March 11, Coolidge testified before the House Subcommittee on Government Information that the press had provided the enemy with key information in printing a picture of four bombers being refueled. But on March 12, he voluntarily corrected the record on this so-called "leak" by stating he had learned the picture had been cleared for publication by both the Navy and the Department of Defense.

Over the years, I have perused thousands of pages of government documents, testimony and charges, all involving the question of national security and the press. Despite the charges of the bureaucrats, I have found not a single case wherein the press, on its own volition, printed a national security secret that gave aid and comfort to the enemy. On the other hand, time and again I have run head on into a curtain of unnecessary secrecy that barred the American people from rightful knowledge of their government.

THIRD: It would take a super-Houdini to navigate the mushrooming maze of Federal bureaucracy which today places a restraining finger upon every phase of living of every free American citizen. If you doubt this, let any one of you try to find out the exact number of Federal bureaus, agencies and departments.

Back in 1951, I wired the Comptroller of the United States, the man who pays all Federal salaries, to give me the exact number of the major Federal bureaus. He wired back that he could not do this, that to the best of his knowledge there were approximately 1,875, not including the new ones. There have been many new bureaus created in the last nine years and I would hazard the guess, after numerous sorties into bureaucracy, that there are approximately 2,000 major Federal bureaus today.

Then, in addition, there are approximately 5,000 Federal advisory commissions, all of which wield tremendous power in the lives of average American citizens. It is of added interest that in 1957 Florida's Representative Dante Fascell introduced and got passed in the House of Representatives a bill that would force these 5,000 Federal advisory commissions to reveal to Congress the identity of membership and to keep minutes of their secret meetings. This, of course, is tantamount to the people forcing their secret governors to reveal themselves. But the U.S. Senate declined even to consider this bill and these 5,000 Federal agencies still are a deep, dark secret insofar as the American people are concerned.

American bureaucracy, operating in secrecy, has built up absolute power not only over the private lives of American people, but also over the legislative proceedings of free American government. And this has been mushrooming in both Democratic and Republican administrations.

On June 14, 1951, David Lawrence, conservative editor and publisher and long-time student of Federal Government, printed in his weekly magazine, the *United States News and World Reports,* the following ten steps showing how bureaucracy in the Truman Democratic Administration achieved its programs:

1. Policy makers, meeting, decide that the public should be conditioned for a new desired policy.
2. Orders go out to all affected officials and public relations officers instructing them on the "line" to be taken in talks with outsiders.
3. A story about the policy is "planted" with a columnist, radio commentator or news writer.
4. The story prompts questions at a Cabinet officer's press conference. He develops the new "line" and gets headlines.

5. Speeches on the new "line" are made by a Cabinet officer, by assistant secretaries, by other Government officials before groups in different parts of the country.

6. The stories and speeches lead to questions at a White House press conference. The President backs the new policy and gets big headlines.

7. Handouts, more speeches and policy statements are prepared and delivered.

8. Friendly senators take up the new "line" in speeches around the country.

9. The new "line" is spread all down through government departments, local officials in various states, in hundreds of communities.

10. The public, with the viewpoint hammered in, accepts the new "line." Opponents are driven to cover.

The Eisenhower Republican Administration came into power in 1952, but there was no slackening in the buildup of the bureaucratic power. In 1954, two years after the Republicans had taken over in Washington, former Senator William E. Jenner (Rep., Ind.) wrote me as follows:

> Another reason for the "railroading" of legislation through Congress is the very large role played in legislation by the bureaucracy of the Executive Branch. They frequently draft the bills. They write the arguments for the bills. They fill the record of hearings on bills. They have supporting groups which come in and testify to the approved "line." Ordinary citizens cannot meet such well-financed, well-organized competition. It may appear as if the sentiment is all in one direction on a bill, and Congress hears little or no objection, and so moves quickly to pass it.

Senator Jenner did not offer himself for re-election in 1958, perhaps because of the disillusionment over the proceedings of free American representative government evidenced in his letter to me.

At any rate, in 1959 and 1960 the Democrats had overwhelming majorities in Congress. Each January this Democratic majority talked long and lustily of how it was going to put the Republican President in his place. Yet every time the Democratic majority balked over the Administration's program, the propaganda mills ground out favorable publicity and Congress quickly folded its tent, rubber-stamped the President's program and, in some cases, left the American people uninformed and utterly confused.

Theoretically, an informed public opinion is supposed to direct the people's representatives in their law-making. That is the very life-blood of free legislative government. But if people are uninformed, through bureaucratic secrecy, and confused, through bureaucratic propaganda, on the major issues of government, how can a citizen make an unprejudiced decision and let his congressman know how he feels about any one measure?

A case in point was the bureaucratic debate of 1960 over our defense budget. Our President, arguing for a balanced budget, told the American people we were "impregnable." But our military generals, arguing for a bigger and better defense dollar, told the people we are a poor second to Russia in the rocket race. Which one could we believe? Truth indeed would be a great comfort to Americans who are paying for all of this and whose very lives are at stake on the outcome.

FOURTH: There has been developed in Washington during the last 25 years an army of approximately 50,000 Federal Government press agents at an annual cost to the American taxpayers of approximately $100,000,000.

These are estimated figures simply because, like everything else in Federal Government, bureaucratic press agentry is beclouded by bureaucratic secrecy.

In 1941 a congressional investigating committee reported that the Federal Government was spending $28,000,000 a year on press agentry. In 1949 the Hoover Government Report put the cost of Federal Government press handouts at $74,829,467 a year, with some 45,000 press agents on the payroll.

The Truman Administration, acting upon the Hoover report, ordered a 10 per cent reduction in appropriations for Federal press agentry. But the bureaucracy simply laughed at this, changed the names of many of its press agents to high-sounding governmental titles, and went right ahead developing its luxurious propaganda. Today veteran Washington newsmen estimate there are at least 50,000 Federal press agents, regardless of what they are called, and that this is costing the American taxpayers at least $100,000,000 a year.

Officials explain that this army of government press agents is necessary to tell the American people the details of the expenditure of their tax dollars. Yet in my 35 years of newspapering, I never have heard of a single government press agent who ever issued a government "handout" that was critical of his political boss. Every line written by a government press agent is designed to reflect glory upon his government agency and to prolong the political life of his boss, regardless of whether it is the truth, half truth or no truth.

If you doubt this, let me tell the story of my good friend, Herschel Schooley. For several years, Mr. Schooley served as Director of Public Relations at the Pentagon, that maze of an office building wherein the Federal Department of Defense censors everything but the toilet tissue. But in 1957 he made the great mistake of assisting members of the Washington press corps to obtain legitimate information of government, instead of propaganda, and was twice reprimanded by his superiors. And early in 1958 he got the axe, all for the great sin of giving reporters at Cape Canaveral, Florida, accurate information on our rocket flops as well as our satellite successes.

A questionable case may be argued in behalf of a bureaucrat who insists that his press agent ballyhoo his good deeds, but no case at all can be argued for the bureaucrat who seeks through press agentry to gouge or hoodwink the American taxpayer. Records show plainly that this is done all too frequently and that Democrats and Republicans are equally guilty.

A House Subcommittee on Expenditures in the Executive Departments, headed by Representative Clare E. Hoffman (Rep., Mich.), reported on the Bureau of Reclamation, Department of Interior in the Truman Democratic Administration, on August 7, 1948:

> Upon the evidence adduced, the most shocking and amazing story of bureaucratic intrigue has been unfolded. Incompetency, evasion of the intent of Congress, disregard of the truth, deliberate withholding of material information from the committees of Congress, and willful violation of Federal law, are a part of the sordid story thus far presented to your committee.

At that time, Congress had appropriated $200,000,000, which was in President Truman's budget, for development and construction of the great Central Valley project in California. The Bureau of Reclamation, which builds flood and irrigation projects for the government, had estimated that an additional $200,000,000 was needed for the project. On the best estimates obtainable, it had been shown that the congressional appropriation was sufficient to carry the project through 1948. But the Bureau of Reclamation was not satisfied. On the false plea that it had exhausted available funds, the Bureau shut down all work on five important projects as of November 30, 1947.

The Hoffman Committee, reporting on this deliberate and needless shutdown, said in its report to Congress:

> Upon the shutting down of the projects, the Bureau of Reclamation propaganda machine went into action. The Congress was villified and charged with

failure to provide sufficient funds for construction in a studied attempt to divert blame from themselves. These attacks were made in spite of the fact that in excess of $7,000,000 was available for construction; in spite of the fact that Congress had made available substantially the amount of funds requested by the President; in spite of the fact that Richard L. Boke, regional director in charge of the Central Valley project, himself had on Nov. 1, 1947, stated sufficient moneys were on hand to operate until Feb. 1, 1948.

American bureaucracy, which got its start in the Roosevelt Administration, had not yet attained its maturity in the following Truman Administration. The Hoffman investigation, and others like it at that time, helped to knock the rough edges off the bureaucrats.

These brief illustrations give you the modern trend in Washington toward Federal Government control of the public mind, and there is strong evidence that the same trend is developing in the lower levels of American government. We have a lot of secrecy in city, county and state governments from coast to coast. We also have the same "hostility of attitude" toward the press, the same bulging bureaucracy and the same army of press agents.

The best way for me to give you a hint of the bulging bureaucracy on the state level is to relate California's fight against secret government. In 1953, the California Legislature, prodded by newspaper editors, adopted a general law for open records and open government meetings. That should have been sufficient, but it didn't turn out that way. Bureaucrats so badly abused the law that in 1957 the California Legislature adopted 64 new laws, one for each state bureau and stipulated by name that it must conduct the people's business in the open.

The state of Florida had 35 press agents in 1950 and the cost of the state's "handouts" was estimated at that time at $265,000 a year. Today we have nearly 100 press agents working out of Tallahassee and their "handouts," much of them propaganda, cost the Florida taxpayers more than $500,000 a year. My own city of Tampa got its first press agent a few months ago when the mayor installed a former newsman in his office. But give us a chance. The city of Los Angeles has more than 75, including 25 in the police department alone, and you can imagine what would happen in the event of a police scandal.

Thus, I present to you the foregoing as more than ample reason why all of us in American journalism today should rededicate ourselves to the very great American heritage of crusading newspapering, and I earnestly urge each and every future journalist to kneel at the altar with Thomas Jefferson and swear to God "eternal hostility against every form of tyranny over the mind of man."

2.

The City
Without a Soul

TAMPA IS A BEAUTIFUL CITY, surrounded by blue bays and blessed with a magnificent year-round climate. A friendly city, it offers a newcomer a combination of life in a bustling industrial community, a colorful Latin quarter with some of the world's finest Spanish restaurants, and Florida's finest beaches only 30 miles away. Furthermore, during World War II, Tampa proved itself when its three shipyards worked day and night and its five Air Force bases processed more than a million young men for the death struggle with the Germans and the Japanese.

Because of its great industrial potential and its rich back country, Roger Babson, the noted financial expert, repeatedly proclaimed to the world that Tampa eventually would surpass the Gold Coast of Miami and would become Florida's No. 1 metropolis.

But let us go back to the Tampa of 1944–45 and peer into its closets and rattle its skeletons. For one thing, its 125,000 citizens were jammed in 21 square miles of which 2 square miles were water. This left a city area of 19 square miles, which was the smallest for its size in the United States and less than a third of the area of Jacksonville or Miami.

Because of its small size, the city was dominated politically by Ybor City, its Latin quarter whose inhabitants for many years voted in a solid bloc, mainly to keep its power. At this time, Tampa's Latin citizens were of the first and second generation and had not yet become completely Americanized in democratic procedures. Newcomers moved into suburbs, worked in the city but had no political voice in City Hall, and consequently received little municipal services. The suburban septic tank problem, alone, menaced the health of the entire community.

In 1928, this politically inspired municipality kicked out the city manager form of government and, through political chicanery, installed the aldermanic ward system, which autocratically ruled the city for the next 17 years.

Under this ward system, the mayor was elected citywide; the 12 aldermen chosen one from each of the 12 wards. Proponents of this system claim it is the only true representative government; that each district is guaranteed its rightful representation in the government; that the mayor will look after the city as a whole. But it didn't work. The city as a whole suffered; the wards gained nothing.

Seven of the 12 aldermen organized into a majority bloc with the shrewdest alderman as chairman of the board. These seven majority bloc aldermen were elected by a combined total of only 5,623 votes in their seven wards. This represented less than 20 per cent of the registered city vote and about 4 per cent of Tampa's official population. In other words, these 5,623 voters, many of them feeding on special privilege, governed the remaining 120,000 through a despotic majority bloc of ward heelers.

This majority bloc quickly became the arrogant boss of the city. It overrode the mayor on important projects; it blocked his appointments; it ruthlessly trampled the rights of the minority members of the board; it cast aside petitions from the people as a whole.

It perpetuated itself in power through political slush funds and special privileges. Publicly, city employees would say nothing because of fear of losing their jobs but privately they confessed they were forced to kick into a slush fund just before each election. Population of the red-light district increased tenfold before each election; and these "ladies of the night" always voted for their aldermanic masters.

Key political figures in the seven wards had their streets patched, their sidewalks built; free earth was dumped into their yards, cement poured for their private driveways. If they owned lake or country places, city trucks transported free gravel, and city prisoners built their private roads. Their friends received free medical care in the city hospital; their kin grabbed the fat political jobs. If they got into trouble with the police — which was often — the charges always were removed from the blotter with an aldermanic eraser. For this, all they had to do was to get out the vote.

This is an old story of municipal corruption, common in many American cities, but difficult to expose. Several members of the majority bloc gained control of Tampa's taxicab companies. Businessmen kept whispering that the ward heelers exacted tribute from new enterprises seeking city licenses. Liquor licenses were a pet football of the aldermanic bloc. The number of Tampa's barrooms jumped by the scores, and the law on distances separating barrooms from schools and churches was totally disregarded.

The majority bloc did the people's business in secret sessions with the press barred. Public sessions of the board were turned into disgraceful near riots. Dignity was unknown: ink bottles were hurled, curses exchanged. Often members were drunk. Procedure was a farce. Good citizens soon learned to stay away.

One drunken member of the majority bloc staggered from a board meeting to a nearby restaurant and shot at a political enemy. On the night before one election, the chairman of the board was arrested in an adjoining county while in the act of marking city ballots. Neither ever served a day of time in jail for these crimes.

During these 17 years, 1928 to 1945, these ward heelers gave the people of Tampa not one thing except a big municipal headache. Tampa was steadily gaining in population but during those 17 years not one major municipal improvement project was undertaken by the city government. The only major city-wide paving project was a WPA job on Tampa's Bayshore Drive. The only municipal addition was a small city airport, which was outmoded in three years because the big air liners could not land there.

The city water works just couldn't do the job. In dry seasons the pressure was not sufficient to lift a stream of water through a fire hose to the second story, and I watched a business building burn to the ground across the street from *The Tampa Tribune* because of this lack of water pressure. People couldn't water their lawns; only a dribble dampened their sinks. In wet seasons, Hillsborough River overflowed into residential sections. A new dam up the river would have ended this menace, but the ward heelers did nothing.

Taxes kept climbing year by year, but the sewer system, bursting at the seams, all but broke down. Raw sewage was pumped into Tampa Bay, the beauty spot of the Florida West Coast. Stench from the low places in the city was terrific; streets cracked and crumbled, and public buildings were unkempt. Political appointees flooded city offices but the police force was inadequate and corrupt, and crimes continued to increase.

On top of all this, a strong organized underworld was developed and eventually became the ruling element in politics. Gambling ran wide open; the bolita business was built into a $10,000,000 a year racket. Gangsters murdered gangsters, often in cold blood in downtown areas, yet none went to jail. Good citizens declined to offer themselves for public office because they were unwilling to compromise their integrity by getting down on their knees to the underworld in order to be elected.

That was beautiful Tampa in sunny Florida from 1928

to 1945 — a perfect picture of political stagnation, careless and corrupt, the happy hunting grounds of ward heelers. It was a city with all the potentials of great growth but hamstrung by petty politicians. It was indeed "a city without a soul," as it was labeled by Karl A. Bickel, retired president of United Press, who lived at Sarasota.

Here is the problem of the leading newspaper: Should it take off its wraps, roll up its sleeves and undertake all the headaches of crusading for the benefit of its community? Or should it stand disdainfully aside, content itself with the printing of handouts, and permit its editor to keep his hair and grow fat and sassy?

The first aspect of this problem is the people. Where were they during the 17 years when Tampa's government went from bad to worse, with them as the victims? Why didn't they rise up and throw out their corrupt rulers? Why didn't they demand that their tax funds be used for water works improvement, new sewers and better street paving?

After all, an informed public opinion not only is the lifeblood of free government but it also is the most powerful force possible in legislative government. But it is difficult to arouse this force, whether it be in a cleanup of a corrupt Tampa government or against wild spending by our Federal bureaucrats in Washington.

The people of the United States are the most heavily taxed of any people on the face of our globe, and there is considerable question as to whether our tax funds are being wasted, stolen or spent wisely by our Federal public servants. Representative James A. Haley (Dem.) of Sarasota, who represents the congressional district to the east and south of Tampa, sat in my office recently and I asked him this question:

> "What would happen if every householder in America should devote three minutes of time and spend four cents to write a letter to his Congressman

stating that unless he reduced taxes by 20 per cent he would not vote for him in the next election?"

"Why," laughed Mr. Haley, "all of us would rush back to Washington, call a special session of the Congress if necessary, and we would vote a general tax reduction of 20 per cent within a matter of hours."

Such is the latent power of the people, the sleeping power of the lowly citizen, the inherent power of your next-door neighbor, who perhaps worries more over his broken lawn mower than over broken-down integrity of elected officials. But that power of the citizen to topple governments is like the power in an atom bomb — the bomb is powerless unless the uranium is exploded, and so is the power of the lowly citizen useless unless there is leadership. Our leading historians are just now reaching the conclusion that there would have been no American War of Independence and perhaps no American freedom today had it not been for the 33 Colonial newspapers who teed off against the royal English government and triggered the seven-year explosion that was culminated at Yorktown.

People always have been apathetic toward their government. Otherwise, man never would have been put into slavery during his troubled course down through the centuries. Recently in Tampa, our city board of representatives called a public meeting to discuss a $20,000,000 bond issue for municipal improvements. Such an issue meant additional taxes on every citizen, yet not a single citizen appeared at the meeting to discuss the matter. A few weeks later the chairman of a Tampa Junior Chamber of Commerce committee to get voters registered, plaintively complained that the campaign was a fizzle simply because too many citizens were afraid to register because they then would be called to jury duty.

Furthermore, politicians discourage, whenever they can, the participation of the average citizen in the business of government. Otherwise, we would not have the present curtain of secrecy draped over most of Federal Government and particularly over the expenditure of Federal tax funds. On October 4, 1957, Tampa's City Board of Representatives called a public meeting to discuss a record city budget of $24,045,961. There turned up at this public meeting several delegations of city employees asking pay increases and one lone tax-paying citizen, who bitterly protested the record budget. Whereupon, our city fathers respectfully bowed and scraped as they received the requests of the city employees for higher pay, then sharply belabored the lone taxpayer for daring to question their proposed expenditure of taxpayers' funds.

Separation of the average American citizen and his government is becoming wider due to the complexities of modern American life. The development of new and better farm machinery has sent millions of Americans to the cities during the last 25 years, and this has produced that new American phenomena called "suburbia." American prosperity has doubled the number of automobiles, with all of the traffic problems, and has put a TV set into almost every home. The average citizen is willing to beat his way through traffic and parking difficulties twice a day to get to his job, but you can't lure him away from his life in suburbia a second time in a day to attend a political meeting. He groans under heavy taxation but, insofar as his government is concerned, he has adopted the philosophy, "Let John do it."

The historian De Tocqueville warned his French people 100 years ago against centralization of government which made a person "... a kind of settler, indifferent to the fate of the spot which he inhabits. The greatest changes are effected there without his concurrence. The condition of his village, the police of his street, the repairs of the church or parsonage, do not concern him; for he looks upon all these things as unconnected with himself and as the property of a powerful stranger whom he calls the government." This may give you a faint idea of the basic cause behind the 25 changes of government which the

French people have had since the close of World War II, and it may also give you an idea of what is ahead for America unless the ordinary citizen awakens to his responsibility in free government.

So much for the people; now let us examine another aspect of the problem. After some years of crusading against governmental corruption in his community, a New Jersey editor and publisher roared his disgust as follows:

> Crusading is a rich man's game. You lose advertising, you lose circulation, you even lose prestige.
>
> People begin thinking you have a personal axe to grind, and that the publisher, himself, is working for some ulterior motive. And when you have thwarted the plans of scheming politicians and have saved the city or county millions of dollars — what happens? No one gives a damn.
>
> The friends appreciate the service you have done for a few minutes, and then forget it immediately and completely. But the enemies you have made never forget. No, and neither do their brothers, sisters, fellow lodge members, and everybody else connected with the culprit or culprits.
>
> The good will you generate in a crusade is short and fleeting, and the ill will lasts forever.
>
> I have discovered that the people hate a crusader and love a pussyfooter. Since I adopted my new policy of barring crusading, everything is running along smoothly and without any fuss or bother. I used to have a string of politicians a block long waiting outside this office to argue and threaten and express their contempt or elucidate their ambitions. Now it is quiet. Everything is routine. Everybody slaps you on the back and says you're a good fellow. We just shut our eyes to everything, and then everybody's happy.

There can be no doubt but that crusading newspapering is truly a man's job. If you think that the scalawag politcans will let you crusade at their expense without retaliation in one form or another, then you have another think coming. And if you think the dear old public will heap accolades upon your crusading and install you as a permanent hero, then you have a third think coming. And if you think you can get away with crusading without accumulating lifetime scars upon your nervous system, then you'll need a fourth think.

There are some editors and publishers of our 2,301 American daily newspapers who have had their fingers burned in crusading and feel the same disgust expressed by the New Jersey editor. And there are a good many American citizens, usually with axes to grind, who like to castigate the American press as a whole for not taking up every little cause and beating the bushes mightily over it. Yet, by and large, the free American press is living up to the responsibilities imposed upon it by the free American people. It is riding herd on our politicians from the White House down to the lowly member of the community school board. It is arousing the public mind to the welfare needs of the individual American citizen. More important, it is the sentinel of danger and the guardian of American freedom. And it is only fair to report that, after a few weeks of the peace and quiet and boredom of being a good fellow to all men, the New Jersey editor whom I quoted, returned to the serious business of ripping the cover off government and arousing public opinion of his community to the corruptions of their public servants.

A good many Americans like to hurl the charges that American newspapers in their news columns are guided solely by the profit motive. Of course, newspapers must be profitable; the more profits they make, the more independent they can be. And the more independent they are, the more they live up to their obligations to the people. I have never heard of a bankrupt newspaper conducting a crusade, with all its headaches, for the people's benefit. Profits are important to newspapers, but they are not everything. There was the case of the scientific report that cigarette smoking contributes to lung cancer. News-papers from coast to coast printed that report, largely on their Page 1, as a public service to the American people and even though publishers well knew that it would have a direct effect upon their advertising revenues. There was an immediate drop in newspaper advertising by all the big cigarette manufacturers.

Time and again the American newspaper has crusaded in fields that have cost it profits. It pioneered in the demand for a Federal food and drug act to protect the American people from greedy business interests. It has exposed a thousand different kinds of business gyps and it bars its advertising columns to those who would violate the ethics of honesty. We in the American newspaper profession today have our faults, of course, simply be-cause we are human, but professionally we equal or exceed any group in our land in business ethics, moral consciousness and the awareness of the rights of the in-dividual American citizen.

What is the alternative to crusading newspapering? It is simple. You confine your ringing editorials to such topics as the flag and mother's love; you polish up your news columns with all the routine news, much of it pro-paganda handouts and political pap, as it develops in governmental boards, in the police court and on the poli-tical platform; and you top this off with a few snappy fea-tures, including a puzzle or two. Finally, you loosen up your belt for a lot of "free loading" at cocktail parties and friendly little dinners, and hunch out your back for the enthusiastic pats of the politicians.

I don't know that you will sleep well, because man's conscience is a funny thing, but I didn't sleep well either for a solid year while Tampa's underworld telephoned me on the hour, every hour, every night, week after week, in an effort to drive me off a crusade against gambling.

A noncrusading newspaper must close its eyes while our public servants cart off City Hall and likewise it must stop up its ears to the plaintive complaints of free citizens whose rights have been trampled on by arrogant politicians. It must be blind to political privilege and to corruption within the government, and it must be deaf to the cries of danger to our freedom from within as well as from without our gates.

If a crippled youngster in the polio ward writes a heart-wringing letter that the hospital has not the sufficient equipment for his cure, a noncrusading newspaper must carefully toss that letter into the wastebasket. Also it must kick out a widowed mother who dared to come in and appeal for help in paying hospital bills for her boy who had a Christmas arrow buried in his brain.

Such a newspaper also must close its eyes, while holding its nose, at the sight of outdoor toilets in a squalid shanty section in the heart of a city, spreading disease and preventing prosperity in the community; it also must ignore a broken-down sewer system, bursting septic tanks, and the general danger of pestilence to the public; and it must dismiss as incidental the case of an old Negro, a witness in a murder case, who was deprived of his liberty and kept in jail for six months while the politicians delayed the trial.

Just as casually, it must close its mind to the fact that its schools rank forty-seventh in the nation and its school lunchrooms are full of rats; that its tourists are being taken for a tax ride in a speed trap in a nearby county; that its politicians and contractors are ignoring the state law, which calls for public bids on all contracts of more than $1,000, by breaking up a $90,000 bridge-painting contract into 100 jobs of less than $1,000 and awarding it on the basis of political privilege.

Such a newspaper, fearful of crusading, must water down its leadership in community drives. It must forego the business of putting its community over the top in charity drives and it must likewise look the other way when its community seeks new roads and industry. Instead, it must concentrate on the printing of the handouts, and by doing this in the sacred name of objectivity, it becomes a part and passel of the sorry spectacle of propagandizing the people for the benefit of the special interests.

Such a newspaper reminds me of certain men I have met in life — smart-talking men who have been impeccably dressed and perfectly mannered; and yet one look into their eyes tells you that they have no soul and are going nowhere in life because they have ducked all of life's real responsibilities.

Give me crusading journalism with the sneers of the politicians; with all of its headaches and its sometimes lonely life.

Give me crusading journalism that lends a constant and willing ear to the pleas of the unfortunate.

Give me crusading journalism that heeds all pleas for help, regardless of whether they concern conditions in a nursing home for the aged, juvenile drinking on Skid Row or a war veteran whose home burned down three days after he bought it.

Give me crusading journalism that provides the initiative and enterprise of leadership for its community, whether it be for a new courthouse or to throw the rascals out of City Hall.

Give me crusading journalism that makes a newspaper an integral part of the community, sharing all the fortunes, all the sadnesses and the joys, all the adventures, big and little, of the citizens in its community.

Give me crusading journalism just so long as it is measured by honesty, fairness, integrity and responsibility.

That is real newspapering, and the editor can sleep at night if the thwarted crooks will let his telephone alone.

3.

Routing
the Ward Heelers

IN THE SUMMER OF 1944, *The Tampa Tribune* decided to do something about its ward-heeling city government. New residents were pouring into the city. Climate and location favored a great future. But polluted politics can stunt the growth of any community. Who wants to raise a family in the middle of smelly municipal corruption?

The decision was not made in haste. Careful consideration was given every angle of the problem to ascertain the best way of going about ridding the community of the ward-heeling leeches. A veteran staffer was assigned for three months to study city government. On the basis of his study, it was determined to advocate city manager government.

The *Tribune* fully realized that there would be opposition to city manager government, even from those citizens who opposed the ward heelers. But our study showed city manager government to be the most successful. And we realized that we had to shoot for the best, even in the face

of political opposition, in order to achieve our real goal —
the elimination of the ward heelers.

A three-point attack was carefully mapped out. This
can be summed up briefly as follows:

1. *Exposure of the shortcomings* — big and little — of
Tampa's ward government, based on the record, but
using ridicule wherever possible, made easier because
the facts often were ridiculous within themselves.

2. *A comparison of Tampa's ward-heeling government
with the more successful governments of other cities.*
This always arouses readership since the average
American loves his home and hates to see it put at a
disadvantage with his neighbor.

3. *The arousing of public opinion.* This is most important. I doubt whether any newspaper can achieve any
project unless it can persuade the public to support
the project, even though, as I have pointed out, the
average citizen is apathetic toward his government.

Our City Hall reporter was assigned to dig into the
city's records, and he spent three months on this before
he wrote a word. At the same time, another veteran staffer was assigned to visit other Florida cities and look into
their governments. From city managers of 25 cities from
coast to coast he also obtained facts and figures on their
governments. Three other staffers, who covered civic
clubs and organizations, were alerted.

I held frequent conferences with these five men, both
before and during our campaign. All three points of
attack, along with the editorials, were perfectly coordinated. This is called the "conference" type of newspaper
crusade as contrasted to the "lone wolf" type, wherein one
reporter is assigned to a leisurely project.

We began our campaign gradually and quietly on
September 4, 1944. There was no fanfare and no drum
beating. The kickoff was an editorial, not even given

great prominence. It was entitled "Time for Organized Action," and it congratulated St. Petersburg, our sister city across the bay, for having obtained the services of a city manager, who had made an outstanding record. This editorial concluded by declaring that the unquestionably large number of Tampans who desired a change in their form of government, should not wait too long to start an organized movement toward that end.

I would like to point out here that throughout our campaign we avoided the sensational and relied altogether upon a calm recital of the facts. The *Tribune* is a conservative newspaper and we do not go for the sensational. In our opinion, the sensational usually is based on half truths. We prefer to seek out the whole truth and pass the sensational. We rarely used more than a two-column head on any of our city government stories.

Because we pushed our three points of attack simultaneously, it would be confusing to try to give a chronological account of our campaign. Therefore, I shall divide it into the three parts outlined above. But keep in mind that we fired at the ward heelers from three sides at the same time, and on some days we ran as many as five different stories. And I can assure you that they were read.

Here in brief, as follows and by dates, is the story of our news treatment of the campaign, based strictly on the record:

September 6 — A report of how the majority bloc of aldermen squeezed a minority member from getting a much needed storm sewer for his district by blocking bids for pipe.

September 15 — A Page 1 story related how for 17 years the ward heelers had kicked around Tampa's desperately needed new sewer system.

September 17 — A report from the aldermanic files showing how ordinances vital to the city were carefully buried deep in the committees dominated by the ma-

jority bloc. These ordinances included a study of the
city audit; a recommendation to set up a separate city
aviation department; and an investigation of the city's
muddled hospital accounts. On that same day, one
of the majority bloc lashed a *Tribune* reporter at a
public meeting for failure of our newspaper to heap
praise on the ward heelers for their good acts. The
Tribune replied editorially that the aldermen's record
of good acts had been "short and skimpy."

We make a regular practice of printing politicians'
criticism of the *Tribune* and its staff, usually on Page 1,
simply because our readers are entitled to all sides of any
public dispute, the politicians are entitled to their say in
our columns, and this usually dumbfounds our erring
public servants.

September 24 — A Page 1 story outlined four methods
whereby Tampa's city charter could be changed.

September 27 — Story and pictures showed how city's
parkways were waist high in weeds due to refusal of
ward heelers to replace worn-out equipment.

September 28 — A report based on the record refuted the
aldermen's argument that Tampa's progress was ham-
pered by heavy boom-time bonded debt by showing
that Tampa had far less bonded debt than St. Petersburg and other more progressive Florida cities.

October 3 — Factual story related how political pressure
for election "slush funds" was brought on Tampa's
city employees under the ward system despite civil
service, which badly needed revamping.

October 4 — Tampa's city civil service was compared to
that in other Florida cities, pointing up the spoils
system under the ward system.

October 8 — A story traced from the records how the
aldermanic majority bloc controlled Tampa's legislators through their district machines and how this en-

abled the ward heelers to slip special acts through the legislature to strip powers from the mayor and put them into their hands.

October 11–14 — A series of stories reviewed Tampa's city charter fights of 1920, 1927, 1929 and 1937 and showed how difficult it was to oust the ward heelers once they were entrenched in power.

October 15 — A story based on the records traced how the ward heelers down through the years had tampered with liquor laws, enabling themselves to dish out permits at their will, with no consideration for the public.

November 2 — An editorial entitled "Is Tampa in Florida?" hit at the ward heelers for their open disregard of state law in allotting liquor permits to suit their personal and political whims.

November 9 — An interview with the head of the county economic development committee brought out clearly and factually that lack of adequate harbor facilities and promotion of shipping were due to the pulling and hauling by the ward politicians in the city government.

November 27 — Series of seven stories described how city manager government worked, and pointed out that a small council elected city-wide was superior to large legislative body elected from the wards.

December 5 — A story based on records cited small amount of money put in budget during last 10 years for sewer maintenance and then showed crumbling sewer lines and breakdown of disposal machinery as a result.

December 10 — Another story from the records traced how the aldermanic majority bloc time and again overruled the mayor on projects benefiting the city as a whole, and how it ousted the mayor's department heads who opposed district boondoggling.

January 25 — First of series of three stories showed how seven members of aldermanic majority bloc were elect-

ed by a combined total of 5,623 out of 22,495 registered voters in a population of 125,000. I might say here
that rotten government is not a great persuader in
getting apathetic citizens to vote.

January 26 — Second of series cited from the records to
show how majority bloc had retarded the development
of the districts of the minority members of the board.

January 27 — The third story, an interview with members of the majority bloc, in reply to questions and in
the face of the record, brought confessions from the
ward heelers that only a few streets had received a
thin coating of asphalt and that only a few street
lights and storm sewers had been installed.

I have cited only the key stories developed during the
campaign. We printed dozens of others. But throughout,
we relied upon the records. Too much was at stake for
us to gamble on anything but careful, factual and honest
reporting.

Time and again the aldermen lashed at the *Tribune*
and at our reporters. Each time we replied, calmly reciting the record. Once I sent a cameraman to a public meeting to obtain new pictures of the aldermen. The chairman
of the board and the brains of the majority bloc demanded
to know why the camerman was there. The cameraman
told him. Whereupon, the chairman put his feet on the
aldermanic table and thumbed his nose at the cameraman. The cameraman lifted his camera, gave him the
flash and caught him with his hand still at his nose,
although he had tried to remove it. We ran that picture
on Page 1 the next morning with a simple caption that
read: "Chairman So-and-So as he presided at a meeting
of Tampa's Board of Aldermen last night." It was the
height of ridicule, and I can assure you that it attracted
attention. The chairman immediately issued a red-hot
statement to the effect that this was his customary way
of stroking his hair, although he was nearly bald. Furthermore, he called a hurried meeting of the majority bloc
and it, like puppets on a string, also issued a long state-

ment declaring that the chairman often stroked his hair that way. The *Tribune* was delighted to print both statements.

Our second point of attack, as outlined previously, was a comparison of Tampa and its government with other cities. This was most effective.

We began this on September 10, 1944, with a series of three stories on St. Petersburg, our sister city 20 miles across Tampa Bay. Two of these stories showed St. Petersburg's growth was faster than Tampa's, pointed to the difference in city governments and revealed that St. Petersburg was building up a big postwar fund for improvements, whereas Tampa had neither funds nor plans for one. The inference, of course, was that unless Tampa did something about its ward heelers, St. Petersburg eventually would become the biggest city on the Florida West Coast.

The third story of the series was a *Tribune* staffer's account of the quiet, businesslike meeting of the St. Petersburg city council. We ran this on Page 1 alongside an account of the turbulent ward-heeling meeting of Tampa's aldermen. It was an impressive contrast.

The effect of this series was immediate. Both Tampa's Junior and Senior Chambers of Commerce began looking into the city government.

We followed this with two stories on Miami, comparing its fine city hospital operation to Tampa's, and its $4,500,000 postwar fund to Tampa's empty treasury. A third story compared the operation of Port Everglades with Tampa's mismanaged port. A fourth and fifth story, done by staffers, compared the city governments of Orlando and West Palm Beach with Tampa's ward heelers.

By this time, we had obtained information on 25 cities located from coast to coast that had the city manager form of government. Letters asking information from hundreds of public officials throughout the country brought, in almost every case, prompt, courteous and complete replies.

We began this series of 25 city manager stories on our Page 1 on January 4, 1945. From then through March 5, we hammered away with these stories under two-column heads at the bottom of our Page 1. Typical headlincs were:

CITY MANAGER GIVES DALLAS ITS MOST PROGRESSIVE ERA

HAMILTON, OHIO, CUTS EXPENSES 17 PER CENT UNDER CITY MANAGER

PASADENA TRIES ALL BUT PREFERS CITY MANAGER

TOLEDO OUSTS ALDERMEN FOR CITY MANAGER

FORT WORTH HIRES CITY MANAGER AFTER JURY REPORT

FLINT, MICHIGAN, GETS LOWER TAXES WITH CITY MANAGER

BANGOR, MAINE, GETS RID OF CITY POLITICS WITH CITY MANAGER

COLORADO SPRINGS PROUD OF ITS CITY MANAGER SETUP

BOSTON PAPER SAYS CRITICISM OF CITY MANAGER JUST BUNK

These stories quickly got under the skins of the ward heelers. At a public meeting, one of the majority bloc charged that the *Tribune* was painting only rosy pictures of the successful city manager governments, that we were carefully ignoring the failures. We came right back with a detailed survey on Page 1 showing that while the city manager plan had failed in 28 cities, it had been a huge success in 622 cities.

Then one of the ward heelers publicly challenged the *Tribune* to tell the story of Kansas City and its city manager. We promptly accepted the challenge and ran a lengthy story on Page 1 under this headline:

CITY HALL INQUIRES ABOUT KANSAS CITY; HERE'S THE STORY

The story went on to tell how the Pendergast gang controlled both city council and city manager in Kansas City. It left the inference that the Kansas City situation was very much like the underworld control of Tampa's ward heelers. And it shut up the aldermen publicly once and for all on this question.

The Junior Chamber of Commerce was the first civic organization to react to the *Tribune*'s campaign. On September 15, the Jaycees invited two members of the ward council to debate with them the question of a charter change to obtain city-wide representation. After the debate, the Jaycees adopted a resolution declaring its intention to work for such a change.

On October 29, the board of directors of the Senior Chamber of Commerce announced that it would poll its membership on whether it wanted city manager government or the present Tampa ward system. On November 10, the Board of Realtors voted to make a study of the most desirable form of government for Tampa.

This hurt the ward heelers to the quick. The floor leader of the majority bloc of aldermen charged at a public meeting that the *Tribune* was taking advantage of the absence of the boys at war to gang up with war-rich bankers and merchants to sneak by a change in city government in defiance of the will of the people. In an editorial entitled "A Ward Councilman Erupts," the *Tribune* thanked the councilman for acknowledging that it had opened the fight against aldermanic government and declared that it was working in the open in an effort to have a better city for the veterans to return to after the war.

From this time on, public opinion against the ward heelers mounted. Here is a chronological account:

November 24 — Senior Chamber of Commerce voted 447 to 26 for city charter change. Of the 447 affirmative votes, 371 favored city manager government.

December 21 — Senior and Junior Chambers of Commerce united and appointed joint steering committee to work for charter change.

January 19 (1945) — Junior Chamber voted for city manager government.

January 24 — Senior Chamber decided to support city manager government.

February 16 — Tampa Bar Association debated the procedure of putting city charter change through legislature.

February 25 — Presidents of 11 women's civic organizations called for change in city government. Eight espoused city manager government; the other three demanded city-wide election of the council.

March 2 — Twenty-three Latin groups voted to oppose any change in the city government. I might say that Tampa had at that time approximately 40,000 residents of Cuban, Spanish and Italian descent, and that most of the majority bloc of the ward heelers represented their districts. These people usually voted in blocs, which is a perfect setting for the development of ward government and all the evils that go with it.

March 8 — President of the County Federation of Women's Clubs announced that the 2,200 members of the 32 affiliated clubs were strongly in favor of city manager government.

March 20 — Exchange Club came out for city manager government.

March 21 — Lions Club voted unanimously for city manager government.

March 21 — County Federation of Women's Clubs by unanimous vote called on legislative delegation to put through bill for charter change.

March 22 — Kiwanis and Optimist Clubs climbed on city manager bandwagon.

March 23 — Board of Realtors, Taxpayers Association and the City Tourist and Convention Bureau joined the parade for city manager government.

March 24 — Senior and Junior Chambers of Commerce named committees, with attorneys, to draw up city manager charter bill for legislature.

March 28 — Rotary and Civitan Clubs cast their support for city manager government.

March 28 — Pushing aside city business, the aldermanic ward heelers spent longer than an hour lashing at the Chambers and civic clubs. They charged the Chambers with driving business from Tampa, and they accused the civic clubs of failure to work for location of a proposed state medical school in Tampa.

March 30 — Two A. F. of L. Unions — the Technical Engineers and Draftsmen and the Seafarers International — voted to support city manager government.

During the next month, numerous other civic groups came out for city manager government. Speakers pro and con went on the radio almost every night. Everybody discussed it and everybody took sides. For one time, at least, the entire community of Tampa was conscious of its government. I can think of no more healthy sign for any community, and had that been the only achievement of the *Tribune's* crusade, it would have been worth all the time and trouble.

Tampa's charter bill for city manager government reached the legislature at Tallahassee on April 29, 1945. It immediately ran into trouble.

Two days later a delegation representing Tampa's Latin districts visited the legislature and presented its opposition to any change in city government. Tampa's legislators bent willing ears, they owed their election to the support from the ward heelers and to underworld influence. They ached to do their masters' bidding.

Thus began a behind-the-scenes tug-of-war in the state capital that almost wrecked the movement for better city government in Tampa. A delegation of Tampa businessmen and civic leaders called on the legislators, pointed to the tremendous public backing of the city manager bill and demanded that it be put through the legislature. They got no commitment.

Meanwhile, back in Tampa the ward heelers launched a move to get on the ballot a referendum with four types of city government. Florida's attorney general, who hailed from Tampa, quickly ruled this out. Then the ward heelers rushed through the board of aldermen a resolution calling their own charter election. This was perfectly legal and had it been permitted to go through, it would have utterly wrecked the new charter movement. The ward heelers would have drawn up the ballot, supervised the election and thoroughly dominated the situation.

This precipitated a compromise. On May 20, about 10 days before the end of the legislature, the *Tribune* printed a story on Page 1 pointing out that Tampa's delegation had done exactly nothing in behalf of local legislation, including the city charter bill. Not even this stirred Tampa's legislators to action. They had given their word to their ward-heeler masters that city manager government was out, and they stuck by it.

In the face of aldermanic maneuvering at home and the opposition of Tampa's legislators, the Tampa businessmen finally withdrew their city manager bill. A compromise charter bill was drawn, calling for the city-wide election of the mayor and seven city councilmen, the latter nominated by district. This bill stipulated that the Board of Aldermen must, within eight days after passage, call a referendum to be held within 60 days. Since the objectionable city manager clause had been eliminated, Tampa's legislators finally, under renewed pressure from businessmen and civic clubs, put through the bill on the last day of the legislative session.

Even though it was a compromise, the bill represented defeat for the ward heelers; providing, of course, that supporters of good government could carry the election. The referendum was called for July 31, less than a year from the time the *Tribune* first launched its campaign.

Businessmen and civic clubs hurriedly organized a Good Government League, which went on the radio and stayed there. The ward heelers put up a fight, even to the last, but it was apparent by this time that they had shot their wad in the legislature. The mayor, silent up to this time, came out for the charter change. One member of the aldermanic majority bloc broke away and issued a statement endorsing the change. The other six ward heelers got into a secret fight over who was to be boss.

The *Tribune*, meanwhile, kept up its pressure with almost daily stories based on the record. One of these stories revealed that a member of the majority bloc had obtained personal control, through political finagling, of Tampa's Negro taxicab business. Another story related how nine aldermen failed to attend a meeting called by the mayor to map plans for expansion of the waterworks.

Came election day finally, and the vote was:

For the new charter 11,586
Opposed 5,969

It was a complete rout for the ward heelers, and crusading journalism had won a great victory for the people.

4.

Cleaning Up
the Mess

THE CHANGE OF TAMPA'S CITY GOVERNMENT from the ward-heeling aldermanic system to a strong mayor with a citywide elected Board of Representatives did not automatically cure the evils of 17 years of municipal corruption.

Firemen still could not get a steady stream of water to the second floor, in the event of a fire, and there were many weeks during the year when householders could neither water their lawns nor get more than a dribble from their kitchen sinks.

Big airliners still had difficulty in landing at Tampa's tiny airport and, with the end of World War II in 1945 and the shutdown of one shipyard and the slowdown of two others, the future appeared dim for Tampa's port, even though it was the finest landlocked harbor south of Philadelphia and stood at the threshold of great potential trade with Latin America.

The city's sewer system, built in 1926 for a city of 50,000, was so deteriorated that effluent bubbled up in the streets, and the septic tanks in the bulging suburbs presented a major menace to the health of 200,000 people.

Furthermore, the city was still locked into 19 square miles of land, and it still was dominated politically by Ybor City.

After 35 years of experience in Florida newspapering, I can assure you that you have to prod the average politician in such nonglamorous civic improvements as these. The average politician is concerned with just one objective in life, that of getting himself re-elected, and he much prefers civic projects above the ground to those under the ground, and preferably those on which he can inscribe his name for political posterity.

One Tampa politician had spent many years as a county commissioner and all the public funds he could get his hands on were used in building sidewalks in which he inscribed his name in big letters. And Florida had one recent governor who had his name erected in big road signs on every routine road project from Pensacola to Key West.

So *The Tampa Tribune* undertook five new crusades. Three of them bore immediate results, but the other two required full-fledged campaigns of four and eight years of political ups and downs.

The lack of water, of course, was the immediate problem, since it constituted a fire hazard to the entire city, discouragement to new industry, a health menace through inadequately working plumbing, and a constant source of discomfort and nuisance to almost the entire citizenry.

The *Tribune* presented this graphically in stories and pictures of weak streams from fire hoses, of pencil-sized trickles in kitchens and bathrooms, of inadequate treatment facilities at the river intake plant and inadequate storage tanks to build up a supply of water ahead of actual usage, and of technical interviews with water department officials as to the reasons for the low pressure. For a solid year hardly an issue of the *Tribune* went to press without some story pointing up the city's water problem, with all its ramifications.

This relentless newspaper pressure on our public servants finally paid off. Our City Board of Representatives, prodded into action by an aroused public, authorized the mayor to purchase the site of an old electric power dam on the river, and voted in rapid succession $200,000 to repair the dam, then $3,000,000 and $1,500,000 for replacement and expansion of water mains as well as for enlargement and new facilities at the water treatment plant. The impetus of the campaign carried on and in 1955 the board voted $4,300,000 more for waterworks expansion. Today Tampa has as fine a supply of water as will be found in any city in the United States.

The *Tribune* pointed its crusades for a modern airport and development of its port at the legislature and not at Tampa's city government, even though these were municipal affairs. The reason, of course, was politics, with its ugly affiliate of political privilege.

Years before, Pan American Airways had sought to locate in Tampa because it was most accessible to Latin America. But the ward politicians demanded their cut, and Pan American with its multimillion payroll went to Miami. Since then the aviation committees of the City Board and the Tampa Chamber of Commerce had waged a running fight, with nobody able to agree on anything. On top of it all, Tampa's port was slowly stagnating and the possibility of suddenly dumping three wartime shipyards, with rich industrial potential, into the middle of the political pot, would precipitate a boiling-out process that certainly would make some public servants and their friends rich for no reason at all.

So the *Tribune* advocated bills in the legislature calling for the creation of aviation and port authorities; members would be appointed by the governor from a list of leading citizens recommended by Tampa's Round Table of civic club presidents. This would have the effect of removing both our airport and port developments from politics.

At the same time, I assigned two teams of two reporters each to alert public opinion. One team toured Florida and Southeast ports, the other concentrated on the aviation development plans of other Florida cities. This double-barreled attack, carrying facts, figures and pictures, did the job. Both bills safely negotiated the legislature, and the Port Authority immediately began deepening the channel, building up harbor facilities and bringing new industry here. The Aviation Authority developed Drew Field, an old wartime air base, into a great air terminal, built one new airport building, and laid ground work for an $11,000,000 expansion of facilities. Tampa's port soon grew to fourth in the nation in dockside loadings and the airport had more traffic than either London or Paris.

The *Tribune*'s fight for new sewers took four years, from 1946 to 1950, and it produced considerably more headaches. For one thing, it required a bond issue of $12,000,000 to be paid for with an additional monthly charge on the basis of and included in the water bill. Any time you crusade for a new tax, you had better provide yourself with plenty of aspirin.

The rapid increase in population had brought problems that earlier city governments had not been able to foresee. Sewage disposal facilities serving only the downtown section and small older areas of the city, were overloaded to the point that treatment was nil. This meant that much of the city was on septic tanks which, because the elevation above sea level is so slight, refused to work properly during rainy seasons. The result was pollution of the river, the bay and even suburban lakes by the virtually raw sewage. Health hazards were increased when effluent overflowed from inadequate septic tanks into rain-flooded streets.

The *Tribune* graphically reported all this in stories and pictures, and many of the latter sickened our readers at the breakfast table. We even persuaded health authorities to count bacteria of the raw sewage in the river, the bay and even in the streets. But sometimes it takes more than bacteria to offset a new tax. And it took series after series of raw sewage stories before the people were finally persuaded that our city could not possibly prosper without adequate sewers, and then, after the victorious vote, it took more series to prod our politicians into actual building of the sewers. You see, our public servants do not like to sit on the political platform and have their opponents point a condemning finger and shout, "There sits the punk who put the heinous sewer tax on you." But the *Tribune* went on to fight for and win an $11,000,000 additional sewer project for our suburbs, then began fighting for a $3,000,000 sanitary sewer system to carry off the surplus water of heavy summer rains. Such is the life of a crusading newspaper editor.

The crusade for suburb annexation required eight years and we suffered two defeats at the polls before finally winning out in the legislature in 1953. In this the *Tribune* was arrayed against a combination of wealthy suburban home owners and business interests, particularly the oil companies, who objected strenuously to assuming their rightful share of community taxes. The oil companies, owners of many of the key corners in the thickly populated suburbs, on two occasions organized telegraphic campaigns and bombarded Tallahassee with sizzling messages, many of them critical of the *Tribune*.

During these eight years, we printed more than 1,500 stories and pictures on the great need of annexation. We keyed our campaign to the great necessity of building sewers, streets, parks, playgrounds and drainage facilities in the suburbs, and time and again we reminded everybody concerned that those who earned their living in the city were obligated to bear their proper responsibility in government and taxes. We printed series after series on how municipal population often was the basis used by state and Federal authorities in allotting postal and housing funds, and by large industries in selecting sites for new developments. We printed additional stories on how other American cities had benefited through suburb annexation.

Once during the campaign, suburban opponents charged that the *Tribune*'s interest was solely in the matter of getting larger advertising allotments based on the same municipal population. We replied that this was untrue, that newspaper advertising is allotted solely on the joint basis of the total population of a metropolitan area, and not by city limits, and of the newspaper's circulation in that area.

After our second defeat at the polls, due mainly to the apathy of the voters, the *Tribune* changed the direction of its crusade and we made suburban annexation the main issue in the 1952 election. The people responded this time by electing a legislative delegation pledged to annexation. A bill was adopted in 1953 which increased the area of Tampa from 21 to 68 square miles and added approximately 91,000 people to the city's population. The *Tribune* further paid half of the $15,000 cost of a special Federal census, which gave Tampa an official population of 216,781 and made us the second city in Florida and the forty-ninth in the nation.

The police always are the political football in a politically inspired city government, and such was the case in Tampa. During the 15 years following World War II, Tampa had no less than six police chiefs. Three lost their positions in gambling cleanups; the fourth was fired when the *Tribune* uncovered hidden police docket records showing that, while drunk, he had particpiated in several accidents; the fifth, a really competent officer, lost out in a shuffle of administrations; and the sixth went by the wayside through sheer incompetence.

Throughout all this, the department was rocked by scandal after scandal. Several officers were convicted and went to jail for robbing Tampa's business houses; a policeman bailiff was convicted of bribery; his successor was fired in a shady shakedown involving a gypsy girl;

and several more officers were indicted by the Federal government in Negro moonshine pay-offs.

Of course the *Tribune*, with its fondness for crusading, had a field day on its Page 1. On a Sunday in early March, 1955, there walked into our office two men, who said they had stopped in at one of Tampa's Skid Row joints for a Saturday night bottle of beer and had found the place jammed with drunken juveniles. They said they telephoned the police and that five minutes after their call the phone rang in the joint and its bartender, after answering it, shouted to the crowd that there was going to be a police raid. When the police finally arrived, these men said the place was empty.

We informed the men that, while we believed them, we could not accuse our police department of such a serious charge as special protection for a drinking joint without further and more official corroboration. After some discussion, the two men agreed to go to the same joint the following Saturday night and telephone us if they found the same juvenile drinking.

Came Saturday night and the men did telephone us. We promptly dispatched our two youngest staffers to the joint, hoping they would be taken for just two more drinking juveniles. On their arrival, the two men again telephoned police and reported the infraction of the law. A few minutes later, in walked a police captain. While he chatted with the bartender, most of the juveniles quietly slipped out of the place, even though they had to brush past the police captain. There was no raid and no arrests.

The two young staffers returned to the *Tribune* and under my direction each wrote a separate account of what he saw in the joint. But we didn't print one word of the story that night. Instead, we waited until Monday night, giving the police every opportunity to bring a charge against the joint and its operator.

Then, when nothing happened, we broke the story under a modest two-column headline in our Tuesday morning editions, carrying on the inside pages the separate eye-witness accounts of our two young staffers. It created an immediate storm. Our switchboard was jammed all day and we received more telephone calls, all commendatory, than on any other story we have handled in my 30 years with the *Tribune*.

That afternoon, the mayor called a public conference with the police chief and the captain involved. During the conference, the captain admitted that he and other police officers had been receiving free meals and other favors from this joint. The mayor promptly ordered a crack down on all juvenile drinking; a cleanup of Skid Row; the arrest of the operator of the joint; and an end to free meals and free drinks for city police officers.

The crack down and cleanup lasted for several days. The police vice squad, later joined by sheriff's deputies, nightly raided various Skid Row joints and arrested so many, most of them on vagrancy charges, that for two weeks our city and county jails were crammed and the prisoners had to sleep on the floors.

But such crack downs and cleanups were only momentary in the daily life of Tampa's police department. Over the years, the conditions constantly went from bad to worse, simply because the evils in the department were fundamental. Here are just a few headlines of the many stories the *Tribune* printed in 1957 concerning Tampa's police:

SCANDALS FROM "COPS AND ROBBERS" TO NICKEL SNITCHING PLAGUE POLICE

DRUNK COP FIRED HERE, ONE HELPING HIM IS SUSPENDED

COP SUSPENDED 10 DAYS FOR BEATING WOMAN, WHO SHOWS MAYOR HER BRUISES

COP CAUGHT AFTER HIGH SPEED CHASE, SUSPENDED

COP, ACCUSED IN LOVE TRYST, QUITS; ANOTHER SUSPENDED

RAID HERE BARES JUVENILE DRINKING AT NIGHT CLUB UNOFFICIALLY GUARDED BY COP

COURTEOUS COP, FIRED FOR STEALING, SUED BY CREDIT UNION SIGNERS

POLICE HEAD REVEALS NEW COMPLAINTS AGAINST COP

Such stories were almost daily occurrences in the *Tribune*, so in September I detached one of my veteran research reporters and assigned him to dig into the fundamental causes of the apparent breakdown in the city's law enforcement. Early in November, the mayor of Tampa suddenly discovered what my reporter was doing while camping in the police department and the city comptroller's office, and he hurriedly appeared before the city board of representatives and asked for an appropriation of $15,000 to employ Northwestern University to make a survey of Tampa's police operation. This is not unusual since our public servants always, if they can, seek to beat a crusading newspaper to the punch. They like to boast on the election platform that they, and not the newspaper, originated the needed reforms of government.

The City Board approved the mayor's request without debate, but this, of course, did not stop the *Tribune*'s crusading research. On January 1, 1958, we began printing a series of stories under the general headline,

A REPORT TO THE PEOPLE

on our Page 1, and the specific headlines on the stories follow:

BEST U. S. POLICE FORCES SEPARATED FROM POLITICS; TAMPA DEPARTMENT IS NOT

BEST U. S. POLICE OPERATE INDEPENDENTLY OF MAYOR; IN TAMPA HE'S THE BOSS

TOP POLICE FORCES EXPAND TRAINING; TAMPA'S ROOKIES GET ONE WEEK BEFORE DUTY

TOP POLICE FORCES SPEND CONSIDERABLE TIME, EFFORT ATTRACTING GOOD RECRUITS

TAMPA STANDS IN POSITION TO TURN "ADEQUATE" POLICE FORCE INTO ONE OF THE BEST

The tone of these stories remained constructive, even though they resulted from one scandal after another. The secret of successful crusading is to dig into scandal and then supply the constructive answer. That we did this was proved conclusively in May when Northwestern University's report, containing 174 recommendations, substantiated every one of our findings. Tampa's mayor immediately began the big job of putting recommendations into force, with the *Tribune* watching over his shoulder. And you can rest assured that should he falter in the months to come, even in the matter of yielding the mayor's power over the police, we'll be ready to back him up to the fire of public opinion and singe him a bit.

I have given you only a few of the *Tribune*'s many crusades in municipal affairs. We undertook many more, some major and some minor. We campaigned against sorry conditions at Tampa's municipal hospital and in September, 1958, the city opened a handsome $4,000,000 wing, giving our citizens 325 additional rooms. We also took a hand in Tampa's traffic problems and fought for and won new parking facilities and one-way traffic to speed an ever growing number of cars and trucks through our downtown sections. Our stories and pictures of squalid shacks and outdoor toilets in the heart of our city resulted in a public housing project for Negroes scarcely five blocks from our courthouse, and this, of course, brought us the headache of a fight with realtors and owners of the shacks over the question of private vs. public enterprise.

This was only one of many headaches during the bitter

political fight over the restoration of the city government of Tampa to its citizens, and our big question is, "Was it worth it?" And was the *Tribune* justified in giving all-out leadership to this community fight? This can be answered by briefly listing Tampa's municipal achievements during the decade 1950–60:

1. The 1960 population of Tampa was 274,407, showing a growth of 150,334, or 117 per cent since 1950, which led all cities of the United States. The federal census showed 94,771 housing units in the city as compared to 40,614 in 1950, a gain of 54,157 for the decade.

2. Business likewise broke all records in the decade. Employment jumped from 82,250 to 127,591, a gain of 55 per cent; bank clearings from $338,058,655 to $1,764,804,808, up 422 per cent; electric power consumers from 83,699 to 138,537, up 77.5 per cent; port tonnage from 5,436,202 to 13,400,403, up 147 per cent; and even postal receipts from $1,850,206 to $3,545,913, up 146 per cent.

3. During the decade, more than $70,000,000 in new industry moved into the city and there was more than $100,000,000 expansion in existing industry. And in September, 1960, Florida's new state university, the University of South Florida, opened the doors of $8,500,000 worth of new buildings in Tampa's north suburbs to 1,965 freshmen. Meanwhile, a contract was let for a $2,000,000 dormitory and the State Board of Control projected $9,500,000 in additional new buildings for the next four years.

4. The city government meanwhile had spent $5,000,000 on six new bridges spanning Hillsborough River, $1,000,000 on new fire stations, $4,000,000 on a new hospital wing, and was busy constructing a new $2,000,000 police station and a $1,000,000 nurses

home. In addition, City Hall had purchased a 20-acre downtown site from the Atlantic Coast Line Railroad for $5,000,000 and had on its drawing board plans for a $2,000,000 auditorium on this site and an additional $1,500,000 bridge leading to Davis Islands, the swanky pumped-up island suburb in the middle of Tampa Bay.

5. In addition, during the decade, the city government put $28,500,000 into sanitary sewers, $10,000,000 into storm sewers, $15,000,000 into street paving and $5,000,000 into a waterworks addition. On the city's drawing boards were such projects as $11,000,000 more for sanitary sewers, $10,000,000 more for storm sewers, $10,000,000 more for street paving, and an additional $35,000,000 to be used for access streets to the $50,000,000 expressway planned for Tampa by the state.

6. The city also had spent $6,500,000 on Tampa's International Airport in the last decade and construction was underway on an additional $16,000,000 expansion, which promised one of the nation's finest jet airports. Millions also had been spent on playgrounds and swimming pools throughout the city and on a new baseball park for Tampa's professional baseball club and for the use of the Cincinnati Reds during the big league spring training season.

7. But more important, public opinion now counts in our city. Any group of citizens may have a say in our municipal government, and our candidates for city political jobs now work for betterment of the city as a whole and not for political privilege as in the old ward-heeling aldermanic system.

8. Most important of all, however, clean government has renewed the faith of our citizens in Tampa, and a new

civic spirit is rustling the palmettoes from one end of our community to the other. We are a city on the march and I can assure you that there is no finer place in America to live.

As for the crusading newspaper and its editor, let me put it this way. I know hundreds of newspaper editors from coast to coast, but I know not a rich one. But I do know there can be no more complete satisfaction than the knowledge that you have had an integral part in the progress of your fellow citizen in the free American way of life.

5.

Tackling
Syndicated Gambling

IF YOU WANT TO LIVE A QUIET, PEACEFUL LIFE, stay away
from crusading against the underworld. If you want to
keep your hair intact and your nervous system unscarred,
shut your eyes to organized crime in your community.

In the middle of *The Tampa Tribune*'s crusade against
organized gambling, a prominent young businessman telephoned me and asked why a leading local financier had
called and urged that he not participate in the crime commission, which had been organized by an aroused citizenry
to fight organized gambling in our community.

I replied that big business interests often had clients
who rented places as gambling joints and who otherwise
profited from organized crime; but that he owed it to good
citizenry and to his community to make the sacrifice for
the crime commission. This young man fortunately stayed
on the crime commission, but I cite this case to show you
the power of the almighty business dollar, which forgives
most anything that shows a profit.

On another occasion, each afternoon for two weeks a

half dozen hoodlums gathered at the Yacht Club riding stables in Tampa, where my eight-year-old son was accustomed to emulate the cowboy movie star, Roy Rogers; they did nothing worse than pull knives and make alarming gestures. I asked a friend in the F.B.I. to check this and he reported back that it was purely intimidation on the part of the local gambling mob. I promptly called a certain elected official to my office, informed him that I never had owned a gun, but if one hair of my family was disturbed because of what I was printing in the *Tribune,* I would go to the nearest pawnshop, buy a gun and shoot two public officials, and that he could tell the other one. The next day the hoodlums disappeared from the Yacht Club.

But this did not stop the gang's personal intimidation of me. Mystery cars constantly parked at my home and followed me everywhere. And for one solid year, I got little sleep. The cowardly hoodlums would ring me every hour on the hour throughout the night in an effort to crack my nerves. I could not shut off my telephone simply because a working editor must keep his connection with the news wires every hour of every day. One of the racketeers once telephoned me at three o'clock in the morning and demanded to know why I didn't print a story about the president of a bank playing poker at the Yacht Club. It so happened that I knew the wife of the bank president had been ill and that he had not left his home at night for many months, and furthermore, that nobody played poker at the Yacht Club, anyway.

Big law firms took a hand in the deadly game and even ministers of churches added to the pressure, which I shall explain later. The lawyer for a convicted racketeer, in his appeal to the Supreme Court, described Florida's newspapers, and particularly *The Tampa Tribune,* as "vicious," "malicious," "glaring," "sensational," "denunciatory," "odious," "inflammatory," "abhorrent," and a few other similar endearing terms, all because we had dared to print the facts as they had developed in the case involving this underworld character who had flaunted Florida's laws in the face of Florida citizens.

The *Tribune* was threatened with at least 25 libel suits, but none ever materialized, simply because our stories were factual and based on privileged records, and there is an old adage which warns not to come into court unless you come with clean hands. My reporters were constantly threatened. One enraged sheriff, who was hauled before the Governor for a hearing resulting from our gambling stories, publicly threatened to put the reporter who wrote the stories under his jail if he ever caught him in his county.

Another of my reporters was summoned as a witness before the State's Attorney who was investigating gambling conditions as the result of stories written by this reporter. The Attorney demanded to know the source of my reporter's information. The reporter declined. The Attorney then informed the reporter that if he didn't name his sources, under the law he could be put in jail for contempt.

"I'm sorry," said the reporter, "the only thing in all the world owned by an honest newspaperman is his integrity, and I'm damned sure not going to give that up."

I immediately alerted the *Tribune*'s lawyers and then I notified this Attorney that if he dared to put my reporter into jail, the *Tribune* would immediately begin printing on its Page 1 a series of stories by this reporter on the conditions in that jail. This, of course, put a quick end to the Attorney's threats.

After we had watched with more than passing interest the local 1947 election in which the underworld swept into office every one of its candidates, we began our crusade. During the preceding 17 years of corrupt, ward-heeling aldermanic government and two years interlude between changing systems of city government, organized gambling had firmly entrenched itself in every walk of our community. Bolita, the Spanish derivative for the old numbers racket wherein the winning number, chosen from 1 to 100, paid odds of 90, 80 and 70 to 1, and "Cuba," the Cuban national lottery which was "thrown" at Havana every Saturday, were widespread. You couldn't get your hair cut or your shoes shined in downtown Tampa without having to brush off a half dozen peddlers. Every business house had its bolita agent and almost every neighborhood block its peddler, often times your maid or yardman. The racket had spread beyond Tampa's suburbs into the state, and Tampa became the bolita banking capital of Florida, wherein the hundreds of "bankers" in other cities laid off the surplus play on numbers with the hoods in Ybor City.

Federal authorities, who at that time could not intervene but kept a constant watch on the rackets, privately informed us that the total bolita play in Tampa topped $10,000,000 a year and they estimated the pay-off to public officials at $1,000,000 a year. It goes without saying that a criminal racket of this size could not possibly have been built up without the active connivance of public officials. It goes further without saying that a criminal racket of this size also had to control elections, regardless of the cost and even if it took bloodshed. Therefore, candidates in Tampa always looked to the underworld for the winning support, and always we had a list of at least 20 unsolved gang murders, some of them done in cold blood in front of terrified spectators.

I assigned virtually my entire staff to the story, and they spent weeks checking every available record, which consisted largely of figures on police arrests (which were few and far between) and they talked with hundreds of characters, from the snootiest bolita "banker" down to the lowliest peddler and everybody else even remotely connected with the rackets. We finally printed a series of 16 stories under modest two-column headlines on Page 1 and under the by-line "By the Tribune Staff," simply because all of them had worked on them and I did not want to expose any one man to the vengeful wrath of this bloodthirsty mob. These stories showed clearly:

1. That Tampa's blood-drenched underworld was ruled by a gambling syndicate of the dreaded Sicilian Mafia,

popularly known as the "Black Hand," which special-
ized in kidnaping and arson before it got into the
gambling rackets.

2. That this syndicate reaped huge profits from its
   $10,000,000 a year numbers racket.

3. That it spent an average of $100,000 on each local
   election and that it was easily the No. 1 political power
   in our community.

4. That its leaders never were arrested and that its hoodlums never went to jail and thus had to have the earn-
   est cooperation of law enforcement officers and public
   officials.

Our stories may have been printed under modest two-
column headlines, but the explosion that followed was
anything but modest. And it started a bitter fight for good
government in Florida that is still going on. Twice during
the summer of 1956 Governor Leroy Collins publicly called
upon Florida's 67 sheriffs to comb the state for the bolita
racketeers and put them in jail.

Public officials denied our stories. A grand jury, under
domination of officials who owed their election to the
underworld, investigated and also denied them. And on
top of it all, a committee of preachers from Tampa's Ministerial Association investigated and in a public statement
declared that there was no such thing as an organized
gambling underworld in our city. I did not particularly
blame these men of the cloth, as their information had
come from those Sunday hypocrites, who fatten the church
coffers both for a show and for the political privilege that
it may bring them. As a whole, newspaper editors are
much closer to life in the raw and therefore are not so
naive in accepting the word of others.

Anyway, it looked bad for the *Tribune* and you would
be amazed at the number of political hangers-on, some
even respectable, who joined in the rock throwing. We had
been forced out on a limb with this crusade, and as the
limb began to bend a little they became braver. Then, in

December, 1948, one of Tampa's bigger gambling bosses, the political fixer for the syndicate, was mowed down in typical gangland style by sawed-off shotgun blasts in one of the city's downtown sections. And that really blew the lid off. In effect, it neatly transposed the *Tribune* and the hypocrites on the limb, and did we saw it off!

Since this particular gambler was the political fixer for the syndicate — and by "fixer" I mean the man who arranged the payoffs to the politicians — I reasoned that he must have kept some sort of records. I set out to get those records. I sent three reporters, all veteran newsmen, one after the other, to see the slain gambler's wife and his two brothers. But the family was suspicious and refused to talk, which was not unusual. It has been my experience over the years that all those connected even faintly with the Mafia are, for reasons of blood, intimidated. But finally, one of my columnists came to me, said he had some connections in Ybor City, and volunteered to make a try at the gambler's family.

Several days later — on the Saturday night before Christmas — my office telephone rang. It was the columnist telephoning from the home of the widow of the slain gambler. He reported that both she and the gambler's two brothers were willing to tell all. I roused a public court reporter from bed and sent him, a notary public and another veteran reporter out to the home. And there, over the kitchen table, the gambler's widow and brothers told the whole story of Tampa's underworld, how the gambling was conducted, how the pay-offs to the politicians were made, and revealed the names of leaders and the small fry of the syndicate. Furthermore, the family turned over to my reporters a shoe box filled with the dead gambler's records.

The result, of course, was a new series of stories that threw utter confusion into the massed ranks of the underworld, and once and for all convinced the people of Tampa that the *Tribune* was absolutely right in its original series of gambling stories. From that time on, public opinion rode with us.

In the slain gambler's shoe box of records, there was a list of political pay-offs, which included the names of no less than eight of our public officials with the weekly amounts paid to them. We could not, of course, print these names, simply because of the law of libel. The fact that they were found in the gambler's shoe box and were purported to be political pay-offs did not constitute either privilege or proof. But just the same, that pay-off list made political history in Tampa and served as the actual springboard for our plunge into the turbulent surf of clean-up journalism.

In our series of stories based on the slain gambler's shoe box of records, we made much of "the list," using quotes around the two words throughout, even though we did not use the actual names. This caught the imagination of our public opinion and aroused so much public discussion that the police committee of the City Board of Representatives requested it. After photostating it for our own private records, the *Tribune* turned "the list" over to the police committee, which promptly placed it in the city clerk's office as a public record. We announced all this in a Page 1 story, whereupon Tampans by the hundreds trekked into the clerk's office to look at "the list." Each day we printed the approximate number of citizens who had viewed "the list" until this finally became too much for some of our public servants. They suddenly swooped in, seized "the list" and buried it in the confines of a grand jury, which at that time, because of the pressure of our stories, was casually "investigating" — and I deliberately put quotes around this word — gambling.

When the furor from "the list" eventually died down, we followed in early 1949 with a new series of Page 1 stories, prepared by the entire *Tribune* news staff, which traced the pattern of Tampa's unsolved gambling murders over the last 20 years. There were at least 15 of these killings directly due to gambling and another half dozen mysterious murders that certainly were due in part to the manipulations within the underworld. This series tied the murders definitely to the Mafia and also to a national arson gang and an international dope ring.

Right in the middle of our gambling crusade, a Federal narcotics report originating in Kansas City had publicly fingered a number of the members of Tampa's gambling underworld as members of the national Mafia. Furthermore, on two occasions, my reporters had watched Tampa leaders of the Mafia assemble in their secret meeting place, and on a third occasion an anonymous letter writer had sent me a list of all the Tampa members of the Mafia.

Tampa's membership in the national Mafia figured again in the national news in January of 1958 when District Attorney Frank S. Hogan of New York issued a nationwide alarm for the pickup of a prominent Tampa racketeer, for questioning in the slaying of Albert Anastasia, the executioner of the old Murder, Inc., mob, who was shot to death the previous October as he sat in a midtown New York barbershop. Furthermore, this prominent Tampa racketeer was also identified as one of the 65 underworld characters who were arrested in a "crime convention" in Apalachin, New York, in November, 1957, even though he used a phoney name.

Meanwhile, as the *Tribune* hammered away at its cleanup of the rackets in Tampa, we also branched out into Florida. I sent a reporter to Jacksonville, 200 miles away, to look into the Federal license records for our State. My reporter thumbed through some 8,000 Federal license records and found 627 license payments on slot machines, which were illegal in Florida. We then printed those 627 names and addresses. I tell you this to show that crusading journalism is not all glamorous work, mixed up with a few threats, but that a lot of it is laborious and meticulous checking of the public records.

We reported 115 slot machines in Okaloosa County, a little county in North Florida, about 300 miles from Tampa. I sent a staff writer there and his story, printed on our Page 1, reported slot machines everywhere, in bus stations, in laundries, even next door to schools. A group of citizens in Okaloosa County, led by churchmen, immediately organized a Better Government League and joined the *Tribune* in its fight for good government. These citizens had the *Tribune* stories printed in pamphlets, which were distributed to every citizen in that community.

During the next few months, the *Tribune* sent four different reporters into Okaloosa County and each in turn reported on wide-open gambling conditions. Finally, the Governor of Florida, under pressure from the Okaloosa County Better Government League, not to speak of continuous Page 1 stories in the *Tribune,* summoned the sheriff of that county and two constables before him in a public hearing. He put them on probation for 60 days. Three weeks later another *Tribune* reporter slipped into Okaloosa County and the next day we printed a story reporting that open gambling still was being operated. The Governor then removed the sheriff and two constables and appointed new law enforcement officers. A grand jury was summoned and it indicted five operators of gambling casinos.

Altogether, various *Tribune* reporters visited 20 Florida counties, investigated gambling conditions and reported their findings in our newspaper. Our reporters ranged from Key West to Jacksonville to Pensacola, a distance of a thousand miles. Of the 20 counties investigated, we found only two in which the law enforcement officers were conscientiously on the job and in which there was no organized gambling.

Here are the typical headlines that appeared over our stories from two of the 18 counties in which we found organized gambling:

**TRIBUNE MAN GREETED BY SLOTS IN BUS STATION AND
    HOTEL IN OKALOOSA COUNTY**

**FT. WALTON VIOLATES STATE LAW BY LICENSING GAMBLING
    DENS AND SLOT MACHINES**

FT. WALTON HOPES FOR BOOM BUILT ON GAMBLING DENS, SLOTS AND EASY DIVORCES

OKALOOSA CITIZENS FIGHT HOPELESS BATTLE AGAINST STRONG GAMBLING RULERS

OKALOOSA GAMBLING DENS SHUT; STATE OFFICIAL FINDS SPOTS CLOSED AFTER TRIBUNE STORIES; SAYS THEY'LL STAY CLOSED

LAKE CITY POLICE FORCE GOES OVER HEAD OF CHIEF, MAYOR AND STOPS GAMBLING

ALL TRIBUNES ARE STOLEN IN LAKE CITY AFTER GAMBLING STORY

DISCHARGED POLICEMAN IN BIG LAKE CITY GAMBLING RAID MAY NOT GET HEARING

Once, during this state campaign, the *Tribune* got into the bad graces of some of Gainesville's leading citizens when it sent a reporter into Gainesville's Country Club and reported that University of Florida students were feeding their spending money, sent to them by their parents, into slot machines. The Country Club hurriedly disposed of the machines, but its leaders were quite bitter since the slot proceeds paid the club deficits and kept down the size of the dues.

Whenever a *Tribune* reporter investigated gambling in a county, one of two results usually happened. A group of citizens and churchmen would organize a "Better Government League" and launch an immediate investigation of public officials; or else apathetic public officials would suddenly come to life, a grand jury would be called, and the gamblers and guilty politicians prosecuted.

This again shows the effect of honest, fair and factual reporting against public evil. Most citizens of any country are honest and want to live under honest government in clean communities. And after many years of personally encountering this deep feeling for honest government in the American people, I firmly feel that it is the obligation of a free press to keep its citizens constantly advised of conditions of their government, regardless of whether the politicians like it or not.

Under the pressure from "Better Government Leagues" and the *Tribune,* the Governor of Florida over a period of a few weeks:

1. Removed from office two sheriffs and two constables on gambling charges
2. Put two other sheriffs on probation against continued gambling operations in their counties
3. Warned the sheriffs of all 67 of Florida's counties that he would dismiss them without a hearing if evidence of gambling in their communities was presented to him.

In addition, grand juries went to work investigating gambling and government conditions in five counties, and in two counties indicted both law officers and gamblers. That investigation of gambling has been going on ever since throughout Florida.

In the middle of this particular investigation, one of the Governor's leading henchmen, a prominent citrus grower, broke politically with him, called in the *Tribune*'s staff writer at Tallahassee and gave out a statement in which he accused two other of the Governor's henchmen, a prominent industrialist and an equally prominent gambler, of trying to take over Florida's state government for the general benefit of big-time organized gambling. Among other things, this man disclosed that the three henchmen of the Governor each had contributed $165,000 to his political campaign. This really opened the eyes of Florida's citizens to the cost of the state's big-time elections. For if three men alone will contribute $495,000 to a candidate's campaign fund, what is the over-all cost of winning a major Florida political office? And, of course, it spotlighted the question of what men expect in return for such contributions.

All of this created great public hullabaloo from Pensacola to Key West, but this was mild compared to the political hurricane which blew over the state when the U. S. Senate's Kefauver Committee, investigating national gambling, moved into Florida late in 1950 and held public hearings at Miami and Tampa. The Committee promptly subpoenaed the Governor to come before it and tell all, but he defied it and announced that state's rights prevailed over the Federal Government in Florida. But many law enforcement officials and hoodlums did parade publicly before the Senatorial Committee and their testimony left no doubt as to the power of the underworld operations in sunny Florida.

6.

Kefauver Joins
the Gangland Battle

I AM STRONG FOR CONGRESSIONAL INVESTIGATING COM-
MITTEES and I do not share in the criticism directed at
them by some of our so-called liberal elements. They are
the people's only protection against national evil and certain abuses in government, and if we eliminate Congress'
right to investigate, how can the people cope with these
evils and abuses? You cannot brush them under the carpet
and retain freedom.

Occasionally a member of Congress, himself, abuses
this privilege of investigating. The most notable modern
example of this was the case of the late Senator Joseph
McCarthy (Rep., Wis.). Yet public opinion always takes
a decisive hand in the deadly game and in the case
of Senator McCarthy it effectively disposed of him politically after a 30-day showing under the TV lights. I have
testified twice before congressional investigating committees and on one occasion I laid an abuse of government
squarely on the doorstep of Congress itself. Yet on both
occasions I was treated most courteously.

The usual procedure is for a newspaper crusade to light the fuse of congressional investigating. This was particularly true in the case of the two congressional investigating committees which dominated our national headlines during most of 1958. The Portland *Oregonian's* expose of the connection of Dave Beck with the underworld and the Des Moines *Register* and *Tribune* series on the abuses in labor-management relations sparked the committee, headed by Senator John L. McClellan (Dem., Ark.), that investigated labor and management. Both newspaper exposes, incidentally, won Pulitzer prizes. Similarly, the constant spotlighting of political privilege within the Federal regulatory commissions in Drew Pearson's column forced Representative Oren Harris' House Subcommittee on Legislative Oversight to rip the cover off Florida's Richard Mack in the Federal Communications Commission and to expose the political privilege of Sherman Adams, the White House aide, in the Federal Trade Commission.

Of keen interest to the newspaper profession were the national crusades of Sigma Delta Chi, the Associated Press Managing Editors Association and the American Society of Newspaper Editors against secrecy in Federal Government. This resulted in Congress appointing special committees headed by Representative John E. Moss (Dem., Calif.) and Senator Thomas C. Hennings, Jr., of Missouri, and in twin investigations that are going on at the present time.

Such was the case in the now famous Kefauver Senate Committee. Crusades against organized gambling and racketeering by *The Tampa Tribune* and other newspapers caused the U. S. Senate to name Senator Estes Kefauver (Dem., Tenn.) as chairman of a special investigating committee. That Senator Kefauver used this eventually to make a strong bid for the Democratic nomination as President is only incidental, but it does show clearly the popular power of congressional investigating with the American people.

In announcing that the Kefauver Committee would hold a two-day public hearing in the Federal courtroom in Tampa December 30–31, 1950, its spokesmen declared they had strong evidence that Tampa was one of the national centers of Mafia operation with definite connections with New Orleans, Chicago, Kansas City, Cleveland, Los Angeles and other cities. They pointed to a Mafia "convention" at Cleveland in 1928 and named two Tampa hoodlums as delegates.

Immediate result of this announcement was that seven of Tampa's leading racketeers took to their heels and two of them, the actual leaders of the gambling syndicate, never have returned to permanent Tampa residence. The *Tribune* also reported that a Tampa lawyer, who was secretary of the Florida State Racing Commission, and who had been summoned as a witness, had suddenly taken to his sickbed.

Newspaper coverage of a congressional investigating committee, of course, presents a first-rate problem. I assigned most of my staff in relay teams to report the questions and answers. In the case of key witnesses, I made arrangements with the official court reporter to buy his official reports at one dollar a page. On the day before the hearing, they were betting 3 to 1 in the courthouse that, because of the tremendous pressure on the *Tribune*, we would print only a lackadaisical report of the proceedings. We responded by printing 18 columns of testimony the first day and 16 columns the second day, a total of 34,000 words.

Actually, the Kefauver hearing really warmed the hearts of the *Tribune* newsmen, who had been on the firing line for many months and who had been subjected to untold pressures. We had written of the shadowy Mafia, the secret society of sudden death. The Kefauver Committee put the Mafia into the privileged records of the Federal Government. We had written of gangster murders and of our law enforcement officers' aversion to doing anything about them. The Kefauver Committee carefully spelled this out in the records. We had written of purported pay-offs by the gamblers to law enforcement officers and the Kefauver Committee wrote this into the Federal records.

Reference to the Mafia ran throughout the hearing. Here is part of the testimony of Tampa's police chief on this secret murder society:

Q. Do you believe there's a Mafia?

A. I believe it does exist.

Q. Can you give us a conception of what Mafia is?

A. I believe it consists of Italian people from the southern part of Italy and Sicily who emigrated to this country through immigration channels in the early part of the Mussolini regime. They came over here and as a result we have the Al Capones and all these other people organized into a crime syndicate. They got themselves into power through a lot of political maneuvering on higher levels. I'd be small fry to the connections they have.

Q. Do you think these killings are the direct result of Mafia activity?

A. I can only assume that it was. One would have to have testimony that would stand up in court to prove it.

Q. As to the actual gunmen, do you believe they were local or imported?

A. I always judged they were imported because the Mafia had far-reaching activities. It would be too difficult for someone known in Tampa to do, and we have traced the implement of death in one case to New Orleans as you will see in one file there.

Some months before the hearing, the *Tribune* had discovered and had printed that Salvadore ("Red") Italiano, Tampa's top gambling racketeer who had fled town before the Kefauver hearing, had purchased a new Cadillac and had taken it with him on a mystery trip to Italy. Our story also reported that he did not bring the Cadillac back to this country on his return.

The Kefauver Committee placed the president of Italiano's beer distributing concern on the witness stand and here is part of his testimony:

Q. When did Red go to Italy?
A. In May, 1950.

Q. Did he take a car to Europe?
A. He took a Cadillac.

Q. Did your company pay for it?
A. No.

Q. What reason did he have for taking it? Haven't you heard that he turned it over to Charles (Lucky) Luciano?
A. No.

Q. Well, you don't know that Italiano left that Cadillac with Luciano?
A. No.

Luciano was the notorious vice gangster and Mafia leader in New York, and this testimony was the first official hint linking the underworlds of the two cities.

In the matter of the aversion of Tampa's law enforcement officers toward investigating the numerous gang slayings in our community, the following testimony by the police chief was extremely interesting:

Q. I want to ask if you have a file on the killing of Angelo Lazzara, filling station owner and undercover agent for the fire department, killed early on the morning of July 26, 1931, while driving south on 29th Street, 10 minutes after leaving a gambling establishment. Two loads of buckshot fired from a sedan struck him in the face. Officers said he "knew too much." There was no arrest. Do you have the records?

(The chief searched briefly in his briefcase.)

A. I do not have the Lazzara records, although I do have some records since 1932. There have been a good many changes in the police department through the years.

Q. Do you have the records of the slaying of Mrs. Fernando Serrano, killed in a parked car at 10 o'clock on the night of January 10, 1932, on 15th Street near 11th Avenue, by buckshot blasts evidently intended for her husband, fired from a moving car? There was no arrest there, either.

A. No sir.

Q. How about Gus Perez, Ybor City furniture dealer, murdered with shotguns as he drove along 15th Street, near Buffalo Avenue, early on the morning of July 24, 1936? No arrest there, either.

(The chief handed over a file folder.)

A. That's all we have on it.

Q. This seems to consist merely of a report of the murder. There should be more file than this. What's become of the records of who was questioned?

A. I don't know.

Q. What disposition was there of the case?

A. There were no arrests.

So it went down through Tampa's long list of unsolved gambling murders. The police chief produced few records and it was clearly indicated, as had been reported by the

Tribune time and again throughout its crusade, that Tampa's law enforcement officers had little heart for the investigations of the bloody shotgun blasts that echoed and re-echoed down through the years in the build-up of organized gambling.

At that time, the slaying of Jimmy Lumia, Tampa's businessman gambling chief, near the business section in broad daylight, was the latest echo of gangland's shotgun blasts in our community, only a few months before the Kefauver hearing. Here is the police chief's testimony:

> Q. Tell the committee any possible chance you have of solving this murder.
>
> A. I don't know. People have fear of talking; nobody has seen it. Even people Lumia was talking to at the time he was killed hesitated to talk about it. It seems to be even in cases of robbery a dreadful element of fear. Especially in the cigar factory robberies witnesses hesitated, refused to identify anybody.
>
> Q. What is the cause of this fear?
>
> A. The shotgun shootings. In the Gradiaz-Annis robbery we got witnesses who saw the escape car, saw the man who used the stepladder to go through a window and take a $25,000 payroll. News reporters following the police got names and addresses of two witnesses for the paper. Yet we couldn't get either of the witnesses to say anything. One told of getting a telephone call that if she wanted to live and be happy not to say anything about it.

Charlie M. Wall, a native Tampan and a member of prominent business and social family, long had been a key figure in Tampa's gambling. But at the time of the Kefauver hearings, he had been pushed out of control by the Mafia and was approaching his seventieth birthday. Everybody who had read Florida newspapers since the roaring twenties and the bloody thirties had heard of Wall, the gambler, the political fixer, the dapper man-about-town, who hobnobbed not only with sheriffs and judges but with senators and even greater political figures. But few knew that 20 years before, he had fought and presumably won a fight against narcotics addiction. So his testimony was of more than passing interest.

He was called as a witness on the first day of the hearing and the committee treated him as the "elder statesman" of the rackets. The questioning was somewhat gentle and there was much laughter in the Federal courtroom throughout his testimony. Here is part of it:

Q. When were the attempts made on your life?
A. I imagine that was about, oh, maybe 1938.

Q. Our records show the first time was in 1930.
A. Well, that is possible. I don't remember.

Q. You mean you were shot at so often, you don't remember?
A. I don't remember the date. When it first happened I came out of my garage to the sidewalk. The folks came up in an automobile. A fellow was shooting, and I didn't realize it.

Q. Hit you?
A. They limbed me a little.

Q. Shoot you with buckshot?
A. I think — I was so scared — I think I shot at him. Then I got in my house.

Q. Was there an investigation?
A. Oh, yes.

Q. Did you go before a grand jury?
A. No, but the authorities came out. But I was

so scared I wasn't able to give them much information.

Q. Was anyone arrested?
A. No.

Wall then was asked about a second attempt on his life in 1939, and he said he was returning from downtown when a fellow drove up in a truck and he could see a gun sticking out of the back.

> "I heard a shot, and it burnt me a little," he told the committee, "and I ducked down as best I could. Then a gent tried to climb into the front seat beside me. I thought maybe he wanted to shoot at me, and I guess he did. But I was down. I put my foot on the accelerator and pulled at the wheel and my car went up on the sidewalk. Then I heard a car leaving, and I was glad to part with it."

In describing the third attempt on his life, which was in 1944, Wall testified he was on the way downtown, and a young fellow who was driving him put on the brakes so fast he was thrown against the windshield. He said he saw another automobile stopping, and something sticking out that looked like the end of a hoe handle or fishing rod. Someone shot and he ducked and a bullet went through the windshield of the Wall automobile.

Q. Had the car been following you?
A. I don't know.

Q. Did you continue on?
A. We started back and they started backing, too.

Q. Was there an investigation?
A. Yes, that afternoon some city detectives came out.

Q. Did you go before a grand jury?
A. No, I didn't testify.

Q. No arrests?
A. No.

Q. No suspects?
A. No.

You would think that an underworld character in his seventies, benign and intellectual, who had escaped the roaring shotgun blasts of the gangsters three times, would have chosen to die a natural death, if he had been given a choice. But such was not the case and I might say, after 35 years of newspapering in the middle of bloody underworld assassinations, that a natural death is a rarity with the hoodlums.

On the morning of April 20, 1955, five years after the Kefauver hearings and at the age of 75, Wall was found in his old-fashioned nightshirt at his home in Ybor City, his head battered in and his throat slashed from ear to ear. On the table by his blood-soaked deathbed was a lone book — *Crime in America* by Senator Estes Kefauver (Doubleday, N.Y., 1951).

An investigation revealed that Wall had visited two night spots the previous evening, then had been driven home in a somewhat intoxicated condition. Somebody apparently had relieved him of the key to his heavily barricaded home, sneaked in while he was in a drunken sleep, and wreaked bloody revenge. There were, of course, no arrests.

Although our paths had crossed many times in my Tampa newspaper career, I had never met Wall personally. Once, early in my career when I was sports editor of the *Tribune*, I wrote a story charging that Charlie Wall had fixed a certain prize fight in behalf of gambling interests. The fight turned out exactly as I had predicted and three days later one of the fighters sat in my office and confessed the details. I printed this confession, too.

But despite this lack of a personal meeting, Wall telephoned me on the average of three times weekly during the last two years of his life. I suspected that he started the telephoning in the hope of getting information. But veteran newsmen are old hands in this little matter, and in the end Wall turned out to be a garrulous old man with a wagging tongue. A wagging tongue is the unforgivable sin in the underworld, and I strongly believe this is the real reason he was murdered.

But back to the Kefauver hearings. There was no such thing as pleading the Fifth Amendment in the two days of testimony in Tampa. The attorneys for the communistic fellow travelers had not yet given this to a palpitating American public as the neat little excuse for not answering legitimate questions affecting the public. Each and every hoodlum and public official called as a witness before the Kefauver committee in Tampa was accompanied by an attorney, but nevertheless they answered all questions reasonably well.

Three of the lieutenants of the slain hoodlum, whose shoe box of gambling records served as the springboard for the *Tribune*'s crusade, testified to pay-offs to law enforcement officers. Here, in brief, is the testimony of one of the hoodlums, who previously told the committee he had been arrested eight or ten times on gambling charges:

Q. How much money this time?
A. $1,000.

Q. Where was the money going?
A. To the campaign, state and local.

Q. Some was campaign and some was rent?
A. Yes.

Q. Where did you take the money?
A. To the sheriff's office back of the jail.

Q. What did you say?

A. I said, "Jimmy sent you this," that's all.

One law officer spent three sweating hours upon the stand on the second day of the hearings, and all of the testimony dealt with his income and much of it with a tin lockbox, in which he kept cash at home. This is a sample of his testimony:

Q. What was the widest spread — what was the minimum and maximum amount you possibly had in the tin box?

A. I may have had $30,000.

Q. What was the least amount you might have had?

A. Maybe $9,000 or $10,000.

Q. Between $9,000 or $10,000 and $30,000?

A. I'm trying to pin it down.

Q. That's it — that's what we want; we want the exact figure.

A. I can't figure it any closer.

At the conclusion of the testimony, the Kefauver Committee totted up on a blackboard in the courtroom this law officer's assets and announced that his income for the last 10 years was $97,698, which was $34,684 more than his legitimate net income reported to the government for income tax purposes. The law officer bitterly assailed the Senate Committee's proceedings as unfair.

But fair or unfair, the Kefauver Committee's swing around the country eventually produced new Federal antigambling laws adopted by the Congress, which:

1. Restrict interstate transportation of slot machines

2. Require all gamblers to take out license stamps, either personally or in the name of his principal

3. Require all gamblers to pay a monthly federal tax of 10 per cent on his gross revenue.

This, of course, broke the back of the national gambling syndicate. It brought the F.B.I. into the gambling picture for the first time and it resulted in a nationwide clamp down by the Federal Government on the racket. Periodically, I send my reporters to the Department of Internal Revenue at Jacksonville and we print the names and addresses of the purchasers of gambling stamps as well as the amount of gambling taxes paid. There are pending constantly in our Federal courts cases against the gamblers and a goodly number have taken vacations in the Federal penitentiary.

On the Tampa front, the results of the *Tribune*'s gambling crusade topped off by the Kefauver Senate Committee hearings, were:

First — an aroused public went to the polls, threw out our erring public officials and elected a new set of five law enforcement officers, all pledged to a clean-up fight against the underworld.

Second — and most vital, our free elections and free government were wrested from the underworld and restored to the free people of our community.

Third — bolita, which once was rampant in our city, is now played only on the sneak basis.

Fourth — the underworld leaders who fled the Kefauver Committee never have returned to their Tampa homes, which is a good riddance in any man's town.

There are still some hoodlums in Tampa and in all of Florida, but I can assure you they are stepping softly these days. And I am getting better sleep than I did in the late forties and early fifties.

7.

Spotlight
on Schools

LIKE A FREE PRESS, free schools are essential to a free
people. Therefore, a free press is obligated to keep a
watchful eye upon the schools of a free people.

You would think that, due to the presence of a Parent-
Teacher Association in every school, interested mothers
and fathers would see that the quality of education provided their children would at least meet the standards.
But such is far from the case, as was developed by the
blockbuster crusade of *The Tampa Tribune* in 1945, 1946
and 1947, and also has been indicated time and again by
the sidetracking of sound education for the frills and
foibles based on John Dewey's fancies.

Parent-Teacher Associations are composed largely of
mothers simply because their meeting hours, usually in
the afternoon after school, prohibit the fathers from attending. Locally they had been completely dominated by
the principal of each school, and if you doubt that this
is true in many communities, let me point out that it is

rare indeed that you ever hear of a P.T.A. revolting. In Tampa, most principals carefully doled out the honors of the frills and foibles of modern American education to those pupils whose parents hewed to the official educational line. If a mother should rise up in the P.T.A. and charge that her child was not being properly educated, rest assured that her Johnny would be penalized.

School principals, themselves, were in no position to lead a drive for better education. For one thing, they usually were chosen solely on the basis of their cooperation with the school superintendent and the school trustees and board. And should a principal revolt against the dictates of this educational hierarchy, his or her head would certainly have gone on the block.

The *Tribune* noted early in 1945, from Federal and other official educational sources, that, while the people of Florida ranked 27th among the 48 states in the ability to pay, Florida's schools ranked anywhere from 43rd to 47th, depending on the specific measurement, among the 48 states. Florida teachers, for instance, were paid on the average about $1,500 a year, which was pitiful when you consider their educational requirements and the fact that they wield such a powerful influence upon the lives of all young Americans during their formative years.

We wanted to know why, so I assigned my best research reporter to the problem. He spent a solid year in research before writing a line, and when I say research, I mean exactly that. This reporter, J. A. Murray, a careful Scotsman who was born in Nova Scotia and was graduated in journalism from the University of Missouri, assembled so much material that the *Tribune* today has one of the finest libraries of school information among American newspapers. He studied every phase of school operation, including that in other states, keeping in mind always Florida's poor standing and seeking out the answers. He paid particular attention to the California and New York school systems, which had done an outstanding job of correcting the problems that beset our schools.

We printed our first story on the condition of Florida schools in May, 1946. During the next year, the *Tribune* carried 647 school stories, including 27 different series on different phases; 202 photographs of school scenes; 198 photographs of school leaders; 41 cartoons on Page 1; 67 editorials; and 64 letters to the editor.

Our stories were produced by plain, old-fashioned re-porting, from observation, interviews and public records. They were written in honest, factual style. Every effort was made to avoid the sensational and scarehead type of journalism. We simply reported the facts fairly and with-out catering to any political group or educational clique. We attempted to draw no conclusions in our stories; the conclusions were left to the readers.

It is difficult to conceive of scandal swirling about the heads of shining tots studying in our schoolrooms and particularly so with a P.T.A. in every school. Yet it didn't take us long to root out scandal, and it flared up through-out the year's crusade. Actually, our reporting project finally resolved into four phases, which were:

1. A general report on Florida's lagging school progress from Key West to Pensacola

2. A report on the broken down physical conditions of Tampa's schools

3. A report of corruption on the part of school officials in some of Florida's smaller offbeat rural counties

4. A report of conditions in the summer strawberry schools in the agricultural counties surrounding Tampa, which the *Tribune* labeled as nothing more than an excuse for child labor.

We opened the general campaign with a series of five stories on Florida's schools, based on Murray's interviews with 75 persons who had some expert knowledge of the schools and on numerous official reports on national edu-cation standards. The headlines on these stories were:

FLORIDA'S SCHOOLS RANK 34TH IN EFFORT IN UNITED STATES

FLORIDA SPENDS BELOW AVERAGE SUM ON SCHOOLS

ONLY TWO CENTS IN DOLLAR GOES FOR EDUCATION

89,024 FLORIDA CHILDREN NOT IN SCHOOL;
STATE HAS HIGH RATE OF ILLITERACY

FLORIDA RANKS LOW AMONG STATES IN SCHOOL SURVEY

There was nothing sensational in either these headlines or the stories under them, and actually they did little
to arouse Florida's taxpaying parents. But they did lay the
groundwork for our crusade, and we fell back on them
time and again, simply because they contained key information based on official national facts and figures.

We followed this with an expose of the physical conditions of Tampa's 40 schools at that time, and it immediately erupted into a scandal, caught the eye of the parents,
and from that time on, throughout the 647 stories in the
next year, we had public support in our crusade.

I sent a reporter into every one of the 40 Tampa
schools and he carried with him detailed standards of our
county health department on safety and sanitary conditions for a school. With him also went an expert plumber
and an expert architect, both of whom we had interested
in the project as a civic duty. The reporter carefully
checked the health and sanitary standards against each
school, then asked the plumber and architect for their ex-
port opinions on what was wrong.

Here is just a part of what this reporter found: dead
rats in lunchrooms; sewer gas escaping in school toilets;
loose plaster hanging over children's heads; fire escape
doors that stuck; toilets out of order; drinking fountains
broken; and jagged and broken steps on fire escapes. In
each school, the reporter doggedly opened doors, tested
water taps, counted broken panes of glass, peered into
closets, flushed toilets, looked under buildings for ter-
mites, and counted rat nests.

Where schools were in good condition, we said so in our newspaper. Where they had been neglected to the detriment of the safety and health of the children, we meticulously listed each evidence of carelessness and neglect. We carried pictures daily on this evidence.

All of this was reported simply and calmly as straight news. When a professional rat exterminator firm, at the suggestion of the *Tribune*, went into one school and poisoned 22 rats in one night, the *Tribune's* position was dramatically verified. The picture of the string of dead rats caused more comment in one day than years of protests from individual citizens had stirred in the past.

In the middle of this phase of our crusade, a ceiling collapsed, through faulty architecture, at one of the schools during recess hours; only a miracle saved the children from physical injury, if not death. Our story and pictures of this created a new stir among the parents.

When you reveal dangerous conditions affecting a people's children, you really hit home. Parent-Teacher Associations took up the discussion of the unrealized and ignored conditions. Civic clubs called for investigations. School officials began defending their positions, but they couldn't defend such incidents as dead rats in lunchrooms and collapsed ceilings in school rooms.

Public pressure so mounted that the key member of Tampa's Board of School Trustees and the superintendent of buildings suddenly resigned. This really put scandal in the middle of our crusade. The school board followed with an extraordinary public session in which, with much political pomp and flourish, it voted $5,000 for an immediate clean-up of rats and $250,000 for the repair of the physical weaknesses of Tampa's long-neglected school buildings.

But the *Tribune* kept right on with its crusade, simply because we had learned through bitter experience that the politician often announces elaborate cleanup plans to get a newspaper off his back, then when the heat is eased, he forgets all about them. By this time, our investigating reporter had moved into Tampa's Negro schools and what he found almost defied the worst adjectives of the English language. Here we relied largely on the news camera, and even the most ardent segregationists were stunned by our pictures of the dilapidated shacks in which Negro children were getting their education.

Public reaction was immediate. The school board again met in extraordinary session, resurrected an ancient dust-covered plan, and in 60 days Tampa was launched definitely into a long-range program of Negro school construction. And today you will find many of the Negro schools in our community superior to white schools in physical accommodations.

I have referred repeatedly to the apparent callousness of the politician toward such crying public needs as our schools, and perhaps you have gotten the idea that I am prejudiced. But consider this little incident, which flared in the middle of our Tampa school crusade. The chairman of our school board rose at a public meeting and severely criticized the *Tribune* for revealing the deplorable conditions of the schools and declared this would prevent people from moving to Tampa. "I know I wouldn't move to Tampa after reading what the newspapers have had to say about our schools," he sanctimoniously grumbled.

But in the next election, a few months later, the voters of Tampa retired this esteemed public servant to private life.

There was a similar reaction in Hardee County. At the request of citizens there, I sent a staff writer to look into its schools, and his stories carried the following headlines:

HARDEE, WITH POOR SCHOOLS, LIKES TRIBUNE CAMPAIGN

LOW ASSESSMENTS PENALIZE SCHOOLS IN HARDEE COUNTY

PETTY POLITICS HANGS LIKE CURSE OVER HARDEE SCHOOLS

The Hardee politicians immediately pooh-poohed the *Tribune* stories, but in the next election the Hardee voters, using the difficult operation of the write-in vote, retired two veteran members of their school board.

While the *Tribune's* crusade against faulty physical conditions of schools actually was pin-pointed in Tampa, it attracted wide attention throughout the state. At the request of The Brooksville Woman's Club, the Junior Service League, the P.T.A., the American Legion Post, the Legion Auxiliary and the South Brooksville Country Club, I sent a staff writer to do a series of stories on Hernando County's schools. Headlines on his stories were:

BROOKSVILLE WOMEN SEEK SCHOOL CLEANUP

ORGANIZED MINORITY OPPOSES HERNANDO SCHOOL CAMPAIGN

HERNANDO ROADS GET MORE ATTENTION THAN ITS SCHOOLS

Again the reaction was immediate. Hernando's state senator and representative in the legislature announced they would seek a state survey of its schools, more school funds and support of a general plan to improve Florida's schools.

Meanwhile, I had sent Murray, our veteran research reporter, out into Florida in a big way. He visited Miami, which reputedly had Florida's best schools — mainly because a booming economy was producing more tax funds for education and of an advanced outlook on the part of its citizens. He talked with school departments and plowed through a survey of the Miami school system by 40 educators. He looked up assessed tax valuations and studied a tax survey to show the source of income in various Miami school districts. He checked enrollment figures. Then he searched out comparative figures in Tampa, and his stories printed in our newspaper showed that, while Tampa was spending $79 per pupil each year, Miami was spending $170.

From the best Florida school system, Murray then traveled to the worst — in rural Holmes County in northwest Florida. There tax records showed that Holmes County collected in real estate taxes only 77 cents per pupil as compared to $4.06 in Tampa. He studied teaching records and found that Holmes County had 58 teachers who were not qualified to teach. He checked payrolls and found that Holmes County paid an average teacher salary of only $750 a year as compared to $1,700 in Tampa.

Holmes County boys and girls obviously were being penalized, and out of these two series of stories on the best and worst school systems in Florida came the *Tribune*'s slogan for its entire school crusade — "Equal educational opportunities for all Florida children, rural and city, poor and rich, black and white."

This slogan really was crystalized when Murray moved into rich Polk County, the world's greatest citrus and phosphate county, and found the children of the county receiving varied educational opportunities through a mixture of petty school politics, revolving around too many little school districts, and inequalities in school tax financing, due largely to the outside phosphate interests in the county. Headlines on his Polk stories were:

POLK PUSHES ITS TEACHERS AND PROGRESSES IN EDUCATION

POLK COUNTY TRIES SCHOOL CONSOLIDATION; HAS SOME SUCCESS; TRIES FOR MORE

POLK COUNTY SCHOOLS FIGHT HOOKWORM AND INSANITATION

POLK COUNTY STRUGGLES WITH INSANITARY SCHOOLS

By this time, much of Florida was aroused over its schools. Citizens in various counties hurriedly organized, then sent frantic appeals to the *Tribune* to send our reporters into their communities and dig out the real facts on the schools. Our newspaper cooperated with every appeal. In the middle of this, we did two comparative series on the school systems of Hillsborough and Pinellas Counties, separated 20 miles by a bay, and this proved most effective in our crusade.

Our series on Holmes County had exposed a 50-year scandal which was prevalent in some of the smaller rural counties, far from the beaten path of crusading newspapers, and this had alarmed a good many citizens and had enraged a lot of politicians. We found a blind man as the new superintendent of schools, a very fine public servant, seeking to rid Holmes of its school scandal. With the aid of a retired County Judge, our reporter went into the county records and disclosed:

1. That there was constant political interference in school operation
2. That teacher jobs were bought and paid for
3. There was considerable graft in school purchases
4. There was padding in the school enrollment figures so that the politicians could get more state funds for their own use, not for the school children

In the matter of the bought-and-paid-for teacher jobs, we disclosed that other persons took the examinations for the teacher applicants, who themselves could not possibly attain passing grades. And we printed the fact that in several cases, when these outside persons failed the examinations, the disappointed teacher applicants later were arrested for making moonshine.

In four of Florida's counties — Hillsborough, Polk, Hardee and Sumter — we found what was known in our state as "strawberry schools." Florida grows its strawberries in the winter. Children make good strawberry pickers because the work is simple and you can hire them cheaper than adults. We found that the strawberry growers had so rigged their school terms that the children had their vacations in the winter months, so they could pick the berries, and went to school in the summer, during Florida's warmest weather. We dug into the records

and proved that these "strawberry schools" were ineffi-
cient as compared to regular schools; that they did not
give their pupils the "equal opportunity" to get an education; and that they were nothing more than an excuse
for child labor.

This naturally aroused many citizens, and the school
boards of Polk, Hardee and Sumter Counties hurriedly
met, abandoned their "strawberry schools" and arranged
to have all their children attend schools under the same
conditions. The school board of Hillsborough County
remained stubborn until the next election, when the
voters removed the "strawberry school" member, and
then surrendered.

By this time the pressure from Florida citizens for
better schools was terrific. As a direct result of the *Tribune*'s searching stories on state-wide education, the new
Florida Citizens Committee on Education, appointed by
Governor Millard Caldwell, suddenly threw off its apathy,
called in seven outside school experts and went to work
in behalf of Florida's children for the first time.

The *Tribune* responded by printing in November,
1946, a list of 20 points of improvement for legislative
action and a second list of 29 general recommendations,
all designed to provide "equal educational opportunities
for all Florida children, rural and city, poor and rich,
black and white." In a subsequent series of meetings,
this state Citizens Committee adopted all except one of
the *Tribune*'s recommendations for its 1947 legislative
program.

That major exception involved the appointment of
school superintendents. The *Tribune* had found throughout the state that the election of school superintendents
put the schools into the middle of politics and often contributed to their dereliction. We proposed to take the
schools out of politics altogether by eliminating the salaries of school board members (which eventually was
done) to get a better class of citizens interested in active
school direction, and to make the post of school superintendents appointive on the basis of educational merit.

Since many of the school superintendents could not pass that test of merit, they hurriedly held a special meeting at the University of Florida and organized a political campaign to eliminate this from the school bill. We opposed their move, but we did not persist in demanding the whole loaf, since we were completely victorious in all our other recommendations. Florida still elects its school superintendents, regardless of merit.

The school superintendents were not the only members of the educational hierarchy whom we irritated during this successful block-buster crusade. We got under the skin of the school lunchroom officials with a special series of stories, the headlines of which were:

SCHOOL LUNCHROOMS SERVE 2 MILLION LUNCHES IN YEAR

**SCHOOL BOARD HAS NOT CHECKED ON LUNCHROOM
COSTS HERE**

SCHOOL LUNCH PROGRAM HERE IMPROVES HEALTH STANDARDS

SOME SCHOOL LUNCHROOMS OPERATED WITH FRICTION

**FEDERAL LUNCHROOM AID PLAN INCREASES IN FAVOR IN
TAMPA**

**P.T.A. LEADERS OPPOSE COUNTY SUPERVISION OF
LUNCHROOMS**

Similarly, we ruffled the egotistical feathers of the Tampa high school football coaches when another of our special school series pointed up how football and not scholarship dominated certain school circles. The headlines of our stories were:

**FOOTBALL IS BIG BUSINESS FOR THREE TAMPA HIGH
SCHOOLS**

**FOOTBALL BUSINESS IN TAMPA FOLLOWS COLLEGES'
PATTERN**

FREE PASSES REDUCE PROFITS OF FOOTBALL BUSINESS HERE

HIGH SCHOOL FOOTBALL REVENUE HITS NEW RECORDS

FINANCIAL DRAMA IS PART OF FOOTBALL HISTORY HERE

But the wrath of the school lunchroom officials and football coaches were gentle zephyrs compared to the hurricane of teacher ire that whistled about the *Tribune* when, in another special series, we dwelt at length on teacher tenure. The headlines were:

COUNTY TEACHERS TAKE PART IN POLITICS OVER SCHOOLS

COUNTY'S SYSTEM OF PAYING TEACHERS CALLED "DETRIMENT"

CAREFUL STUDY OF TEACHER PAY SETUP SEEN AS BIG NEED

EDUCATORS SAY GOOD RATING WOULD PROTECT TEACHERS

FLORIDA EDUCATORS FAVOR MERIT TEACHER PAY SYSTEM

TAMPA NEGRO TEACHERS PAID MORE THAN WHITE TEACHERS

SOUTH CAROLINA ADOPTS MERIT SYSTEM OF PAYING TEACHERS

TAMPA TEACHER TENURE ACT IS LOOSELY ADMINISTERED

TEACHER TENURE HERE GIVES PROTECTION TO INCOMPETENTS

Under tenure, a teacher could be fired for only four causes: (1) immoral character or conduct; (2) violation of the law; (3) failure to discharge duties of employment; and (4) dishonesty. Any one of these causes would be exceedingly hard to prove, and the *Tribune* clearly pointed out that few teachers had ever been removed under tenure; that once a teacher gained it, she was in for life; and that Florida's system was crowded with incompetent teachers, all at the expense of Florida's children.

The teachers, one and all, grabbed for a microphone and for weeks Florida's ozone increased no end with the thunder of their orations in behalf of tenure. So vociferous were these orations and so powerful was — and is — the teacher legislative lobby with the politician that our little side-issue crusade came to naught. Instead, we reaped the suspicion of the teacher and it has not waned, although it was more than 10 years ago that our blockbuster crusade doubled teacher pay in Florida. Such are the many fruits of a newspaper crusade.

8.

Teachers and Parents Outwit Politicians

AN AMERICAN STATE LEGISLATURE is a unique body of human beings. There is no other organization on the face of the earth like it.

Some years ago the *Saturday Evening Post* printed a series of articles on the Illinois Legislature which detailed just about all the political chicanery in the book. You could substitute the name of Florida for Illinois, and you would have the proper picture of springtime in Tallahassee in the odd years.

Strange currents flow through the legislative halls of any state capitol, all of them motivated by political privilege and guided by conniving lobbyists, who are the real dictators of the people's state laws.

There are lobbies for every special interest except the people, and all of them are armed to the teeth with money, whisky and threats. And they are so chummy with the politician that it is difficult each day to separate them so that our legislators can assume their law-making seats to do the lobbyists' bidding.

Unquestionably, the American taxpayer is the most lovable character in all the world. Otherwise, he long since would have armed himself with a shotgun, hied his way to his state capitol and scattered legislators and lobbyists all over the premises.

Florida's new deal school bill, sponsored by the Citizens Committee on Education and supported by hundreds of citizens' groups throughout the state, was introduced into the legislature at Tallahassee on April 10, 1947. Including most of the reforms highlighted in *The Tampa Tribune*'s block-busting crusade, the bill provided for the following major provisions:

1. It doubled the state's annual appropriation for schools from $18,000,000 to $36,000,000.
2. It set up what was called the minimum foundation formula which provided that the children in the poorest Florida counties could have the same educational advantages as the children in cities and the larger and richer counties.
3. It doubled the pay of Florida teachers, from an average of about $1,500 to a minimum scale of $3,000 a year.
4. It eliminated salaries of school board members and took this particular governmental function out of the hands of the politicians and handed it back to the citizens.
5. It improved the professional status of Florida's system of universities and provided for coeducation at the two big state universities.
6. Over all, it would raise Florida's school standards, according to all the professional ratings, from 47th to about 22nd among the 48 states.

There were many other minor technical provisions, designed to improve the educational opportunities of Florida's children, but these six key changes were the points which provoked a senatorial revolt. Even though they had been espoused by groups of citizens from Key West to Pensacola, citizens who would pick up the bill for extra taxes needed to carry out these provisions, senators opposed the bill vigorously.

The *Tribune*, which had crusaded all the previous year for the program, could not lobby for the bill, once it was laid before the legislature. But we could print in detail all the developments at Tallahassee, which we did, and on our editorial page, we could hammer at the senatorial dissenters, which we also did. In the end this proved sufficient, simply because, through factual reporting the previous year of the great weaknesses in Florida's schools, we had aroused the people of the state. We had one final crusading fling just before the legislature met, and the headlines of our stories were:

CALIFORNIA 1ST, FLORIDA 47TH IN EDUCATION; HERE IS WHY

CALIFORNIA VOTES $2400 FOR TEACHER; FLORIDA PAYS $750

CALIFORNIA COURT UPHOLDS MERIT PAY FOR TEACHERS

CALIFORNIA GIVES 15 YEARS SCHOOLING; FLORIDA ONLY 12

CALIFORNIA GIVES GUIDANCE TO PUPILS; FLORIDA NONE

CALIFORNIA, TOO, TAKES STEPS TO MODERNIZE SCHOOL SYSTEM

Our school bill got off to a deceptively smooth start. The Education Committee of the House of Representatives, with a minimum of debate and no major changes, approved it unanimously on April 15 and it moved onto the floor of the House on April 17.

This was not particularly unexpected. House members are elected every two years and are far more amenable to the pressure of public opinion than are senators, who are elected every four years and feel a little more secure from the emotions of the voters. No House member would have wanted to go back to the polls in 1948 and have his political opponent charge him with letting down the children, while his action still was fresh in the minds of the Florida parents.

Senatorial storm signals were hoisted on April 17 at the first meeting of its Education Committee. The Orlando member, a realtor who was of the senate's controlling bloc, rose and said he was not opposing the school bill, but that it was "absurd" and he warned the P.T.A. and the teachers that they would be disappointed with it.

But the big blow came the next day when the *Tribune* revealed in a lead story that 30 of the 36 senators had signed a telegram to the Florida Education Association, in convention at Tampa, urging that the teachers agree to separation of the pay provisions from the rest of the school bill. Text of the senatorial telegram was:

> We members of the State Senate, including members of the Education Committee, sincerely urge every school teacher to demand a separate bill providing revenue and salary increases for teachers. We are fearful that your legislation we are so anxious to enact into law will be lost or jeopardized in the omnibus bill of school committee. We respectfully ask that this telegram be read to delegates attending convention and advise what, if any, action taken.

The *Tribune* answered this on its editorial page. We pointed out that this implied promise of a pay increase made by 30 Senators no doubt would be attractive to Florida's long-suffering teachers. Then we said:

> But there is a point the teachers cannot afford to overlook. As members of a profession held in high esteem, they have a vital part to play in building a progressive school system. They will be failing their own end if they concentrate on a plan of action around their own demands and forget the needs of children and education in general.

School teacher pay long has been a political football of state legislatures, and this perhaps explains why the profession in general ranks low in the American scale of living. Many a time in American history, the teacher has sacrificed real gains for the profession by accepting the political sop of a small pay raise, and the teacher's perpetual cry for more pay has been permanently attached to education in general in the mind of the average citizen.

But in this case, the Florida teachers measured up completely and nobly to public responsibility. The Florida Education Association convention abruptly refused to consider the senatorial telegram and told the 30 objecting Senators to proceed with dispatch the enactment of the whole school bill into law. The teacher reply then said:

> Any decrease in the Citizens Committee's recommended program for financial support of schools will jeopardize the functioning of the minimum program and will adversely affect the educational opportunities of Florida school children. We recognize the necessity for controls which will insure the proper administration of these funds. The FEA urges the Legislature to use the best possible methods to expedite the enactment of this program into law.

Financing of the new school program had not yet entered into the senatorial picture, but everybody in Tallahassee knew that the Senate was getting ready to tie it up in one of those permanent legislative knots. So, to forestall this, Governor Millard Caldwell plumped a compromise into the pot, which immediately eased off the threatened steam.

This compromise called for a reduction of county school taxes by one mill, with the state making up this difference. The Governor wired his proposal to the Florida Education Association convention, which promptly accepted it, and this most effectively robbed the senators of the opportunity of beating their breasts over the pitiful picture of their constituents back home having to sell the old homestead to put the teachers and school children in Cadillacs.

Meanwhile, Western Union was doing a landslide business and should have declared an extra dividend to its stockholders. More than 8,000 telegrams from enraged parents, all directed at the 30 objecting Senators, poured into Tallahassee and this stunned the Senate and left most of them speechless. It was a magnificent illustration of the power of public opinion in democratic processes of free government, and it seems a great pity that we do not have more of it directed at our Congress in Washington.

Four days later there was a colorful interlude at Brooksville. The County Commission of Hernando County had absolutely ignored the series of stories which the *Tribune* had done on Hernando's poverty-stricken schools, in response to a plea from half a dozen women's organizations. So, on the morning of April 21, just as the Commission was sitting down at its regular meeting table in the courthouse, there resounded over the courthouse square the notes of band music. A glance out the courthouse windows showed the entire school population of Brooksville, led by the teachers, parading behind their school band and waving placards which read, "We want better schools in Hernando County."

A *Tribune* staff writer and cameraman were on hand, and we carried a 1,000-word story and a big picture of the parade the next morning for the benefit of our thousands of readers. Under this pressure by the school children themselves, the opposition of the political-minded commissioners caved in and a few days later they voted their approval of the new Florida school plan and agreed to provide the necessary funds in Hernando County.

On the same day, the *Tribune* printed a feature story from J. A. Murray, its expert school writer at Tallahassee, under the headline,

EVERYBODY HAS LOBBY BUT THE CHILDREN ON FLORIDA SCHOOL BILL

This story concluded with the following paragraph:

> During the last few months this reporter has attended meetings in Tampa, called to consider recommendations of the Florida Citizens Committee on Education at which all the educational issues were discussed, but not one voice was raised for the barefoot boy. Which may be the reason why his lobby is not strong in Tallahassee.

This apparently wrung the hearts of quite a number of Florida citizens because the trek of parents to Tallahassee started the next day and the final deliberations of the legislature on the school bill were held within a ring of silent, forbidding and determined-looking faces of Florida's first people's lobby.

Murray's story apparently angered Senator Raymond Sheldon, whom we had tagged as one of the signers of the senatorial telegram to the teachers, for the Tampan rose before a crowded gallery in the legislature and spent some 30 minutes ranting and raving that the *Tribune* reporter was guilty of lobbying. Under Senate rules, a reporter found guilty of lobbying could be expelled from the chamber and denied access to its proceedings. But the veteran Murray, although his research reporting actually had fathered the school bill, had carefully steered clear of anything that approached lobbying, and nothing came of Sheldon's windy attack, even though the 30 objecting Senators would have liked to have penalized the *Tribune*.

You will find that politicans who oppose a newspaper's program or policy on any public matter are always eager to rawhide the editor or reporter with adjectives and adverbs. But when the chips are down and the newspaper is stalwart in its sincerity, the politician shies away from a positive decision on the matter simply because he is unwilling to risk a public defeat which possibly would have an effect on the next election.

The school bill formally moved onto the floor of the House of Representatives for a vote on April 24, amid cries of "railroading" and "steam-roller tactics." These cries came from the small rural county representatives, and for an hour and a half they sought in a bitter debate to reduce the bill to a meaningless piece of paper with a score of crippling amendments.

Small-county men had led the revolt in the Senate, too. In every state legislature in our land you will find this small vs. big county, or country vs. city fight. Usually, the small or rural county is on the side of status quo, and there often is a very good reason spelled out in a five-letter word called "power."

The legislator in the small county or rural community has far more political power, and the political privilege that goes with it, than does his political brother in the large county or big city. For one thing, there usually is no daily newspaper on hand to report political skullduggery to the voters. And there always is the "local legislation" process wherein a legislator has supreme control over the introduction of any and all laws pertaining to any changes in his local government. This can be used viciously.

Through this legislative courtesy, a legislator without integrity can become the political dictator in his community, simply because he has an effective club to pound the heads, through vindictive use of this process, of the other politicians in the community. Thus the rural legislator, more than his big city compatriot, entertains the belief that his local political scene is his private domain.

The *Tribune's* research in Florida school affairs had uncovered considerable corruption, most of it in the smaller counties and some of it involving the sale of teacher jobs as well as graft in the purchase of school supplies. And you can be sure that the legislators of those communities either had fingers in the political pie or else condoned corruption in exchange for their election.

So a rural county legislator heatedly proposed the first crippling amendment in the House debate, but the ad-

herents of the school bill, led by Representative Neil Mc-
Mullen of Tampa, chairman of the House Education Committee, shouted it down in an overwhelming voice vote.
And so it went through a score of such amendments until
the final official vote, which was 91 to 0.

The legislators who had bitterly fought the bill looked
at the handwriting on the wall and they lacked the cour-
age to vote their convictions. They had fought viciously
for their political privilege but in the final public show-
down, when they knew they were beaten, they wanted
their names listed on the people's side for political posterity.

The *Tribune* had this editorial comment:

> It is clear, of course, why the House took such
> emphatic action. Members accurately judged the over-
> whelming public demand that the general level of our
> public schools be elevated. They knew that Floridians
> were solidly behind the measure designed to provide
> a comprehensive and continued remedial school pro-
> gram which will give to every child in every section
> of the State a public education opportunity of the
> highest standard.

The overwhelming House vote had a decided effect
upon these 30 Senators. On April 29, the school bill
came before the Senate Education Committee, most of
whom had signed the telegram to the teachers, and it was
voted out unanimously without a single word of debate.

There was a definite reason for this action, which was
curious in the face of the senators' opposition to the bill.
All of the debate of the Education Committee revolved
around a new bill, introduced by a small-county Senator
which would raise the teacher pay and which was designed to split the over-all school bill in such fashion
that its opponents could wreck it.

The *Tribune* promptly alerted the state to the danger,
and Parent-Teacher Associations from Key West to Pensa-

cola sent feminine delegations to what always had been a man's Heaven. This feminine pressure was so effective that two days later the small-county Senator surrendered, withdrew his teacher pay bill, and announced publicly that he would vote for the school bill.

On May 2, the school bill finally moved onto the floor of the Senate, and Florida was treated to a steaming four-hour debate over the fate of the school children. The debate itself was curious in that it quickly developed into a two-pronged affair.

The big-city Senators, who by this time had yielded to public pressure and were for the bill, got into a verbal fight over the matter of whether or not to increase the scholarship program which the bill provided. This thoroughly overshadowed the rural-county Senators' efforts to hamstring the bill. There was only one official vote on a crippling amendment proposed by a small-county Senator, and it was defeated 30 to 7. Thereafter, the Senators settled all amendments with a voice vote. Under the expert floor generalship of Senator LeRoy Collins of Tallahassee, chairman of the Education Committee, the Senate finally voted 35 to 1 for Florida's first progressive school bill, with no changes in it and with one stubborn rural-county Senator abstaining.

The one vote against the bill was by Senator Charlie Johns of Starke, and this had its political aftermath. In 1953, after the sudden death of Governor Dan McCarty, Senator Collins, the leader of the fight for the school bill, and Senator Johns, who cast the lone vote against it, were pitted in the special election for Governor.

Senator Johns, who then was acting Governor by reason of being president of the Senate, came to Tampa and campaigned against me personally. In speaking to political rallies he would thoroughly excoriate me by name and his henchmen would boo lustily. Senator Collins campaigned with the support of the grateful teachers and P.T.A.'s and won handily. And it was a great source of personal satisfaction to me that Tampa and Hillsborough County turned out a huge vote against Senator Johns.

There was another aftermath that was pleasing to the entire *Tribune* personnel. On June 5, the House of Representatives adopted the following resolution:

> WHEREAS, for the year preceding the 1947 Session of the Florida State Legislature, The Tampa Tribune devoted more than 650 columns of news, pictures, cartoons and editorials to the development of the Citizens' Committee on Education reports and other items for the improvement of our schools, and

> WHEREAS, during this time newspapers were forced to ration advertising because of newsprint shortage, and had The Tampa Tribune sold the space granted to schools, it would have been valued at approximately $50,000,

> THEREFORE, BE IT RESOLVED that The Tampa Tribune be commended for its unselfish efforts for the benefit of the children, the teachers, and the school system of the State of Florida as a whole.

This is now just a slightly yellowed piece of paper hanging framed in my office, but I still look at it occasionally. I look at it when crusading gets rough and the headaches mount, and I remember the barefoot Florida boy who had no lobby in the Tallahassee arena of political privilege. I remember also the rats scampering in the school lunchrooms and the inferior education dealt out by the politicians to the future leaders of Florida. And I remember also that good public education is the only solution to the responsibilities imposed upon us by freedom. And I have great satisfaction in my soul, because that is the only reward ever reaped by a crusading newspaper editor.

9.

Waste and Corruption in State Government

STATE GOVERNMENT IS CONSIDERABLY FARTHER from the people than city and county government, and this imposes considerably more responsibility upon the free press. It goes without saying that the ordinary citizen can hardly journey to the capitol, tap the shoulder of the Governor, surrounded with political pomp and glory, and shout forth: "Say, bud, you're taking me for too big a tax ride." Neither can the ordinary citizen plumb the depths of complicated road budgets running into the hundreds of millions of dollars, nor can he dig into the mess of a prison scandal.

It is rare indeed that government, itself, will voluntarily investigate government, and this is usually done only after the press, in a concentrated crusade, has so alerted the people that the elected public servant begins to feel the hot breath of an aroused public opinion upon his neck. In Florida, the state collects and spends more than $250,000,000 in taxes each year. And if the press does not keep a watchful eye on this, then, pray, who will?

Tallahassee, the capital of Florida, is 250 miles from Tampa; yet *The Tampa Tribune* was the first Florida newspaper to establish there a news bureau, manned by a staff writer. That was in 1948, and repercussions of this are still shuddering through the palmettoes. We found a newspaperman's gold mine there, particularly in the office of the State Comptroller, where my staff writer camped for a solid year. His research proved conclusively that a government unwatched by the press will take the people for a ride.

There were two immediate results. At that time, the *Tribune* was delivering less than 100 papers to subscribers in Tallahassee, all by mail. But within six months, we were delivering more than 1,500 papers daily to Tallahassee subscribers, simply because our state politicians had to take our newspaper to find out what new trouble they were in with the taxpayers.

Our staff writer was greeted with open political arms on his arrival at Tallahassee, and you've never seen such enthusiastic back patting. That lasted about two weeks. Thereafter my staffer lived a lonely life; he lunched alone; he walked alone; he dined alone. Only when he wrote his stories did he have company and that was in the form of numerous state press agents who buzzed about his typewriter, peeking over his shoulder to ascertain what new scandal he had dug out of the records.

I can't stress too strongly that all of our stories were nothing more than reports from the State Comptroller's records. Yet the politicians apparently thought that "traitors" within their midst were slipping the information to my staffer, and they avoided talking with him publicly as assiduously, as they would the plague. Here are just a few of the many hundreds of reports from the State Comptroller's office which we printed in the next three years:

1. Florida Supreme Court sits in plush elegance — $3,570 table, $1,800 desks, $560 telephone cabinets, $45 waste baskets.

2. Woman, who supported Governor in his election, gets two state salaries — $150 a month from the Florida Attorney General's office and $150 a month as a clerk in the Governor's office.
3. State Beverage Department expenses high — single employees sometimes turn in expense accounts of $500 a month.
4. Records in Comptroller's office showed the state paid the Governor's staff fat pay bonuses, although he previously had announced that the state could not pay his $1,000 monthly salary.
5. President of Florida State University spent $900 of state funds on party for state legislators; president of University of Florida bought orchid corsages with state tax money for wives of Florida cabinet, members of which decide the university's annual budget.
6. Despite the fact that the Secretary of State voted with other cabinet members to reduce all state spending by 25 per cent in an emergency, he recommended five employees of his department for special pay bonuses.
7. Washington lobbyist for Florida's Commissioner of Agriculture draws up to $1,200 a month in state funds for expenses and entertainment, including, of course, his share of hosting at the cocktail swing in Washington, D. C.
8. Refurnishing of swank new office of State Beverage Department cost the state $4,193 for such items as a $16 glass bottle, $108 arm chairs, $26.50 name plates, $6 letter openers, $4 ash trays, an $18 calendar, a $469 davenport and a $346 desk.
9. Attorney for State Citrus Commission draws $100 a day expenses when he is outside the state.
10. Expenses of State Commissioner of Agriculture totaled $7,700 for four years. The average was $1,925 a year, or 21 per cent of his salary. This figured to $37 a week, which was more than the average Florida worker drew in pay at that time.
11. Personal expenses of the state's auto tag inspectors totaled $13,104 for one month, an average of $230

per employee. Average salary paid the inspectors was $250 a month.

12. The state paid $4,500 for 30,000 booklets urging increased appropriation for schools. These booklets were distributed to legislators. This was tantamount to the politicians spending the taxpayers' funds to get more tax funds to spend, which is not unusual in American government.

13. Despite a state financial emergency, the State Board of Control and the State Department of Education each spent $1,785 in tax funds for air-conditioning units.

14. The State Attorney General and the 20 attorneys in the state's legal department drew $110,000 in salaries during one month. At the same time, the 31 private attorneys employed by the various state departments drew $150,000 in special fees and salaries.

15. Budgets of the three state universities included $118,000 for press agents and their expenses. This was an increase of 50 per cent over the previous year. The University of Florida budgeted $42,950 for press agents as compared to $28,540 the previous year, including the creation of a new post of public relations director at a salary of $8,000 a year.

16. An executive assistant of the Governor wrote the Governor's patronage advisors in each of Florida's 67 counties for a thumbnail analysis of the political attitude of each weekly and daily newspaper. The state, at that time, spent about $50,000 in legal advertising and the Governor proposed to ladle this out only to those newspapers which supported him. The *Tribune* printed the text of his assistant's letter.

17. A rural legislator's wife was on the payroll at $10 a day for both regular and extra sessions of the legislature, although at the time she was working regularly at a secretarial job in private industry 200 miles from the capital.

18. One legislator and five members of his family drew a total of $4,845 for the 78 days of the legislative ses-

sion, although Florida has a law that stipulates that no state official, including the legislator, may hire directly or indirectly more than one person who is a member of his family or even as close as third cousin.

19. The State Industrial Commission paid a $350 salary to a special investigator who a few weeks before had been arrested as the manager of a Tallahassee gambling casino.

20. Following the passage of Florida's first sales tax, a perusal of the Comptroller's records showed that $4,000,000 in pay raises and new state employees had been foisted upon the shoulders of Florida's taxpayers.

21. Expense records of nine state departments in Tallahassee showed nine different prices paid for toilet tissue, with the plush Supreme Court using the fluffiest.

22. A printing concern owned by a state legislator was awarded $34,000 in state printing contracts in spite of a state law which reads: "No member of the Legislature or other officers of the State shall be interested, directly or indirectly, in such contracts."

23. Certain members of the State Game and Fish Commission were fired by the Governor for the simple reason that they declined to give the Commission's insurance to friends of the Governor.

24. Seven newspapermen and radio commentators, all friends of the Governor, turned up on the state payroll, even though they did not resign their private jobs. These included two Spanish newspapermen in Tampa, who landed jobs as state road and tag inspectors at $175 and $275 a month, and a check showed that they did exactly nothing in return for these state salaries.

25. While Governor Fuller Warren was authorizing special bonus payments for his office staff, he announced he had to borrow money on his Cadillac in order to

live. The *Tribune* inspected state records and uncovered an involved procedure which included the
trade-in of four cars and the purchase of Lincolns
for the State Road Department; plus a "loan" of
$3,000 made by a Panama City banker friend of the
Governor on the Cadillac. Tampa bankers and loan
firms declared a car of that vintage was worth no
more than a loan of $1,800. The Governor hit the
ceiling, calling the *Tribune* story "sly" and "irrele-
vant."

Such stories, even though they are based purely on
the records of government, itself, are not good for the
blood pressure of our public servants. We continued printing these revelations from the Comptroller's office throughout 1949 and 1950 and into 1951, with the Tallahassee
atmosphere getting cooler and cooler toward the *Tribune*.
In fact, there were icicles hanging from the door of many
a state official insofar as we were concerned. Finally,
on October 23, 1951, Governor Fuller Warren, one of the
greatest orators Florida has ever produced, flew to Tampa
and made a special speech in our courthouse square.

It was a speech to end all speeches. Before a crowd
mostly of his political henchmen, the handsome Governor
spent two hours raking the *Tribune* and its editor fore and
aft in as magnificent outburst of adjectives as I have ever
heard. I strolled the three blocks between the *Tribune*
and the courthouse square, stood in the crowd and listened. It does one's soul good occasionally to hear someone, and particularly a political bigwig, plaster you from
head to foot with stirring vituperation.

The Governor teed off by repeatedly calling the *Tribune*
"foreign owned" and by charging that its policies were
dictated by "multimillionaires in Richmond, New York and
Chicago." Then he really warmed up. He lashed at us,
with much flinging of his arms, as "a soulless corporation," "a personal house organ," "organ of falsehood,"
"small, petty, mean and crummy," "organ of vituperation

and villification," "run from Wall Street," "organ of mis-information" and "untrue, mendacious, twisted and tor-tured pages." This went on and on, and each time the Governor would let fly one of his steaming adjectives, he would pause and his henchmen would whoop and holler with much glee.

Finally, he ticked off the 22 planks of his election platform of three years before and sanctimoniously pro-claimed that he had fulfilled 20 of these 22 promises. Then he charged that the *Tribune* had failed to inform its readers of his great triumphs and accomplishments, and he accused us, quote, "the foreign-owned, Wall-Street-controlled organ of scurrility" as being responsible for Florida's first sales tax. Actually, the Governor had op-posed the sales tax in his election campaign but had signed it into law instead of vetoing it, as he could have. It was indeed a sparkling evening down on the moon-kissed shores of beautiful Tampa Bay.

But this only began it. Governor Warren had inaug-urated a practice of giving a weekly speech through the means of a state-wide radio hookup to all of Florida. Thereafter, until the end of his term, he lambasted us and occasionally he would deposit some of those magnificent adjectives upon my shoulders, even though we had been friends and fellow students at the University of Florida years before. He also began to lump other Florida news-papers, such as the Miami *Herald* and the Tampa *Times,* in the same low category with us but, of course, the *Trib-une* being his first love, he really concentrated on us.

In one of his speeches in November, 1951, he singled out the columnist of the Tallahassee *Democrat* for special attention. This writer had picked up for comment several items from the *Tribune*'s news accounts of wasteful spend-ing. The Governor told his state-wide audience that the Tallahassee *Democrat* had dealt fairly with him and that its publisher and managing editor were "nice people." But, he said, the *Democrat*'s columnist operates under an alias and is a "professional character assassin," "a professional falsifier" and a "chronic smear writer." Then he offered to guarantee the people of Tallahassee more state road funds if they would shut up the columnist.

It went from bad to worse. At that time *The Tampa Tribune* and the St. Petersburg *Times* were competing for a TV permit. Whereupon, the Governor wrote an official letter to the Federal Communications Commission, in which he repeated all of his old charges and included a new one, "journalistic schizophrenia," and then he called upon the commission to turn down the *Tribune*'s application. This upset the St. Petersburg *Times* no end, and it hastened to write an editorial in which it said the Governor's remarks were "a reiteration of the monotonous harangue of accusations of falsehood which the Governor has kept up against the *Tribune* ever since it started exposing the irregularities and inanities of the Warren administration. The Governor is so vengeful toward the *Tribune* that he once made a preposterous charge that it was communistic controlled." This, of course, so angered the Governor that he wrote a new letter to the Federal Communications Commission urging that the St. Petersburg *Times'* TV application also be turned down.

But this was not all. On October 25, Governor Warren called on the Solicitor of Hillsborough County to investigate if the *Tribune* had violated an old state statute against publication of anonymous letters which seek to bring ridicule and disgrace on any person. And on December 28, 1952, he called a public hearing for January 2, 1953, four days before his term expired, and directed that the publisher of the *Tribune* bring his records and defend himself against the Governor's charge that the capital stock of the *Tribune* company was undervalued for taxation purposes.

Even in his final meeting with his cabinet on December 21, 1952, the Governor closed out his official administration with a stinging blast against the "lying" of the *Tribune* because one of our news stories revealed his secret firing of a member of the state livestock sanitary board. And such are only a few of the headaches of a newspaper which crusades in behalf of the taxpayers.

Governor Warren's feud with the *Tribune* continued after he was out of office. We have received scores of blistering letters from him and on several occasions he sought to purchase advertising space in which to "read our title" from A to Z. In June, 1958, he wrote us a letter, which we printed, that an anonymous member of the *Tribune* organization was a member of the Klu Klux Klan. And he made this charge in the face of the fact that in a crusade of many years before, the *Tribune* broke the back of the Klan in Florida.

A large part of any state's annual tax budget is spent on roads. Throughout the stirring years of the Warren administration when the *Tribune* was bringing to its readers in Florida their first on-the-spot report of their state government, we devoted considerable space to accounts of the official monkeyshines in the business of spending hundreds of millions of taxpayer funds. Some of these stories made political history and all were extremely interesting to Florida's taxpayers simply because they stirred up more than passing hullabaloo. Here are just a few of our stories:

1. Florida has stringent state laws barring public officials from sharing in the state's business and stipulating that all state purchases and jobs involving more than $1,000 must be let at public bidding. Despite these state laws, a company owned by Representative George Tapper of Port St. Joe received a $94,000 contract to paint the long Apalachicola bridge packaged in 100 separate orders, each of less than $1,000.
2. The State Road Department built a $54,000 road into an uninhabited river-front area, owned by wealthy men with political power in Hernando County — the home county of the department's chairman — while ignoring the pleas of poor people for a road into a heavily populated area in the same county.

3. Favored political attorneys time and again carried off lush financial hauls in obtaining rights-of-way for new roads. The *Tribune* revealed that, among others, a member of the State Supreme Court received a $12,700 fee shortly before his appointment, and that the law partner of a former Governor received an $11,000 fee.

4. Booming Tampa was badly in need of a new highway to the north but despite the need shown by surveys, the Road Department refused the highway, on the grounds that it was too expensive, but at the same time spent millions in new highways criss-crossing Hernando County, sparsely inhabited but the home of the department chairman.

5. The Road Department became the dumping ground for political patronage. Time and again, the *Tribune* revealed in news stories how certain of the politically favored received fat side jobs, for which they rendered very little work in behalf of their taxpayer employers. One of these, a former legislator from Hernando County, had a regular job at $300 a month with the State Real Estate Commission and pulled down an extra $250 a month as a statistician for the Road Department.

6. The *Tribune* disclosed also that the Road Department had purchased four big cars — three Lincolns and a Cadillac — for its department heads in violation of the state law requiring public bidding. This was a common practice in Tallahassee until the *Tribune* opened its news bureau and focused the public spotlight upon the practice. In this case, two of the Lincolns were purchased from a company owned by one of the Governor's principal henchment.

7. But the big political patronage haul came in the bulk contracts, usually granted without public bidding, also. The *Tribune* obtained from the records and printed letters from rich contractors showing that they bought all their oil and gasoline from political friends

of the Governor only, regardless of the cost. Our crusade on this particular political patronage brought a cleanup early in the next administration which saved Florida taxpayers hundreds of thousands of dollars.

This kind of reporting, of course, brought quick response from our public servants. In a July 4 Independence Day address at Bushnell, Alfred McKethan, chairman of the State Road Department orated as follows:

> "I see with alarm today a trend in public life that can only give comfort and satisfaction to the enemy; that will, perhaps, not intentionally but nevertheless actually, intensify the threat that now confronts us. I refer to the unwarranted attacks and undeserved abuse that are being heaped upon public officials in torrential proportions. It has attained such pitch and volume that it seems, in my opinion, almost inspired.
> "I do not stand here and tell you that all men in public life are honest — but by large, most of the people in government are honest and they, like my fine associates on the road board, were called to duty seeking no personal gain and with a single desire — to serve Florida."

These and similar stories in the *Tribune* all but marred the pomp and glory of the Governor in his road dedication ceremonies. In dedicating four new bridges in Hernando, Pasco, Sumter and Lake Counties, he really opened up on the *Tribune* and accused it of doing " . . . subversive work by printing malicious lies about public officials." Then he said: "This newspaper swindles the people of Lake and other counties."

But lies or no lies, Clarence Gay, Florida's State Comptroller, declared, after the four hectic years, that the *Tribune* had been exceedingly fair in its reports of Florida's government.

"It is like an intangible matter," he said. "But I believe that *The Tampa Tribune,* by its Tallahassee reporting, saved Florida's taxpayers at least $10,000,000."

That statement came from the man who, at that time, paid all of Florida's government bills with the taxpayers' funds, and I'll rest my case on his evaluation.

10.

"Pork Chop Gang"

THE STORY OF FLORIDA'S "PORK CHOP GANG" is nationally known. It is a story of rural political domination over the modern suburbia of the big cities; a story of taxation without representation which was the colonial evil that resulted in the Revolutionary War and American independence; and, last but not least, a story of outrageous political privilege for the few at the expense of the many.

Florida's "Pork Chop Gang" is a group of 22 state Senators who dictate what laws are passed or not passed by the 38-member Senate and the 95-member House of Representatives in the state legislature. These 22 rural county Senators represent only 18 per cent of Florida's population, who pay only 14 per cent of the state's taxes and get back 27 per cent of the state's benefits.

Stated another way, the 685,000 people in Florida's 40 small, rural "Pork Chop" counties paid state taxes of only $95,250,792 in 1959, and got back in state benefits, $175,689,828. Florida, the fastest growing state in the Union, has a 1960 population of 4,893,000.

The Tampa Tribune hung the name of "The Pork Chop Gang" on these 22 rural Senators in the heat of Florida's unsuccessful reapportionment fight of 1955. It is a derivation of the old southern Negro expression of "eating high on the hog" and, based on the above figures, together with other startling figures from the records, Florida's "Pork Chop Gang" certainly is "eating high on the hog" in every way possible, politically, financially and in special privilege.

Yet Florida can lay no particular and special claim to its "Pork Chop Gang." California has its "Cow County Senators" and Alabama its "South Black Belt Lawmakers," both of which are composed of tightly knitted groups of rural legislators, who dominate the two legislatures.

To give you an even better look at the misrepresentation of the people in the Florida Legislature, little rural Jefferson County has a population of 9,483 and is represented by one state Senator. But Dade County (Miami), with a population of 917,851, also is represented by a single Senator.

Similarly, Los Angeles County has 40 per cent of California's population but only one vote in the state Senate. Northern California Senators, from the so-called "Cow Counties," control 32 votes. And Lawndes County in Alabama's "South Black Belt" — named for its dark, loamy soil — has a population of a little more than 18,000 whereas Tuscaloosa County has well over 100,000. Yet each county is represented by one Senator and two Representatives in the state legislature.

In Georgia, 121 legislators from the small rural counties rule the state politically and otherwise. The eight largest counties, including Atlanta and Savannah and which have the bulk of Georgia's population, have only 24 Representatives in the legislature. The 1874 Constitution of Pennsylvania limits Philadelphia to six Senators, one for about 300,000 people; whereas, many rural Senators in the state represent less than 50,000 constituents.

It can readily be seen why the big Florida rumble for

reapportionment actually is a national fight in 48 main-
land states, which has been accelerated by the modern
movement to the suburbs.

The Florida Constitution stipulates that the legislature
must reapportion itself every 10 years according to Federal
census but this hasn't been done in 35 years. But Alabama
hasn't effected reapportionment since 1901; Iowa since
1904. (except for a slight change in 1928); Indiana, 1921;
Nebraska, 1938; Oklahoma, 1910; North Dakota, 1941;
Mississippi, 1890; and Vermont, 1920.

Minnesota citizens took the question to court and lost,
but their action persuaded their legislature to agree to
some sort of reapportionment in 1962. A New Jersey newspaper publisher sued and won, but it remains to be seen
whether that rural-dominated legislature will actually
agree to a fair reapportionment. There have been similar
legal actions in Oklahoma, Tennessee, Florida, Indiana
and Michigan in recent years, yet there are no positive
signs that our rural legislators are abashed by our courts.

Late in 1960, the United States Supreme Court finally
agreed, after ducking the question for many years, to
hear the reapportionment case in Tennessee.

The feeling persists in many quarters that the actions
of these rural legislators, in defying the reapportionment
laws, make all actions of the legislatures suspect legally
because of improper representation of the people. And
many would like to see the issue settled in Federal Court
on the simple legal question of taxation without representation. After all, the Federal Constitution stipulates national reapportionment after every Federal census, and
Congress has meticulously followed this.

The Florida fight began in 1945, but it was short-lived.
South Florida, bulging with a huge war-time population
gain, clamored for fair representation amid great talk of
splitting the state. Leaders in West Palm Beach, on the
southeast coast, suggested that this area secede from the
state. Central Florida urged that the state capitol be
moved from Tallahassee, at that time a sleepy old town

in northwest Florida, just about where progressive south Florida began. But the cards were stacked against reapportionment at that time.

Governor Millard Caldwell, a Tallahassee lawyer, gave only vocal support to the state Constitution which stipulated that the legislature must be reapportioned every 10 years. He did ask the 1945 Legislature for reapportionment and, when it could not agree, he did call an extra reapportionment session which lasted a record 53 days.

By this time the ranks of rural legislators had been solidified by all the talk in south Florida about moving the capitol from Tallahassee to Orlando, some 250 miles south. They simply voted down any and all proposals that would give south Florida more legislators. Meanwhile, Governor Caldwell launched a building drive in Tallahassee and spent so many millions of tax dollars in new state government buildings that it forever made it impractical to move Florida's capitol from rural north Florida into the more populous regions of central Florida.

Thus, with the first serious attempt for reapportionment killed off and the state capitol firmly anchored in Tallahassee, the matter of reapportionment rested in peaceful slumber for 10 years. Then another Tallahassee lawyer, Leroy Collins, was elected Governor, but he turned out to be a different kind of man. Under his administration a real knock-down, drag-'em-out reapportionment fight broke out that rocked the Sunshine State over its 1,000-mile length from Pensacola to Key West.

In the first place, the populous cities of south Florida helped Collins win over Charlie Johns, a north Florida state Senator and leader of the rural legislative bloc, and Collins' sympathies naturally rested with those who had put him into office. In the second place, he belonged to that progressive modern school of politicians who cater to the great masses of people rather than to the special interests.

So Governor Collins took personal leadership in the fight for reapportionment and demanded of the 1955

Legislature that it do something about the Constitutional problem. Most south Florida newspapers, including all in the big cities, joined in the free-swinging fight and promptly reaped a public denunciation from the "Pork Chop Gang" as the "scandal mongering press."

That 1955 Legislature twice adopted the same reapportionment bill, which would have given one new state Senator each to south and north Florida, and each time Governor Collins vetoed it with a ringing demand for a reasonable solution. The Legislature finally adjourned, whereupon the Governor promptly called it into a special reapportionment session.

Then resulted one of the classic political wrangles of all time in Florida, which cost Florida taxpayers $300,000, and got exactly nowhere. After 115 days of the special session, broken by a cooling off period, the Legislature adjourned on September 29, 1955, to meet again on June 4, 1956. It met again on the appointed day but promptly voted to recess until November 7, 1956. Throughout all this political wig-wagging, the "Pork Chop Gang" steadfastly stuck by its guns, declined one and all compromise measures, and talked long and earnestly of a plan that would call for 67 state Senators, one for each county, which would have given the 40 rural counties an even greater political control of the legislature than the six-vote margin which the 22 "Pork Chop" Senators then held.

Came the election of November, 1956 which changed the complexion of the "Pork Chop Gang" not one whit, and the reapportionment fight was dropped, by consent of both sides, until the regular 1957 spring session of the new legislature. Governor Collins promptly opened the session with a stern and strong demand for reapportionment. Again the "Pork Chop Gang" thoroughly dominated all matters and the regular session was adjourned in late May with no reapportionment agreement.

Governor Collins again called a special reapportionment session and, after many millions of oratorical words, none of which meant much, the Florida Legislature on October 8, 1957, finally agreed upon the State's first reapportionment in over 35 years. The bill called for 45 state Senators and 114 Representatives, compared to the legislature's membership of 38 Senate and 95 House members at that time.

This would have given south Florida a slight gain in both the Senate and the House of Representatives, but before the bill could be voted on by the people, the "Pork Choppers" took it to court. Florida's Supreme Court, at that time dominated by arch conservatives, promptly ruled the bill out of order on one of those legal technicalities.

Thus, the fight began all over again in the 1959 Legislature, with Governor Collins just as sternly and just as strongly demanding reapportionment. After 60 harrowing days of much political oratory and more editorial comment from virtually every newspaper in the state, a maverick reapportionment bill that pleased nobody was spawned. It called for a 44-seat Senate, with south Florida gaining four seats and north Florida two, and a 103 member House, with the big cities gaining eight seats.

Governor Collins immediately proclaimed the bill to be unsatisfactory both to south Florida and to the Constitutional requirements, but he said that it was probably the best that could be obtained under the circumstances and he called upon Florida voters to get behind it. But his message was brushed off by the populous southeast Florida coastal area, including Miami, and the leader of this dissenting factor announced to the state: "Not only does it not give citizens of Florida's populous counties half a loaf — it doesn't even give them a crumb."

It was a desultory campaign, even though the Governor spoke earnestly and often in behalf of the bill. Just prior to the November election, he appeared before a meeting of southern Governors at Asheville, N.C. and denounced the "Pork Chop Gang." In that memorable speech, he said the "Pork Choppers" took "blood oaths" to support each other, and he charged that Florida's big business interests were fighting the reapportionment bill because they like to "work with" the rural legislators.

All of this aroused only great disinterest among south Florida's populous areas, even though fair representation and fair taxation were at stake, and in the November election hardly more than one-fifth of Florida's 1,600,000 registered voters took the trouble to vote. Thus, the united "Pork Chop Gang" and their constituents scored a somewhat easy victory, defeating reapportionment by 31,354 votes.

Florida newspapers faithfully reported all of the foregoing on their Page 1, but the fight, itself, was largely conducted on the editorial pages. Over the years, dozens of reapportionment plans had been suggested, and the knights of the ivory tower got themselves completely bogged down in higher mathematics, much to the confusion of everyone concerned. What this reapportionment fight needed perhaps was another Boston Tea Party.

The one thing that impressed me, as an interested observer of the Florida political scene, during this 15-year fight for proper representation of the Florida people, was Governor Collins' charges before the meeting of southern Governors at Asheville. If the "Pork Chop Gang" were "blood brothers" and if Florida's big business preferred to "work with" the rural legislators, then these charges should be proved publicly for the great benefit of the Florida taxpayers. Furthermore, an investigation of the charges might furnish a clue as to why the rural legislators dominate virtually every state legislature in our land.

Immediately after the 1959 defeat of reapportionment at the polls, I assigned my veteran staff reporter at the state capitol in Tallahassee to look into the personal financial dealings of the "Pork Chop Gang." He spent the next three months camping in the records of the rural county courthouses.

The result was a greatly enlightening series of nine stories, which we printed in 2-column type on our Page 1 in March 1960. The best way for me to give you these revelations is to sum up our findings briefly story by story, as follows:

STORY NO. 1

The 22 Senators of the "Pork Chop Gang" hold frequent social meetings at the fishing camps of a lobbyist for some small loan companies and a private utility company.

The "Gang" keeps a firm grip on the "killer" committees in the legislature, through which it "kills" all bills it does not like. These "killer" committees are Appropriations, Finance and Taxation, Federal Legislation and Governmental Reorganization, Miscellaneous, Temperance, and Judiciary "C".

In the 1959 session of the legislature, these "killer" committees killed legislation before it reached the floor, which would have provided the following: central purchasing, chancellor for the state university system, regulation of unethical business practices, urban renewal, state control of unclaimed bank accounts, regulation of billboards on highways, aid to libraries, integrity in government, and provisions for less costly purchase of highway rights-of-way.

One of the leaders of the "Pork Chop" Senators also serves as prosecuting attorney for Calhoun and Liberty Counties, school board attorney for Calhoun County and city attorney for Blountstown, Fla.

STORY NO. 2

A run-down of the personal business occupations of the "Pork Chop Gang," which includes millionaire bankers, millionaire cattle ranchers, millionaire potato growers and a number of prominent and wealthy lawyers.

One wealthy northwest real estate Senator had participated in a number of huge land deals with the

U.S. Congressman representing that area of the state.

The "Pork Chopper" called the "old gray fox" of the Senate campaigned ceaselessly for a law which would relieve candidates of the legislature from having to report campaign contributions.

STORY NO. 3

President of the Senate and a leader of the "Pork Chop Gang" is attorney for the powerful St. Joe Paper Co., a DuPont industry which controls most of north Florida, and over the years borrowed a quarter of a million dollars from such big business interests as the DuPont banks, a Tampa cigar company, and Lykes Bros. Steamship Co. of Tampa.

Another "Pork Chopper" serves as attorney for the Florida Light and Power Co., which doesn't operate within 250 miles of his home.

A third is attorney for Florida Public Utilities Co. and West Florida Telephone Co.

A fourth member, an attorney, borrowed thousands from DuPont banks at Jacksonville, Ocala and Bushnell and finally became a director of the last one.

As an example of business "working with" the rural legislators, a bill which would have established a tax on minerals mined in Florida was killed by the "killer" committee. The Senate president is attorney for and director of the Floridin Co., which mines fuller's earth.

STORY NO. 4

A millionaire banker member of the "Pork Chop Gang" loaned $71,181 over the years to a fellow "Chopper," who was a former president of the Senate and a former acting Governor of Florida.

When the latter organized a new bank in his home city in north Florida, the former became chairman of its board.

STORY NO. 5

The records show that over the years the millionaire "Pork Chop" banker had held 700 personal mortgages in a dozen rural north Florida counties.

One of these mortgages was a $10,000 loan to the lobbyist for the small loan companies and in the 1959 Legislature, this "Pork Chopper" pushed through bills which permitted small loan companies to lend up to $600 instead of $300 and to make real estate loans.

STORY NO. 6

One "Pork Chopper" borrowed $4,000 from a bank in his rural county just before the opening of the 1959 session of the legislature.

Ten days later this "Pork Chopper" introduced a number of banking bills sponsored by the president of this bank who also served as the lobbyist for Florida's banking interests.

All nine members of the Senate Banking Committee were "Pork Choppers" in the 1959 session and they quietly killed in committee a bill that would have permitted the state to take over unclaimed deposits and funds in banks, savings loan companies, utilities, insurance companies, etc., worth an estimated $100,000,000.

STORY NO. 7

One "Pork Chopper," sued for dozens of unpaid bills, borrowed several thousands of dollars from a fellow "Chopper" and then endorsed his $100 a month legislative pay check to him.

A second was sued by a wealthy Tallahassee printing company for non-payment of a 60-day $4,000 loan, then borrowed $10,000 from a DuPont bank.

A third made a deal to rent a building to the State Beverage Department before he even bought the land and erected the building.

STORY NO. 8

The 22 Senators in the "Pork Chop Gang" zealously guard Florida's racing law, which splits up the horse and dog racing tax intake into 67 equal shares, one for each county. A county's share now amounts to about $180,000 a year.

In some small rural counties, this is half as much money as the county pays in all state taxes and means that half its tax money comes directly back in one whack from the big, populous counties in which the racing tracks are located.

Liberty County, with a population of about 2,400, paid state taxes of $235,934 and got back state benefits of $1,907,502.

Wakulla County, with a population of about 4,700, paid state taxes of $384,130 and got back state benefits of $1,604,478.

STORY NO. 9

"Pork Chop" Senators, one and all, say their record in the Florida Legislature is a proud one.

"What little progress the state has made, the credit must go to the 'Pork Choppers,' " declared one member of the gang.

"We have held down spending and held down taxes," said another.

But the minority members of the Senate, representing the big, populous south Florida cities, just won't talk.

"I've got to get along as well as I can with these men if I want anything for my district," said one minority member, who asked that his name not be mentioned.

But Senator Joe Eaton, of Miami, in announcing that he would not offer himself for reelection, told his friends he was "the most disillusioned person in the world."

This is the sad story of Florida's "Pork Chop Gang." And I leave it to you to decide whether or not Governor Collins was telling the truth when he charged that the "Pork Choppers" are "blood brothers" and whether Florida's big business prefers to "work with" rural legislators. I leave also to you the question of the probability that this sad Florida story applies in the rural-dominated legislatures of most of our states.

Anyway, our "Pork Chop Gang" series had a terrific reading impact upon Florida's public, but that was just about all. One Florida east coast newspaper asked and got our permission to reprint the series. And one of the six candidates for Governor in Florida's Democratic primary in May reprinted the series in a pamphlet and distributed it widely among south Florida voters.

But in the May primary, which is tantamount to election in Florida, the three candidates supported by the "Pork Chop Gang" for Governor, Secretary of State and Commissioner of Agriculture, scored easy victories, although they were opposed by the editorial page of every big newspaper in south Florida. This gave the "Gang," already dictators over the legislature, control over the Cabinet and a firm hold on the Governor's office.

I noticed in this campaign that most of the prominent lawyers and law firms in south Florida supported the "Pork Chop" slate. So I asked one of the lawyers why.

"Ah," he said, "don't you understand that our business clients get a better break with the 'Pork Choppers'?"

Thus, you can see that political privilege is decaying the grass roots of free democratic government in America and that if it is permitted to mushroom into the higher levels of government at Washington, the United States is doomed to stroll down the road that led to the fall of Roman civilization.

11.

Corruption
in Lower Levels

I HAVE GIVEN YOU, in brief, the details of four block-busting crusades, in which *The Tampa Tribune* fired all of its guns against general evils in government. Three were successful, and the fourth is far from finished. Now I shall outline a half dozen single-barrel crusades in which we exposed to the taxpayers specific evils connected with Florida's state and county government.

In mid-1949, I sent one of our staff writers into Hernando and Citrus Counties to look into a road contract held by a Tallahassee contractor, who had been chairman of Governor Warren's inauguration committee the previous year. There this writer found that a tractor, rented by the contractor to the state, was listed in the records as working 23 hours a day, with the State paying a specified rate per hour rental and in spite of the fact that Florida roads are built in the daytime and not at night. He also found that the contractor had received $3,516 rental for one tractor for the month of August.

I then sent another staff writer into Wakulla County to inspect another state road project. This contract was held by a Chipley contracting firm, but my writer found that all machinery on the job was owned by a state senator, one of a small group who had switched their votes overnight on the administration-supported sales tax the previous year. He found also the same lush road machinery rentals paid by the state.

These made wonderful Page 1 stories and particularly so since Governor Warren had pledged in his campaign speeches to abandon the old practice of the state renting road machinery without bids. Neither of the two rental jobs, which *Tribune* writers inspected, had been let in public bidding, which, of course, was in violation of Florida law.

We then really dug into the records at Tallahassee and disclosed that during the 18 months of the Warren administration, the state had paid out more than $3,000,000 in road machinery rentals without bidding and that this was just $300,000 short of the state's entire road machinery rental business for the previous 10 years. The Governor's inauguration chairman, the Tallahassee contractor, had collected more than $700,000 in rental fees.

All of this created quite a stir out among the ordinary Florida citizens, whose taxes paid these fabulous sums; and of course it also stirred the wrath of state officials. Alfred McKethan, chairman of the State Road Board, immediately issued hot statements that such road machinery rentals were essential to the state's $79,000,000 road program. He also declared there was an old state law authorizing these rentals without public bidding, but when the *Tribune* reporter sought to pin him down on this, he ducked it by saying that this would come out in court.

Right in the middle of his controversy, a group of 180 taxpayers in St. Lucie County filed a petition with the State Road Board against the machinery rentals in the construction of a three-mile stretch of road near Ft. Pierce. And a few days later, two young officials in the Road

Department suddenly resigned and filed suit in circuit court at Tallahassee against the state's rental of road machinery without public bidding.

This brought the matter to a head. State Comptroller Clarence Gay refused to issue checks for $411,328 in pending rentals, and Attorney General Richard Ervin called the rentals "a camouflage used to evade state laws requiring competitive bidding." The State Road Board hired 13 leading Florida attorneys, including two former Governors and the president of the state bar association, but Attorney General Ervin, aided by two young assistants, scored a complete victory. On August 18, 1950, Circuit Judge Hugh Taylor issued a decision banning once and for all the state's rental of road machinery without public bidding. There was no appeal.

On a hot summer afternoon in 1955, the head of one of the feeble wings of the Ku Klux Klan sat in my office and related how he was in the process of disbanding his end of the hooded order. This, of course, made a news story but it wasn't what really interested me in the conversation. During the talk, this man dropped in a sentence that a Negro had been secretly flogged by a mob at Live Oak within the last few days.

I didn't let on to this Kluxer that this sentence particularly interested me, but the minute he walked out of my office, I called in one of my staffers and dispatched him to Live Oak. It was a difficult story to get, simply because Negroes in the South just won't talk about a flogging, regardless of the circumstances, and particularly to a white man. My staffer talked to scores of Negroes and whites in the Live Oak area before he finally got the name of the victim.

We broke the story on our Page 1 on June 21, 1955, and it was a sensation. It was very much like the old-time Ku Klux Klan floggings except in this case the floggers put a sack over the Negro's head so he could not identify them. The Negro, hesitant at first, finally broke down, and we related the gruesome story of how a mob of white men took him from his home to the banks of beautiful Suwannee River and flogged him with leather straps. The Negro told also the reason for the flogging. He had nine children and wanted them to work on his own farm, but the mob told him he had to let them work for white farmers when they needed them.

While investigating this case, my staffer ran across another incident wherein a white bill collector had pistol-flogged a pregnant 18-year-old Negro woman. We made this a Page 1 story on June 22, and on June 23 Governor LeRoy Collins called for a thorough investigation of the two cases. A grand jury was called but Suwannee County's Sheriff Hugh Lewis and other officials plaintively pleaded that they couldn't get anyone to talk. The *Tribune* replied editorially that it was strange why the sheriff and other officials, armed with the law, could get no information, whereas, a lone *Tribune* reporter, armed with nothing but his pencil, could get the whole story. The bill collector was finally indicted, but no arrests were made in the case of the flogged Negro farmer.

There the case rested for three years until on June 26, 1958, a committee of the Florida Legislature opened an investigation of the Ku Klux Klan. The same Kluxer who sat in my office and gave me the original tip appeared before the committee at Tallahassee and testified that Sheriff Hugh Lewis knew all about who flogged the Negro farmer but had done nothing about it. The committee promptly called Sheriff Lewis as a witness, disclosed that he was a former member of the Klan, but could not get him to answer 15 questions concerning the flogging of the Negro. The committee then voted contempt procedures against the Sheriff, and Governor Collins called upon all 67 Florida sheriffs to go after the Klan. We're still waiting for the next chapter.

A letter from a woman late in 1956 put the *Tribune* in the middle of a controversy involving the Ringling Art Museum at Sarasota which is operated by the state. The woman, an employee of the Museum, wrote that there were "strange things going on," and she urged that we send a writer to look into them. Our writer did find a lot of "strange things," we printed them and, as usual, this immediately blew up a political storm.

Among the "strange things" found by the *Tribune* staffer were: extreme waste and extravagance; a very loose payroll in which excess employees were running all over the place; the director was taking a five months vacation; such ridiculous expenditures as a $300,000 theatre to house $7,000 worth of ancient Italian theatrical trappings, and more than $3,000 spent on reweaving a tapestry; declining gate receipts due mainly to the public being pushed around; and a lot of highhandedness and arrogance. We brought out clearly that the museum officials were accustomed to going ahead with their various projects and then, after they were completed, ask for permission of the State Board of Control to do them. We also disclosed a secret plan of the museum to add an expensive purchasing agent, although such a job was not needed in so small an operation.

Art people are just naturally superior in their outlook toward the rest of the human race, and my reporter was exposed to considerable artistic arrogance during his investigation. And the minute we printed his first story on the museum, a group of Sarasota citizens led by Karl A. Bickel, retired president of the United Press, issued a public blast at the *Tribune* for daring to look into the museum. Mr. Bickel admitted that he had not read the stories and he said he did not question the right of the reporter to investigate and the right of the *Tribune* to print his findings, but he declared that the *Tribune* was ". . . looking down the wrong barrel."

Notwithstanding this, however, Governor Collins called for a cleanup and appointed a citizens' committee, headed by former Governor Doyle E. Carlton to make a thorough investigation. The result, of course, was a complete shakeup in the management of the museum, elimination of much waste and extravagance, and a better deal in every way for the public, which was paying all bills with tax dollars.

There was a curious aftermath in which the *Tribune* had no part other than to report the various developments. Representative James A. Haley of the Sarasota congressional district bitterly protested the action of Governor Collins in removing several of the fine paintings from the Ringling Museum to the new Governor's mansion at Tallahassee. Finally, Haley sued on the grounds that the will of the famous circus man, John Ringling, stipulated that all of the paintings which he had bequeathed to the state, must remain in the museum. The court finally ruled that the paintings must be returned to the museum, and on June 1, 1958, the *Tribune* printed on its Page 1 a picture of Governor Collins personally taking down the paintings in his Tallahassee mansion.

Another woman put the *Tribune* in the middle of Florida's system of prisons, brought down on our heads the wrath of the Governor, but resulted in a cleanup and the beginning of the modernization of our state prisons. At first, we politely brushed off this woman's telephone calls because we get many calls from many citizens, including crack-pots, and these came in the middle of a busy season in 1955. But she was so insistent that I finally sent a staff writer to her home and she turned over to him the letters of her 15-year-old daughter, who was an inmate of the Florida Industrial School for Girls at Ocala. I took one look at the girl's letters and rushed my writer to that institution.

The writer interviewed the woman's daughter and other inmates, and his first story graphically detailed the contents of the girl's letters, including relations with other girls, beatings and riots. It was sensational, and in the immediate explosion at Tallahassee Governor Collins rawhided the *Tribune* verbally for accepting and printing without corroboration the girl's letters to her mother. The Governor, like many politicians I have known, sits augustly upon the pinnacle of perfection, and resents any criticism of government as a personal attack upon him, regardless of its truth.

Our second story carefully documented the following:

1. Evidence of abnormal behavior among the girl inmates.
2. A score of girls had carved upon their arms and other parts of their bodies, the names or initials of their girl friends at the institution.
3. Officers used tear gas to quell a rebellion by some of the girls in the detention ward.
4. A highway patrolman was called into the institution at frequent intervals to beat recalcitrant girls.

We illustrated this story with a picture of the arm of one of the girls, showing plainly the carved initials of her girl friend. Actually, the inmates told my reporter that most of the initial carving was done on the girls' buttocks.

Our third story was based on my writer's 10-hour interview with the woman superintendent of the Ocala institution and developed the following main points:

1. She admitted shortcomings of the institution in respect to rehabilitation of girls deemed incorrigible and those with mental and emotional problems.
2. She blamed the legislature for cutting appropriations for the institution, which she said was inadequate in personnel and facilities.
3. She criticized the juvenile courts' practice of returning girls released from the institution to original homes which bred delinquency in the first place.

Regardless of the Governor's wrath, these stories forced him to call an investigation and he appointed a subcommittee of the Cabinet, headed by Superintendent of Schools Thomas D. Bailey, to conduct it. This subcommittee called in psychology experts from the University of Florida to assist in the investigation, and in December, 1955, Superintendent Bailey announced that it had widened its investigation to include all of Florida's prisons.

Subsequently, the Governor created a new post of Director of Prisons and this man, a veteran expert, began the tremendous task of modernizing Florida's antiquated system of prisons.

There can be no question but that newspapers should keep a constant watch upon the people's public servants; otherwise, as the records of Florida's state government plainly show, the politician always will indulge in political privilege, particularly when the almighty dollar is involved.

Let us, as an example, consider the printing business. Florida has an excellent state law which clearly stipulates that all state purchases of $1,000 or more shall be made on public bids. That should guarantee Florida people a fair shake in all state purchases, including the $2,000,000 which the state spends each year on its printing contracts.

Early in 1959, just before the legislature met, the *Tribune*'s capitol reporter looked into the records of the state's printing contracts at Tallahassee, and here is what he found:

1. Three printing companies, including two at Tallahassee, in one way or another always managed to snare the greater portion of the state's printing business, and one of them usually got at least half, or $1,000,000, of the total annual business.
2. These printing contracts were let on bids all right, according to the state law, but records showed that the bidders were especially invited and bids were not advertised for the benefit of all printing companies in the state.
3. Records also showed that the Tallahassee company which got half the state's business was the "low bidder" on 76 of 101 Florida Development Commission contracts and on all 32 of the Florida Railroad Commission contracts.
4. An assistant to the State Superintendent of Education was on the payroll of this big Tallahassee printing company.

5. A check of records of printing contracts of the Florida Crippled Children's Commission showed that dates on three of the printing bids had been altered in the same handwriting, and that in five of the Commission's 36 contracts the bids of two or more of the printing companies had been typed on the same typewriter.

6. Two Tallahassee companies denied there was an agreement to split the State's printing business between them. The manager of one company said he could not explain why printing bids of competing companies often appeared to have been typed on the same typewriter; the manager of the other company said it was possible that he occasionally used the typewriter of a competing firm to type his bids.

7. It was disclosed that one Tallahassee printing company was promoting sale of honorary memberships in the Alabama Sheriffs' Association. This promotion was in the name of charity, of course, but the split of the $10 membership was as follows: $1 to the sheriff in the Alabama county where the purchaser lived to be used for scholarships, etc.; $1.50 for a year's subscription to the sheriffs' monthly publication; $5 for subscription to the sheriffs' yearbook; 50 cents for a membership certificate; $1.20 for the Montgomery office of the sheriffs' association; and 80 cents to the Tallahassee printing company for promotion.

All of this created an uneasy stir in the ranks of Florida's politicians and provoked no less than three separate investigations. The State's Attorney of Leon County (Tallahassee) subpoenaed printing records of the Florida Children's Commission, but nothing came of this. Governor Collins launched an investigation and called for all executive agencies under his direction to ascertain that all was aboveboard in their printing contracts.

The third investigation was by the legislature and it resulted in the adoption of new laws which would require: (1) that all state printing come under regulation of the State Purchasing Commission; and (2) that on big contracts — over $2,000 — legal advertisements would be run in newspapers to alert printers that bids were being taken.

Later Governor Collins complained that these laws did not go far enough. He said they did not prohibit interlocking printing companies owned by the same people from being the only bidder on the state's contracts, and he pointed out there were no penalties for printers who sought to evade true competition in the state's contracts.

All of which clearly indicates that it probably will take a loaded shotgun aimed squarely at the head of our politicians to force them to eliminate political privilege from the little matter of the people's business.

A scandal at Florida State University launched the *Tribune* in a full scale crusade against the secret meetings of the State Board of Control, which directs the policies and spending at Florida's universities. In the fall of 1953, a co-ed accused a professor of improper conversation on sex after class, and the professor's resignation was demanded and obtained. All of this took place in deep, dark secrecy on the part of both the University and the Board of Control.

The professor appealed to the *Tribune* and demanded a public hearing of the charges. I sent a staffer to Tallahassee and there he ran head on into a most rude reception. University officials simply would not discuss it and took the attitude that what took place on the campus was their business and not the business of the taxpayers who were paying all the bills. But we came out of there with a Page 1 story of how the University's burly athletic director had punched the nose of the slender professor in the office of the president for daring to ask questions on the operation of campus athletics. The professor, in asking for a public hearing, made a plea for "fair play and common decency" and pointed to his tubercular wife and two small children.

Acting Governor Charlie Johns finally stepped into the torrid picture and called a public hearing, at which he presided, on December 20, 1954. The whole mess was thereby placed in the public records, including charges by the professor that University authorities were covering up a bold homosexual ring which operated on the campus. The following April, the secrecy-loving Board of Control made history by holding a public hearing on the matter, at which a notarized statement from the girl, who made the original charges, was placed in the records absolutely clearing the professor. Thus collapsed the case against the professor, but it did not collapse the *Tribune*'s case of secrecy against the Board of Control.

Up to that time, no daily newspaper reporter had covered the monthly meetings of the Board in various cities of the state. The Board would meet in its secret "executive sessions" and the only news the Florida taxpayers received as to the operation of their universities and institutions was in the form of handouts, mostly propaganda. I immediately assigned a staffer to cover each and every one of the board meetings, and the fun began.

Human nature being human nature, you can bet that whenever more than two people meet in a secret session, one of them will talk. Thus was the case in the seven-member Board of Control. They would hold their secret "executive sessions," often in a hotel room the night before the scheduled meeting. My reporter always would get the information from one or more members within an hour after the secret session was concluded. He then would write his story about the secret meeting and would detail all the actions of the board. Once, at Sarasota, my reporter wrote of such a secret meeting, then detailed the torrid debate over whether the hedge surrounding the Ringling Art Museum had been clipped too closely. On another occasion, my staffer was ejected from the Board's meeting.

These stories, of course, kicked up considerable political dust. The Tallahassee Press Club formally protested the secrecy; a bill was introduced in the legislature against the closed meetings; and three Cabinet members roundly condemned them. The matter eventually landed on Governor LeRoy Collins' desk in a public hearing and he issued a statement that "Florida's government should be conducted in the sunshine and not in the shade." At the same time, he directed the Board of Control to conduct its business in open meetings.

This came in 1957 and it should have concluded the issue. But Governor Collins went to the annual Governors Conference at Williamsburg, Virginia, and engaged Governor Orval E. Faubus of Arkansas in a debate, all because Governor Faubus wanted the Governors' committees to meet in secrecy. Then Governor Collins came home, jumped the fence and promptly engaged in a public controversy in which he informed the Board of Control that it should not reveal the deliberations and decisions of its secret meetings until this information had first been conveyed to the parent State Board of Education, of which the Governor is a member. The controversy involved the selections of a president and the name of the new University of South Florida in Tampa, and was of wide interest to the people of Florida.

There seems to be a fairly consistent pattern to the rise and fall of corruption. When an exposure ends in a conviction, the underworld goes into hiding for a period of time. There usually is a mastermind who carefully plans a cautious move in a remote spot. If this goes undetected, the next move will be bolder. Success with this one opens the way for a network of small moves that will serve as a snare to entrap a person or a community so that when the strings are pulled, the underworld will have full control. When it is possible to ferret out one of these early moves, the whole chain may be broken up. It is a newspaper's responsibility to spot these leads and run them down.

It was one of these leads that developed into a large-scale exposure of the gambling syndicate getting back into control in this area, in spite of all the previous exposures and convictions.

In May, 1959, the grand jury of Pinellas County, across the bay from Tampa, returned a most curious report. Out of the blue sky, it reported that two Tampa hoodlums, with the connivance of two prominent St. Petersburg citizens, had attempted to bribe Constable Rodenbaugh (who then was the Republican candidate for sheriff) with campaign funds. Purpose of the bribery was to give Tampa hoodlums control of gambling in St. Petersburg and Pinellas County.

The jury's report commended Constable Rodenbaugh, the county's prosecuting officials, and everyone else in sight, but did not indict anyone nor name either the Tampa hoodlums or the prominent St. Petersburg citizens.

The grand jury was composed of ordinary citizens summoned out of private life to sit as a public investigating body. Because of the limited time the jury sits, it must be guided by the State's Attorney not only in the matters it investigates but also in its legal actions. In this particular case, the State's Attorney, a Republican, had advised the jury that there was not sufficient evidence to prosecute anyone in the attempted bribery of Constable Rodenbaugh. It was plainly a political whitewash job.

The naive jury report resulted in a public wave of speculation, which swirled over St. Petersburg, Clearwater and Tampa, as to the identity of the two prominent St. Petersburg citizens and the two Tampa hoodlums. And a number of public officials and community leaders were subjected to the unjust stigma of suspicion.

At this time, there came into my hands from a confidential but unimpeachable source, a photostat of the stenographic report of Constable Rodenbaugh's testimony in the case given to certain prosecuting officers of Pinellas County. This photostat named names and told play-by-play how the two Tampa hoodlums, along with the two prominent St. Petersburg citizens, met with the constable and paid him $4,500 in supposedly campaign contributions.

I immediately sent two veteran *Tribune* reporters, armed with the photostat report, to Pinellas County to contact everyone involved and to get, if possible, some sort of an official admission that this actually was the constable's testimony. They met a stone wall of tight-lipped official silence. They finally tracked down the constable, who had gone into hiding on an island in the bay, apparently afraid of gangland bullets. He talked to the two *Tribune* reporters only in the presence of witnesses, and then said exactly nothing. A heavy-set man, apparently a bodyguard, sat nearby and was never introduced to the reporters.

At the end of a week, my two reporters had gotten not one word that we could print, even though they had talked with dozens of potential witnesses. Stymied for the moment, I sent them to the Pinellas County Circuit Judge, a stern, doughty old jurist with a reputation for great honesty.

I told the reporters to lay our cards squarely on the table in front of the judge. The main thing we needed to know was whether or not this particular photostated document had been placed as evidence before the grand jury. If it had been given to the jury as evidence, then the law of secrecy which surrounds American grand juries would bar us from printing it and, should we ignore this law, we would face charges of contempt.

The judge listened to the reporters, looked at the photostat, then he observed that there was no way for the reporters to know whether it had been presented to the jury, since they weren't present. Then he dryly remarked that the only thing their editor had to worry about was libel.

That was all we needed. The following day we printed on our Page 1 the entire photostated report, deleting only the names of the two prominent St. Petersburg citizens and the two Tampa hoodlums. In the case of the citizens, we tagged them as Prominent Citizen No. 1 and Prominent Citizen No. 2. In the case of the Tampa hoodlums, we left a blank space for their names.

Since the matter had been investigated and reported on by the grand jury, we were safe in printing all the details, just so long as we did not identify improper persons. And in view of the judge's dry comments, we had no worry about contempt proceedings.

We followed this up with an interview with the Pinellas County prosecuting attorney, who admitted he had official possession of the $4,500 in bribe money. "It was placed in an envelope, which was sealed and stored in a safety-deposit box obtained especially for this purpose," he told a *Tribune* reporter.

That, in brief, was the strange situation. The authorities knew all about the pay-offs and who participated in them. They had possession of the bribe money, itself. Yet the State's Attorney had informed the grand jury that there was not sufficient evidence to prosecute.

Our revelations actually blew the lid off the scandal. We ran a series of editorials, illustrated by blank spots for the pictures of the four participants in the bribery, and called for a thorough investigation and justice in behalf of the people of Pinellas County.

Governor LeRoy Collins responded by relieving the Pinellas County State's Attorney of his responsibilities in the case and appointing the State's Attorneys of West Palm Beach and Tampa to conduct a special investigation. A new grand jury was promptly called, seven witnesses testified, including Constable Rodenbaugh, and on June 3, 1959, it returned indictments on charges of bribery, conspiracy to bribe and conspiracy to violate lottery laws against the following:

William H. Bowes, Postmaster of St. Petersburg
Also:
C. Ray Smith, former County Attorney for Pinellas County
Frank Trafficante, of Tampa
Primo Lazzarra, of Tampa

The case had tremendous interest in Florida's First Congressional District simply because Bowes was formerly campaign manager for Representative William C. Cramer, the district's Republican Congressman, and Smith had suddenly resigned the previous January as Cramer's law partner.

And the case had significant interest in Tampa because Frank Trafficante was a brother of Santos Trafficante, one of the delegates to the notorious gathering of Mafia leaders at Apalachin, N.Y. in 1957, and Lazzarra had been questioned in several of Tampa's gang slayings.

Just before the *Tribune*'s investigation of this case, Representative Cramer had delivered to the House of Representatives a ringing piece of oratory in which he urged that the FBI be allowed to investigate gangland-type murders and he described Tampa as a "cesspool of crime" and a center for Mafia operations.

Late in the year the four men went on trial and Constable Rodenbaugh, the main witness, told virtually the same story as the photostated reports which the *Tribune* had printed. He also testified that he had strapped a small tape recorder to his person during the pay-off meetings, but defense attorneys blocked its admission as evidence. But on October 23, 1959, the six-man jury reported it was hopelessly deadlocked after nine hours of deliberation and the judge declared a mistrial.

The case was retried again early in 1960 and again Constable Rodenbaugh testified to the same story. Much of the trial consisted of wrangling by the attorneys over the constable's tape recording, but again the judge did not permit its admission as testimony. However, on Feb. 4, 1960, all four defendants were convicted on the charge of conspiring to bribe Constable Rodenbaugh in his unsuccessful campaign for sheriff. And thus ended Tampa Bay's sensational case of the political whitewash.

Such are the sad ways of the politician.

12.

Florida's
Sweat Boxes

IT TOOK *The Tampa Tribune* AND THE PEOPLE of Florida
13 years to get rid of sweat boxes in Florida's prison
camps simply because Florida's public officials first defended these medieval torture chambers and then hid
behind an iron curtain of secrecy the facts about sadism
practiced by prison guards.

At the very start of our crusade against "Sweat Boxes"
in 1945, we discovered no less than 35 boys from 14 to 18
in Florida's prison camps. Public revulsion against the
brutality of adult prison guards in handling these teen-
age prisoners was such that the state quickly whisked the
youngsters out of the camps. But the sweat box remained
until 1958, even though it often was located only a mile
from plush tourist hotels.

The Florida sweat box was a small wooden structure
with a top for holding prisoners in solitary confinement
ranging from a few hours to many days. Prison guards
could, at any whim, confine prisoners here, sometimes
blackjacking them first.

The boxes were so small that a prisoner had either to sit or stand; he could not lie down. They contained no toilet facilities, or anything else.

They got their name from the fact that little air circulated in them and in the summer the temperature inside often rose to 125 degrees or higher, particularly in south Florida. They truly were sweat boxes.

Guards often would toss a pinch of sugar into the boxes and instantly hordes of ants and sub-tropical insects would march into them. After consuming the few grains of sugar, the insects would turn their attention to the prisoner.

Mind you, I am not beating the drum for the pitiable plight of Florida's convicts. We have just as many murderers, rapists and armed robbers behind our bars as do the other states. And certainly their testimony always is suspect.

Nor am I drawing a particular bead on Florida's prison guards. They probably are no more brutal or sadistically inclined than the prison guards in other states. In Florida, we pay prison guards about $200 a month. You cannot expect to hire a humane genius in psychiatry for that money, and I am afraid that a certain mental personality is attracted to the sordid business of lording it over penned up hoodlums.

What I am condemning is our whole system of prisons. You cannot rehabilitate a gangster in a sweat box or with a blackjack. And I am sure this great problem is at the bottom of all the prison riots that have flashed across our land in recent years.

During the summer of 1960, a terrible tale of prison torture was unfolded before the Florida public, and it is well to interrupt this account of sweat boxes and dwell a moment on it simply because it clearly shows that, while you get rid of one evil, the iniquitous system in all of its evil goes right on. The Federal Government brought charges of cruelty against 14 Florida prison guards for their treatment of 21 convicts in the wild rioting at Florida's state prison at Raiford in 1958. The three main charges, to which a string of witnesses testified, were:

1. The guards chained, handcuffed and shackled the prisoners by their hands and feet to the bars of their cells and kept them there naked and without food for periods of from one to 10 days.
2. The guards assaulted the naked prisoners in their cells with so heavy a stream of water from hoses that the latter suffered physical injuries.
3. The guards spread rock salt on the floors of the cells to an extent that many of the naked prisoners were rubbed raw.

Where, oh where, is our so-called civilization!

Flashes of this terrible human torture leaked to the Florida people in the middle of a political fight in 1958 between the State Director of Prisons and the chief warden at the Raiford prison, but the whole story was withheld by Florida's public officials, which showed plainly the iron curtain of secrecy.

The *Tribune* figured in two incidents during this 1958 scandal. On a tip, we investigated the death of a Negro prisoner, Talmadge Sellers, at Raiford. The prison officials swore to us that the Negro died from pneumonia and a coroner's jury ruled the death resulted from natural causes. But in 1960 Assistant United States Attorney John Briggs told the Federal Court in Jacksonville, Fla., that Sellers died after being made to spend two days in a small room filled with tear gas.

Later in 1958, Governor LeRoy Collins sent what he called a confidential memorandum to members of his Cabinet in which he asked their advice on Florida's penal problems and in which he ordered the State Director of Prisons to stop talking to the press. The *Tribune*'s staff writer at the capitol got hold of this so-called confidential memorandum and we printed a story on it prominently on Page 1.

At his next Cabinet meeting, the Governor demanded that the *Tribune* reporter reveal the source of his story. The reporter, of course, declined. And the *Tribune* supported him editorially by pointing out that a good news reporter does not confine his duties to handling governmental handouts and that he has a duty always to protect the identity of his informants. The editorial concluded with this paragraph:

> But from the time when the first smudged sheets came off colonial presses, American newspapers have been digging out and printing information of public interest, which some officeholder sought to keep secret. Sometimes, no doubt, well-meaning officials are hurt in the process. But more often these disclosures have exposed official incompetence, connivery or corruption and thereby contributed to better government. That kind of let-the-chips-fall reporting is, in our book, responsible reporting.

But let us get back to the sweat box, which you can now see is a dramatic symbol of what is wrong with the prison system of America. The death of a young convict in a north Florida prison camp sweat box, which Florida's public officials sought to hide from the people, put the boxes into newspaper headlines for the first time in 1945. Prison authorities immediately clammed up and greeted newsmen with hostility, but a *Tribune* investigating reporter informed the people of Florida that this convict's death was not a natural death, that he had been cruelly beaten and then kept in a sweat box for days, and deprived of medical attention. Most of the information we printed on this case was hazy, because of the tight official secrecy, but it was not denied.

I immediately assigned my investigation reporter to do a series on the Florida prison camps, spotlighting the sweat boxes. Even though their testimony was suspect, convicts told of experiences in the boxes, and along with this we printed pictures and stories of life in them. We even photographed one of our reporters trying to lie down in one of them. And we revealed that three years before, 18 convicts had cut the tendons of their legs to get into prison hospitals and escape the boxes.

All of this, of course, had a terrific impact on the Florida public, but it actually was a gentle zephyr when compared to the storm of protests which resulted when we got into the matter of boy convicts and the sweat boxes. Letters smuggled to us out of the Raiford prison gave us the first tip that two teen-agers had cut the tendons in their left heels with a razor blade to escape the cruelty, including sweat boxes, of the hulking prison guards at a camp near Chattahoochee, Fla.

My investigating reporter hied himself to Raiford and demanded to see everybody including authorities, doctors and boy convicts. The prison superintendent and physician begrudgingly confirmed everything and finally permitted my reporter to interview the boy prisoners without the presence of prison authorities.

A parade of boy convicts, including two 14-year-olds working in the prison tobacco factory, talked to the reporter and told of work beyond their endurance, beatings by prison guards, use of shackles, and frequent solitary confinement in the sweat boxes.

One of the maimed boys, a 16-year-old from Pensacola (serving a five-year stretch for breaking and entering) said he was beaten with a cane on his first day in the Chattahoochee camp and placed in a sweat box with two other boys. The second maimed boy, a 17-year-old from Daytona (serving two years for unarmed robbery) told how he was beaten by a guard for not keeping up with a man in pulling corn and then placed in a sweat box.

On the day after this story appeared in the *Tribune,* the prison superintendent gave out a statement to news services in which he said the boy convicts cut their heels to escape work. But in an interview with the *Tribune* man on the day after this, he candidly admitted that boy convicts had no place in adult prisons and particularly in prison camp sweat boxes.

Meanwhile, a hurricane of protest blew up all over Florida, mostly from indignant women, and whistled about the heads of Governor Millard Caldwell and Cabinet members at the state capitol. During the next few weeks, the *Tribune* printed dozens of stories with such headlines as the following:

17,000 WOMEN CALL ON STATE TO ABOLISH PRISON SWEAT BOX

3,432 CHURCH WOMEN PROTEST SWEAT BOXES

METHODIST WOMEN HIT SWEAT BOXES

TYPOGRAPHICAL UNION URGES SWEAT BOX END

TEACHERS HIT SWEAT BOXES

25 BAPTIST MINISTERS HIT SWEAT BOXES

This public criticism promptly got under the skin of Florida's public officials, who united in defending the sweat box. The secretary to the Board of State Institutions wrote the Methodist women in defense of the prison camps, declaring the only change contemplated by prison officials was removal of partitions in sweat boxes to permit prisoners to lie down, and said that a decision by the Attorney General prevented removal of the 14-year-old boy from the work camp.

"The letter made it sound as though the prisoners loved the sweat boxes," said Mrs. Elgin Davis, chairman of the Methodist women, in a public statement to the *Tribune.*

The late Nathan Mayo, Florida's long-time Commissioner of Agriculture, who was in charge of the state's prison camps, wrote the Madison, Fla., Woman's Club that there was no such thing as sweat boxes and that the solitary confinement cells in the prison roads camps were most humane.

But it was Governor Caldwell who veritably hit the ceiling over the state-wide protest. In a public statement, he blamed all the uproar to a "frustrated city editor who knew nothing of the facts" and he declared "there are no sweat boxes in the State of Florida."

Since the Governor's public criticism was aimed directly at *The Tampa Tribune,* we ran pictures of the sweat boxes the following day with a caption over them which read:

GOVERNOR, WHAT ARE THESE?

This provoked a new squall of protest directed at the Governor, and a few days later he softened his tune by stating publicly that the critics of Florida's prison system had opposed funds for improvement. Then he said he welcomed criticism "even though it be insincere and founded on distorted fact."

Meanwhile, Commissioner Mayo announced new plans for Florida's prison sweat boxes, which would be in force on the following January 1, and he distributed pictures of them to the press. These pictures showed space for air circulation at the top of the boxes and they were large enough for a prisoner to lie down. But after all was said and done, they were still sweat boxes and sadistic guards could still toss pinches of sugar into them.

At the same time, Florida's public officials erected probably America's tightest iron curtain of censorship around the state's prison system. For the next 13 years, news reporters were barred from all prison road camps and they were permitted only to deal with the Prison Superintendent at Raiford. During this period, every bit of news that reached the Florida people on their prison system was the press handout, which smacked strongly of sweet-smelling propaganda.

However, as one redeeming feature, out of this first newspaper hassle over the sweat box, came a new approach to the great and growing problem of juvenile crime. The legislature quickly voted funds for a system of juvenile courts and the boy convicts were taken out of the adult prison and placed in a more humane institution of their own. But the sweat box remained in the Florida prison system for 13 more years, a symbol of modern sadism.

Came the fall of 1958 and with it a new rumble of sweat boxes. But it was a nebulous rumble. We were tipped only that a young convict had suffered exceptional cruelty in a prison road camp. This was not a particularly good tip, since Florida has 35 prison camps along its 1,000-mile length to which prisoners are transferred from the state prison to work on various state projects.

Prison authorities at the state capital declined to discuss the matter with my investigating reporter. I sent him back to our original source of the tip and he was told to look into matters at the prison camp at Moore Haven, down on the edge of the Everglades. The reporter hied himself there but the Moore Haven warden would not let him into the camp. The iron curtain of censorship, which had been dropped over Florida's prison system 13 years before because of our crusade against the sweat boxes, was just as tight as ever.

Back to Tallahassee went the reporter under instructions to dig, dig and then dig some more into prison records. I reasoned that even the toughest prison camp warden, for his own protection and the protection of the state prison authorities, would be required to keep some sort of records concerning confinement of convicts in sweat boxes. And that turned out to be the case. The reporter discovered there were records, he talked an underling official into letting him see them with the provision he would not reveal the identity of the source, and he quickly made photographs of the records and brought them back to the *Tribune*.

These records were most revealing. They showed that the 35 prison roads camps reported total confinement of convicts in sweat boxes at 11,784 hours in April, 11,776 hours in May, 11,826 hours in June and 10,362 hours in July.

Records for the Moore Haven camp revealed that two convicts, 18 and 23 years of age, had served stretches of 26 days each in the sweat boxes and that a third convict, 27 years old, had spent 35 days in four stretches in them. The records also showed that the 18-year-old convict originally was sentenced to Florida's juvenile institution for 18 months for stealing a purse containing $174 from a residence at Ocala, Fla., but that, upon escape from the institution and subsequent recapture, he was given two years in the adult state prison.

My reporter returned to the Moore Haven camp and asked to interview the three prisoners and to inspect the sweat boxes. Again the warden refused and said the three prisoners were no longer in the camp but had been transferred to the state prison at Raiford. That, it developed, happened just after the reporter visited Moore Haven for the first time.

From outside sources close to the prison camp, the reporter learned that the three prisoners had been stripped naked upon confinement in the sweat boxes and during the first 10 days had been given only bread and water. The sweat boxes, three by six feet, were located in an abandoned warehouse instead of in the open. They had no toilet facilities or running water, and each convict was given two small pitchers of water a day and permitted only two shower baths during the 26 days confinement.

My reporter then went to Raiford and discovered that the three young convicts were in solitary confinement there, on orders from the Moore Haven warden. Under pressure from the reporter, the Raiford authorities begrudgingly permitted him to interview the convicts and they told him they had beaten up a brutal guard in hopes that this would bring their transferral from the road camp to the state prison. Instead, it got them 26 days in the sweat boxes.

The three convicts said they did not get a single night's sleep during their 26 days in the sweat boxes, that the warden, himself, and the guards woke them up all during the nights to taunt them and to threaten them with extra 10-year prison stretches. They said the warden personally participated in this and often brought law books to the sweat boxes to read to them the crimes they had committed.

Back to Moore Haven went the reporter and the prison camp warden denied everything. He said the convicts had been given pajamas, had been fed, had been given shower baths, and he made it sound as if life in a sweat box indeed was a privilege. He also denied that the three men had been kept in the boxes as long as 26 days. The reporter said the *Tribune* would be glad to print his version of the time, but the warden said he "was not at liberty to discuss it."

The *Tribune* printed only two stories on this case. The first quoted from the prison camp sweat box records and informed our readers of the 26-day stretches in sweat boxes served by the three young convicts. The second story carried interviews with the three convicts and the Moore Haven camp warden.

The Associated Press and United Press International picked up our stories and distributed them on their news wires over the country. Official action was almost instantaneous. New York newspaper editors telephoned the Governor's mansion at Tallahassee and demanded to know his thinking on the sweat boxes.

Governor Collins was not at the mansion but was attending a Federal-State Action Committee meeting in New Hampshire. By this time, the Governor had established himself as one of the progressive national leaders of the Democratic Party and he had no intention of permitting Florida's sweat boxes to be placed upon his shoulders. He relayed orders to Tallahassee by telephone to remove the boxes forever from Florida's prison system.

In a hurriedly called press conference, the Governor's executive assistant announced to the press that decent, regulation confinement cells would be erected in each prison road camp but that they would be used only as detention cells pending a prisoner's transferral from camp to the state prison. He invited the press to accompany him on a tour of the camps within a few weeks to prove that the sweat boxes were being destroyed. The *Tribune* reporter took him up on this and later we printed a story showing the state destroying the boxes.

In other words, after 13 long years a newspaper had forced Florida's public officials to admit there were such monstrosities as prison sweat boxes and to destroy them. They are gone today from Florida's prison system but sadistic guards and prison cruelty still remain, as proven by the Federal trial of the 14 Florida guards in the summer of 1960. And the prison riots in other states from coast to coast indicate that something is wrong with our modern civilization, and this should tug at the conscience of every thinking American citizen.

13.

A Strange Brew:

Politics
Industry
Business

THE AVERAGE POLITICIAN intensely dislikes the crusading newspaper. He puts all the degradation of the worst human sneer into the word "crusader," which he plasters at every opportunity upon the newspaper editor who evidences more than passing interest in the improvement of the people's government or in the upgrading of human life.

A dictionary gives the following definition for the word "crusade":

> Mark of the cross. Any of the military expeditions undertaken by the Christians of Europe in the 11th, 12th and the 13th centuries for the recovery of the Holy Land from the Mohammedans; any war carried on under papal sanction; in general, any aggressive movement or advancement of an idea or cause, or against a public evil.

There is nothing whatsoever low in this definition, yet the politician, with his eye usually on the next election, has connoted the meaning of "crusade" as something far below a cockroach's foot. This has caused many newspapers not only to shy away from the word but also to avoid anything that resembles a fight in behalf of a cause or against a public evil. Even in our national journalistic awards, we use the term "public service," which may be a better description. Yet I am one newspaper editor who sees nothing disgraceful in the word "crusade."

Several years ago we received a pitiful letter from a teen-age boy, a patient in the polio ward of Tampa Municipal Hospital, which told in schoolboy handwriting of the lack of the proper equipment for his treatment. I immediately sent a staffer into the polio ward, confirmed the fact that equipment was badly needed to the extent of $10,000, and then ran the boy's letter on our Page 1 with a plea to our readers for the $10,000. Within three days we had the $10,000, and it took us a week to persuade our readers to cease their contributions. We wound up with $32,000 in the fund, bought the $10,000 in essential polio equipment and upon completion of the new hospital wing in the summer of 1958, we spent the remaining $22,000 for warm-water pools for the use of polio and other victims with ailing muscles.

I call this a "crusade" with great pride. And I cannot refrain from pointing out that Tampa Municipal Hospital is under the care of our city politicians, and why didn't they provide the proper equipment for the polio ward? Could it be that this kind of public service would bring in no votes in the next election?

There also were the three cases within a week wherein Tampa taxicab drivers committed rape. I put five reporters checking the records of the 683 men who had been given cab-driving permits by the city of Tampa. We then reported that 118 of them were convicted criminals who had served time for such offenses as murder, rape and armed robbery. The results were immediate. The city Taxicab Commission quickly adopted a new regulation barring ex-convicts from obtaining city permits as drivers.

But why was a newspaper "crusade" necessary to protect women passengers from rape in taxicabs? Let the politicians who condemn newspaper crusading answer this!

We do not, of course, win all of our "crusades." Booming industry needs fresh water, and this became a prime problem as national industry began moving into Florida in the post-war years. In 1954 we launched a crusade against the contamination of our streams and lakes. With stories and pictures we told how the new industrial plants were pumping their refuse into our fresh water, which not only ruined the fishing but also reduced the amount of that fresh water available for new industry. I even made a speech at the University of Florida, outlined the dangers of the contamination and dumped the problem into the laps of our state politicians.

Under the pressure of this crusade, a reasonable law regulating the dumping of refuse into streams and lakes was introduced in the 1955 legislature. But by the time the lobbyists got through with the legislators and the legislators got through with amending the law, it was no law at all. And so I ask Florida's politicians, where was the public service in this public matter?

We lost another crusade in the legislature, or rather, I should say that the Florida public lost. Cost of public welfare is one of the greater state drains on the taxpayers' dollars and it is an evergrowing drain, regardless of whether our economy goes up or down. Recently I assigned a couple of staffers to look into public welfare, and their stories, heavily documented with exact individual cases, showed: (1) that many elderly people were on the welfare rolls even though they owned considerable property, and (2) many elderly people were receiving pensions even though their children were comparatively wealthy.

A bill calling for a state lien on the pension recipient's property and for the responsibility of children for their aging parents was introduced in the 1957 legislature, but it went the way of many such bills for public welfare. Most of our documentary cases were in the small counties, which are largely unpatrolled by daily newspapers, and it was the small-county representatives and senators who put the finishing touches to it. Throughout our nation, you will find the small counties dominating almost all of our legislatures and our small-county politicians frequently take the attitude that it is the inherent duty of the taxpayers in the large counties to assume all financial responsibility for the political monkeyshines in the small counties.

We scored a victory in one of our crusades in south Florida and then subsequently reversed the field and took the other side in a similar controversy in central Florida. Some years ago I received a letter from a businessman in Michigan, who informed me that, while he had enjoyed his winter vacation in Florida, he was burned to a crisp because he had been arrested at Palmetto, required to post a large bond, and his case was put on the court docket so far into the future that he couldn't possibly run down from Michigan to fight it. His bond, far more than the ordinary speeding fine, automatically was forfeited when he didn't appear in court.

A *Tribune* staffer dug into the city court records at Palmetto and uncovered what truly was a speed trap, with winter visitors as the victims. It was based on Florida's ancient and out-of-date fee system, wherein the constable and city officers got their salaries on the basis of the amount of fees they piled up in court. These same records showed that the city was using these bonds plucked from their winter visitors to pay part of their municipal bills. Our series of stories, played on Page 1, put a quick end to this evil.

A few months later the AAA issued a report accusing two communities in Levy and Lake Counties of preying on Tampa motorists. We sent a staffer to each community and they pored over the records, interviewed everybody concerned and made personal checks of the traffic. They found the trouble was caused by Cadillacs and Lincolns racing through the communities at 80 and 90 miles an hour in utter disregard of the law. Here we upheld, through factual stories, the law officers of the two communities.

In one crusade we ran head on into what Max Lerner in his book *America as a Civilization* (Simon and Schuster, 1958), calls "the political eunuchs of the civil service." Heeding the growing protests of Tampa householders that they were not getting the proper mail delivery service, we checked into the post office and got little satisfaction. America moved into civil service to protect the routine functions of government from politics and to give some stability to the great mass of routine government workers. But always in such widespread protection, you pay a penalty, and the penalty of governmental civil service is a marked lack of initiative and enterprise.

Tampa postal workers, of course, weren't concerned over the protests, simply because they were doing their routine jobs, they couldn't be fired and they were taking their orders, not from the taxpayers who paid their salaries, but from people higher up in the hierarchy of Federal bureaucracy. So we keyed our campaign to our congressman and senators, and several staffers did a series of stories based on personal interviews of Tampa householders in various sections of our city who let us use their names. It paid off immediately; orders came down from on high — 50 postmen were added, and the mail delivery squawks ceased.

Some crusades explode into the spectacular sensation; others drudge on through months and sometimes years. On the basis of continuous protests from Florida's businessmen over growing high costs of the state's unemployment compensation, the *Tribune* ran a series of 12 stories putting the spotlight squarely on the weaknesses in the law.

Under Florida law, business firms had to pay into the state's general compensation fund annual amounts ranging from .001 per cent to 2.7 per cent of the first $3,000 earned by each employee. This was in addition to the .003 per cent assessed by the Federal Government in the joint Federal-State program.

The state's percentage was fixed each year on the basis of the previous year's record of payments to unemployed persons, which ranged from a minimum of $10 a week for 10 weeks to a maximum of $33 a week for 26 weeks, depending upon conditions of the worker's length of service and general job specifications. For a number of years, Florida has assessed one and all of its businessmen close to the maximum percentage, which was an expensive business in the case of firms having many employees. Furthermore, the state placed upon the business firm the responsibility of patrolling the program — an impossible situation.

The *Tribune*'s series revealed widespread fraud in the program in all sections of Florida on two counts: (1) many workers, although employed, were collecting unemployment compensation; and (2) some business firms were using the unemployment compensation to pay for vacations for their employees during slack seasons.

On the day the seventh story of the series appeared in the *Tribune,* the state's unemployment office at Tallahassee announced a general investigation, which eventually confirmed our reports of fraud in all of Florida's bigger cities.

The subsequent cleanup not only saved considerable money for Florida's business firms but it also resulted in an improved program wherein the state assumed the responsibility for investigations and the individual business firm was assessed on the basis of its individual record and not on the basis of the whole state record.

Equally sensational was the *Tribune*'s crusade against

the faulty construction of the $4,500,000 State Tuberculosis Hospital in Tampa. We dedicated the beautiful building, which looked out over Hillsborough Bay, with much political pomp and glory in 1951. One year later I sent a staff writer and a photographer through the place. What they found created a scandal. Our stories and pictures of the cracks and collapses in that pile worth $4,500,000 of Florida taxpayers' dollars resulted in a sensational investigation. One man went to jail and the state sued the contractors for repairs.

The crusade with the quickest result involved an old Negro in the Hernando County jail at Brooksville. This Negro had been arrested some six months before as a material witness in a murder case. But since he was a good worker and had a sunny disposition, the sheriff conveniently forgot about his civil liberty and used him on various jobs in and about the county jail. We dug into the case and printed the story on our Page 1. In Hernando County the *Tribune* is delivered in the morning about 6 o'clock. At 7 o'clock that day, the doors of the county jail clanged open and the old Negro was restored his freedom.

Our crusade on meat took considerably longer. We sent our staffers peering into the butcher shops of the grocery stores throughout our community, paying particular attention to the government stamps on the meat. The subsequent series of stories clearly showed that Florida housewives were being gypped in quality of meat they bought. This appeared to be through faulty government inspection. The direct result was a new law adopted by the legislature tightening up state inspection of meat. One year later, *Tribune* staffers again checked meat in the stores, again found faulty inspection, and our new series of stories produced drastic changes by the State Livestock Sanitary Board in behalf of Florida's housewives.

In contrast to these is the *Tribune*'s 22-year crusade against the loose operations of the Florida State Pardon Board. Back in 1936 we ripped the cover off a pardon racket wherein certain "fixers," in exchange for dollars, could obtain the release from prison of almost any criminal. Our expose put an end to this particular evil, but it did not by any means sweep political privilege out of the issuance of pardons by the pardon board, which is made up of the Governor and cabinet members, all elected officials.

Over the 22 years, every administration has had its pardon scandal, wherein some convicted criminal, through political privilege, has escaped the penalty. One prominent case came in February, 1958, and involved a Tampa bail bondsman, convicted of bribery. The *Tribune* ran a new series of stories, reciting a lot of Florida's old pardon scandals. But a number of prominent Tampa citizens wrote letters to the Governor in behalf of the bail bondsman, and the pardon board yielded to the pressure.

We have done a number of crusades involving business, but I would warn the journalism beginner to tread easy in this field. Experienced know-how is essential, for the legal matter of privacy is involved. A safe policy is to look into business research only when the taxpayers, in the form of government, itself, are directly involved and where the business affects the living of a whole community. And always stick closely to the records.

Responsibility for conditions often are not clearly defined. As a result, both businessmen and local officials are apathetic and inclined to pass the buck back and forth. Only when citizens become aroused will either side be forced into accepting responsibility, and taking action to improve the situation.

One of our award-winning crusades resulted from a tip that, at first, appeared to be good for only a feature story.

Most of the nation's winter vegetables are grown in the rich soil of the fringe areas of the Everglades. There owners of vast acreages gamble each winter, winning or losing fortunes on the turn of the weather. If they are lucky in getting a stretch of sunny weather, unmarred by a cold spell, they can harvest a crop of beans in three weeks.

But, to do this, they must have the services of some 14,000 migrant farm laborers. In some cases, the Florida growers import Puerto Ricans for the winter; but largely they depend upon the bands of migrant workers who follow the crops across the country. Most of these migrants earn an average of $892 a year, which gives some idea of their economic standards. Wealthy tourists often spend more than that amount in one week in Florida's luxury winter resorts, a few miles away.

In the fall of 1954, I sent a *Tribune* staff writer down to Immokalee, a migrant-worker community on the edge of the Everglades' winter salad bowl, to do a feature story on a school operated by the Mennonite Church of Lancaster, Pennsylvania, for the children of the migrant farm workers. Among the facts disclosed were that the school had to teach the children, ranging from six to eight years in age, how to eat at a table and how to use a knife and fork.

This intrigued me no end because if any American children haven't learned in their home long before this age how to eat at a table and with knife, fork and spoon, then very definitely they don't have much of the equal opportunity about which Americans like to brag. In short, if these children were eating like animals during their formative years in their homes, then they probably were destined to limited progress in life and could eventually become a drag on American society.

So I sent my reporter back to Immokalee under instructions to do a series of stories to inform the Florida people of conditions among the migrant farmers. These stories, illustrated by dozens of pictures, told how thousands of migrant farm workers were living in squalid, one-room shacks and, to use the exact words of the reporter, in conditions "nauseating" and "not fit for animals." Many of the shacks were of tin with uncovered openings for windows, and families of 12 were sleeping on the floor of one room. There were no toilet facilities and the workers got their water from a central pump. Garbage and refuse were everywhere, a veritable haven for flies and a menace to the health not only of the migrants but to the surrounding countryside. There were no medical facilities and no schools except those provided by church missionaries. The migrant workers got $6 a day for their work in producing America's winter vegetables.

Our stories, of course, shocked the people of the state, and, as a direct result, Representative Ted David, Speaker of the Florida House of Representatives, toured the migrant camp and, after complaining about the smelly conditions, got himself thrown out by the camp manager. Subsequently, David appointed a nine-man House committee to investigate the camps, and Governor Collins followed by naming a citizens investigating committee. Chairman James Vocelle of the State Industrial Commission, launched his own investigation.

These investigations disclosed only that there was a migrant labor racket, with shadowy underworld interests in Miami illegally bringing in many of the migrants from Puerto Rico. This brought on just one more investigation, this time by the Senate of the Puerto Rican Government.

But all the hue and cry of these investigations turned out to be nothing more than a big burst of political noise. Absolutely nothing concrete was done to improve the pitiful lot of the migrant workers, even though the *Tribune* time and again revived the issue with stories and pictures.

Then came the freezes of December, 1957, and January, 1958, which reached deep into Florida, destroyed the winter vegetable crops of the Everglades, and left the thousands of migrant workers stranded in their hovels without food or much of anything else. I quickly dispatched my reporter back to Immokalee and his stories pin-pointed these two facts:

1. The migrant workers and their women and children faced immediate starvation, with no food on hand, no

prospect of their scanty wages, and no means of transportation out of the area.
2. Disease and pestilence, bred in the garbage-littered area and the outdoor privies, were imminent.

Pictures accompanying the stories showed dirty migrant babies, whose main item of food was dried beans.

Florida people reacted to these stories of human misery far quicker than did Florida politicians. Sparked by the women of the churches and American Legion Auxiliary, within hours kind-hearted citizens all over Florida were donating foods, milk and medical supplies in vast quantities. A trucking company agreed to take these supplies free of cost to the Everglades. Air Force planes from Mac Dill Base in Tampa flew medical supplies to the migrant camps.

Florida's Cabinet at first demurred over voting funds for relief of the migrants but, in the face of the daily stories printed by the *Tribune*, finally agreed to immediate spending of $45,000. Governor Collins personally toured migrant camps, described them as "disgraceful," and adding: "There is no place in Florida for a picture such as this." He then threw his potent political weight back of the drive to clean up the blot of migrant farming.

During the next year, the *Tribune* reporter visited migrant camps time and again and we published the progress of the official cleanup. In December, 1958, he wrote a story which, with pictures, covered a solid page in the *Tribune*, and it listed the following definite accomplishments:

1. Two-thirds of all the shanty housing in Florida's migrant farm area had been condemned and torn down, and new housing, approved by state agencies, was being built.
2. All outdoor privies had been destroyed and indoor flush toilets, with septic tanks, had been installed; all housing had been fitted with screens and painted inside

and out; garbage cans with tops had been allotted to each house; gigantic shower and laundry facilities had been built for each migrant camp.

3. A health clinic was opened in each camp.
4. An intensive public nursing program had been launched, which included weekly inspection of all migrant children.
5. A new community center, fitted with showers, laundry and toilet facilities, had been opened in the Negro migrant camp.
6. Schooling, under the direction of the state, was provided for all migrant children.
7. State agencies had begun detailed supervision and inspection over the vast Florida winter vegetable area for the first time.
8. Legislation had been prepared by the various state agencies, subsequently adopted by the 1959 Legislature, which provided for strict health regulations, welfare relief measures and special educational programs for all migrant farm camps.

Thus, a newspaper campaign, stirred only by the heart, had so alerted public opinion of Florida that a big chunk of human misery had been eliminated in the preparation of the winter vegetables which grace the dining tables of America. But equally important, is the new opportunity being offered to a lot of children who had no say whatsoever as to the homes in which they were born.

There were some dissenting voices raised against the *Tribune*'s drive and some sneering at the plight of the migrant farm laborers. A few citizens expressed feelings that the migrant farmer's plight was his own personal responsibility and that the people of Florida had no moral, no financial and no public responsibilities in any way.

I cannot agree with this thinking. The brilliant minds of American society have charted our course into the advanced mechanical era. The majority of American people have profited from this. But a sizeable minority, perhaps one-third of our population — for one reason or another and beyond their control — simply cannot cope with the exigencies of this advanced mechanical age. Therefore, I feel that the majority of us who can cope profitably and successfully with the mechanical age, certainly have a moral, financial and public obligation to help our less fortunate fellow men. We cannot kill them off, as Stalin once did in Russia.

Businessmen sometimes act like politicians. In the late spring of 1958, one of our staffers looked into the state inspection of fertilizer to ascertain if Florida's farmers were getting an even break. Within 24 hours, the manager of the plant of a national fertilizer company threatened to get the staffer's job. And in the next few days, the staffer's telephone rang on the hour every hour during the night, to upset him nervously, and one of the company's cars, wth a leering, shouting driver, parked in front of his home during the daytime. But we went right ahead and printed our story, which showed that this particular company had the worst record in the state inspection of fertilizer.

Tampa's principal industry for many years was the manufacture of hand-made cigars. Early in the history of the industry, old Samuel Gompers, a cigarmaker himself, and his American Federation of Labor got an iron-clad grip in Tampa. The march of machinery vitally affected the entire cigar industry, but Tampa's cigar unions fought it tooth and toenail. The result, of course, was that Tampa's hand-made industry began to lose ground to machine-made cigars produced by plants in the east, and our cigar payrolls began to dip.

So a team of *Tribune* staffers went to work and their series of factual stories brought out graphically: (1) the responsibility of the entire community to this industry with a $10,000,000 payroll affecting 25,000 persons; (2) the need for modernization, and (3) the need for a close study by operators and workers alike of competing methods. Direct result of the series was the creation of a promotion campaign for the first time by Tampa's cigar manufacturers and a warm and cooperative reception by our community.

Tampa is in the very heart of Florida's $600,000,000 citrus industry. For years the small citrus grower had complained long and loudly that the selling price of his fruit was being squeezed below cost. A *Tribune* staffer spent months studying the industry. Then he wrote a series of Page 1 stories that gave the whole picture of the industry. Overnight the series became a best seller in Florida's citrus country. As a public service, the *Tribune* reprinted the stories in a booklet and, upon request, distributed thousands. Immediate upshot of this project was that 7,000 Florida citrus growers, packers, shippers and processors organized into a gigantic cooperative, the Florida Citrus Mutual, to keep a restraining finger upon the proper stabilization of prices.

We did the same thing in the matter of pine seedlings. A *Tribune* staffer spent weeks studying Florida's lumbering industry and his series of Page 1 stories pointed up the great need of replenishing Florida's rapidly disappearing pine forests. Again public demand caused the Tribune to go to the expense of reprinting the series in a booklet. One central Florida bank president distributed hundreds of these booklets to his customers. Today you will find thousands upon thousands of acres of new pine in Florida.

When a newspaper gets the reputation for crusading, it receives many pleas for help from those citizens who are victims of ill fortune. This presents a problem since the average newspaper does not have the trained personnel to ascertain if the plea is genuine. The best procedure is to send the pleader to a social welfare agency and then, if professional welfare workers give him their stamp of approval, the newspaper can appeal for public aid.

But there is danger in even the best of these individual cases. One Christmas Eve the home of a Tampa war veteran, who had a houseful of children, burned to the ground. At the instigation of sympathetic neighbors, the *Tribune* asked the public for help. Overnight warm-hearted citizens, perhaps moved by the Christmas spirit, contributed enough money for a new home. But a week after the new house was erected, the war veteran sold it for a neat profit and left for parts unknown.

On the other hand, a totally disabled war veteran in DeLand appealed to the *Tribune* for help in the run-around being given him by the Veterans Administration in the faulty construction of his home. A *Tribune* staffer inspected the home and found that portions of the construction, including the roof, did not meet the specifications of either the contractor or the VA. His stories hurriedly brought VA intervention, and the veteran's home was satisfactorily completed.

Likewise, a crusading daily newspaper receives many pleas from citizens over the mismanagement of government in the smaller communities. I never turn down such an appeal simply because if I did, where else could the complaining citizens go? In such situations, and there are many throughout the United States, public opinion is the final court of appeal and if a newspaper turns a deaf ear, then it is false to the great traditions of American freedom of the press.

It has been my experience over the years that, once elected to office, the small community politician regards his elevation in society as a short cut to special privilege. Early America was famous for its open town meetings, but such is not the case today. Much small-town political privilege is ladled out in secret meetings, and the weekly and small daily, through the pressure of limited advertising and of small town privilege, usually is in no position to fight this.

There are times when investigation discloses situations that need no correction. Such was the case when a dignified old gentleman of 85 laid before us a tale of dire mismanagement of government in his rural county. I sent a veteran reporter to the county and, after a week's research, he reported back: (1) that the county's government was honest and aboveboard; (2) that young man had assumed control and were seeking to modernize the county government; and (3) that the old gentleman had served 50 years on the county commission and his complaints were based purely on resentment of being pushed out of his position of special privilege by old Father Time. We, of course, wrote nothing, even though the old gentleman once sent a batch of watermelons to our office and continued for weeks his insistence that we wage his battle for him.

But, in answer to citizens' pleas, we have written over the years many millions of words about the mismanagement of small-town government in Florida. And likewise, we have done research and printed many a series of stories in behalf of community improvement in the small towns in our area. Our staffers roamed far and wide in their successful campaigns for school bond issues in eight counties surrounding Tampa; and, in winning new sewer systems for the citizens of Mulberry, Wauchula and Inverness, they dug deeply into tax problems, in spite of outspoken opposition from the wealthy.

At Arcadia, a *Tribune* staffer wrote how the members of the city council, certain favored city employees and privileged businessmen received free driveways and free gasoline, all paid for by the taxpayers, and how the city's public works superintendent presented concrete lawn benches as Christmas presents to the members of the city council. At Sebring, a staff-written series of stories related how equipment of the city-owned air terminal had dribbled away into the unknown.

Under Florida's system of county government, the county is divided into five districts and each of the five county commissioners has his own road-building equipment and crew for work on secondary roads and bridges. Such a system necessitates the watchful eye of newspapers to see that the individual commissioner does not expend his district's share of the county's road funds for driveways and roads for his friends or, in some cases, for personal profit. The *Tribune* exposed to taxpayers of Lake County the facts that one of their county commissioners was using county equipment and receiving special pay for paving the streets of Howey-in-the-Hills.

Another *Tribune* staffer's reports of a widespread moonshine business in Lake City resulted in a big raid by state beverage department agents, and a series of stories on the waste of taxpayers' money in the ancient ward system of building roads in Hendry County was climaxed by a cleanup and a return to good government. At Zephyrhills, we exposed a neat little municipal racket wherein city officials sold their land to the city just before the city tax rolls were made up and bought it back afterwards, thus escaping taxation. The citizens of Zephyrhills reacted by tossing out the erring public servants in the next election. We scored another election victory in Mulberry where the taxpayers, in answer to our stories, threw out an antiquated city government and installed a city manager.

For some strange reason, the minute the average citizen of a small community is elected to his school board, he assumes that education of the children of the community and all business thereof belong to him as his private domain. Thus, much of the business of the average small-town school board is conducted in secrecy, not only in Florida but elsewhere in the United States. We ran head on into this secrecy at Dunnellon and Bonita Springs, and our factual stories of the bitter behind-the-scene fights between principals, teachers and parents cleared the atmosphere and stirred the taxpayers into positive action.

The same secrecy is largely prevalent in small-town government and we encountered it in a big way at Auburndale. There, for many years, the city council had doled out special privileges in buildings, utilities and personnel. Our campaign against this was only partially successful simply because it is difficult to achieve an overnight cure in a long-time cancerous growth in government.

We were the only newspaper to give Florida taxpayers a full account of developments in the fight between the city of Gainesville and the University of Florida over a 1905 contract which calls for the city to give free water to the University. And in the middle of this, a *Tribune* story disclosed that funds specially appropriated for a tank to increase campus water pressure had been used by the University to complete the Century Tower, while buying only a small pump for the pressure.

Thus, regardless of the Florida politicians' dim view of crusading, you can see that over the years *The Tampa Tribune* has been an integral part of the way of life in Florida.

14.

Secret Government Is Vicious

POLICE ESCORTED A TAMPA *Tribune* STAFF WRITER out of an official meeting of the City Commission of Sarasota, Florida, all because he persisted in sitting there and taking notes of a discussion of charges of maladministration which had been placed against that city's police chief.

Florida has a Statute which stipulates that all cities and towns must include in their charters a law for public meetings, and Section 18 of Sarasota's charter reads as follows:

> All meetings of the City Commission and of the Committees thereof shall be public and any citizen shall have access to the minutes and records thereof at all reasonable times.

The *Tribune* reporter was abiding by the laws of both Florida and Sarasota; whereas, the Sarasota police, in obeying the Commission's orders by bodily removing him from the meeting, violated both state and city laws.

This is no isolated example of secrecy in the lower levels of American Government. Rather, it is a running problem that confronts the newspaper reporter from the Atlantic to the Pacific, since our public servants love secret government and are going to have it whenever possible and regardless of laws, and particularly so when they are confronted with delicate problems of the people's business wherein they undergo the risk of public criticism.

School boards often are guilty, and *Tribune* reporters have been tossed out of the meetings of those bodies of our public servants at Clearwater, Dunnellon and Bonita Springs, among others. But the reporters of other Florida newspapers have been excluded from regular meetings of the County Commissions at Fort Myers, Panama City and Miami and the City Councils at Jacksonville and Tallahassee.

Unlike the palms and the palmettoes, these secret government meetings are not a peculiar Florida characteristic. There was the spectacular case in Reading, Pennsylvania, in 1956 where the mayor closed the City Hall press room, arrested a Reading newspaper reporter and had police serve the Reading newspaper delivery trucks with 73 traffic tickets, all because local newspapers exposed a pinball scandal.

When, in my capicity as freedom of information chairman for a national journalistic organization, I protested these dictatorial tactics, the mayor of Reading wrote me that the managing editor and reporters of the newspaper there were "journalistic rodents who have attempted to portray and blacken the City of Reading as a den of unrestrained iniquity." I can observe, on the basis of great experience, that whenever we in the newspaper profession crusade against the political rackets, we always are "journalistic rodents" in the eyes of the politicians, and always we "blacken a community's reputation."

The "country" and the "city slicker" politician are the same in their great love for secret government. The Board of Aldermen of Hamilton, Missouri, had police bodily remove the editor of a country weekly from its regular meeting, while the Common Council of Milwaukee, Wisconsin, made a regular practice of excluding the reporters of that city's great dailies from its meetings, and its aldermanic members denounced the Milwaukee *Journal* with great verbal vitriol for daring to get the facts of the people's business for Milwaukee people.

Politicians of the old, conservative East and the new, progressive West are identical in their affinity for locked doors. The Town Meeting of Selectmen of Andover, Massachusetts, and the City Council of Alameda, California, tossed newsmen out of their meetings with the same political aplomb. And in between, the school board of Savannah, Georgia and the County Commission at Fargo, North Dakota, likewise barred newsmen from their exclusive little societies.

But it is only in communities where you have aggressive newsmen, who seek to live up to their obligation of reporting all facts of government to the people, that you have these public incidents of secret government. In many communities newsmen are apathetic, for one reason or another, and the politicians get away with their secret government and spoon-feed the public with handouts based largely on propaganda, always portraying themselves as God's answer to the people's prayers.

At the instigation of newsmen, who wanted a state law against secret government meetings, the Massachusetts Legislature in 1956 created a Legislative Research Council to study the matter, and its findings were startling to those citizens who labor under the innocent dream that their public servants are statesmen. This study by the Council revealed: of 825 specific town, school and tax boards in 242 Massachusetts towns, no less than 187 did all the people's business in secret meetings and 114 others refused to answer the official questionnaire. Furthermore, it showed that 146 of these boards refused to permit Massachusetts citizens to inspect the minutes of their meetings, and that 45 boards kept no minutes whatsoever of the people's business.

Similar surveys a year later by the journalism schools of the University of Maine and Marquette University at Milwaukee, Wisconsin, revealed similar results. The Maine survey disclosed 18 cases of secret government in 11 branches of city, county and state government, and the Wisconsin survey brought to light 24 cases.

Striking feature of both the Maine and Wisconsin surveys was the revealing apathy of newsmen. Forty-one per cent of the editors in Maine and 34 per cent in Wisconsin refused to participate in the survey, which, sad as it may be, indicated their great lack of interest in the serious business of reporting all the facts of free government to free people.

That this is alarming is putting it mildly. It the free American newsman, sentinel of liberty and guardian of the people's government, shuts his eyes and dulls his conscience to this growing development of secrecy in the lower levels of American Government, which is close to the people, then he simply sounds the knell to freedom and lays the bedrock for a dictatorial government of the future, be it by an individual or a bureaucracy. It is a responsibility that the newsman cannot ignore, regardless of his inner craving for tranquility and his preference for a quiet life.

Always human nature enters into the picture, and an alert press can utilize this to the limit. Always in any government board there is a dominant majority and a minority, even though the minority often is weak and spineless. And always when more than two persons meet in secrecy, one will talk. *The Tampa Tribune* used this device a few years ago in breaking up the secret government of the local Board of Aldermen, and secured factual details of all that took place, including some of the colorful quotes of the arrogant majority faction. This, of course, we published, and provoked anguished bleats of political denials, but under this newspaper pressure an aroused public opinion finally stepped in and forced the ward heelers to abandon their so-called "executive sessions."

Crusading is a constant business and not even the entrance of the citizen into his government puts an end to secrecy. One Tampa mayor attempted to cloak himself with virtue by the appointment of what he called his "advisory committee," which consisted of a group of wealthy business leaders. In recent months, he called a secret meeting of the City Board of Representatives and his "advisory committee" and, with no public discussion, these groups approved his plan of increasing the appropriation of the citizens' tax dollars from $650,000 to $1,300,000 for the construction of a municipal hospital nursing home.

A *Tribune* reporter was waiting at the closed doors when this meeting broke up, and got all the facts of the meeting from a friendly member of the Board of Representatives. The next morning our Page 1 story advised Tampa's taxpayers that allocation of $650,000 of their tax dollars had been agreed upon in secret meeting, and then we printed all the details. The mayor immediately hit the ceiling, beat his breast righteously and denied all over the premises that there had been a secret meeting. "Why," he shouted, "anybody could have attended it." But my reporter pointed out that there had been no notification to the press of the meeting and that it had taken place behind closed doors.

At the same time in our community, the businessmen members of the Tampa Aviation Authority were conducting a series of secret meetings, usually in their lawyer's office, on the little civic matter of investing $11,000,000 of taxpayer funds in the development of our municipal airport. Our reporter, of course, was thrown out of the meeting, apparently on the grounds that the dear old public had no right to any inner secrets of manipulation of citizens' tax dollars.

After two of these secret meetings, the County Commission's member of this Authority came to my office and complained bitterly over the fact that the businessmen members were now leaving him out of their secret discussions.

"What am I going to do?" he lamented. "I campaigned on a pledge that I would never do the people's business in secret meetings. The Aviation Authority wants to hold all its financial discussions in secrecy and, because of my objections, they're leaving me out altogether."

I dryly replied that the solution was simple, that all he had to do was to issue a statement to the voters that the Aviation Authority was planning in secrecy the spending of $11,000,000 of the taxpayers' money, with perhaps a lot of political privilege involved, and that he would not be a part of the proceedings until this part of Tampa's government was restored to the people. I promised to print his statement prominently on Page 1, but this politician shuddered and quickly left my office. He apparently preferred to totter through his political career with the water of both the politician and the public upon his two shoulders.

In defense of secrecy, the businessman in politics tells me that he is not like the politicians and "you know I am honest." Of course, I know the businessman is not like the politician and that he is honest. But I also know that it was the businessman who bought the mink coats and freezers in the Truman Administration and the vicuna coats and paid the hotel bills in the Eisenhower Administration.

Police records, even though they are public records, often are the source of many journalistic headaches. We have had innumerable police scandals in Tampa and in every case the police carefully hid from newspaper reporters the record against themselves. But, also in every case, either a fellow officer or some citizen telephoned the tip to our office and we broke the stories on Page 1.

At Claxton, Georgia, the editor of a weekly, who had crusaded against the Ku Klux Klan — much to the horror of public officials — got into a fist fight with the sheriff over the latter's refusal to make public his records of the people's police business. Both men were arrested and the mayor of Claxton, sitting as the judge, convicted and fined them.

The sheriff of Raton, New Mexico, barred the editor of the Raton *Daily Range* from offical records of traffic accidents and said: "You'll get the news when I am ready." Again in my capacity as freedom of information chairman, I protested and the editor printed my protest on his Page 1. The next day, the attorney general of New Mexico ordered the sheriff to open his records, simply because that state is among those having laws guaranteeing their people the right of constant inspection of public records.

These various public incidents of secret government have caused editors to unite all over the country in the sponsorship of state laws guaranteeing open records and open meetings of government. In 1957, 1958, 1959 and 1960, the Legislatures of 22 states, prodded along by newspaper editors, adopted these statutes, and today 32 states have laws guaranteeing their people the right to inspect the records of government and 25 states have laws guaranteeing open meetings of governmental bodies.

Illinois was among the states adopting the open-government statutes in 1957, but at the start of the campaign many editors were only lukewarm, contending they were getting along all right. Then came the Chicago *Daily News*' crusade exposing corruption in the office of Orville E. Hodge, state auditor, and the laws almost raced through the legislature without opposition.

At the very start of this Illinois scandal, George Thiem, the *News*' Pulitzer Prize winning reporter, found Hodge had closed his records of the state's spending of tax dollars. I issued a public protest and Hodge ironically wrote me that he was fully in accord with the journalistic principles of open government. But he kept his records closed and it took a great piece of newspaper crusading on the part of Thiem to expose that Hodge had stolen more than $2,000,000 of Illinois tax funds. Hodge then became the guest of the American taxpayers in the federal pen.

But some states had no public Hodge case, even though the danger always is there, and the editors' freedom of information laws were beaten. New Hampshire was among these and the Keene *Sentinel* carried this editorial:

> It is indeed a sad commentary on the citizens of the State and New Hampshire newspapers that there was obviously no organization whatsoever of proponents of this bill who might have argued its merits before legislators.

> It seems a bit ludicrous to watch the "Right to Know" bill washed down the drain while considerable effort is devoted to making such weighty decisions as what definition should be given itinerant hairdressers.

The Far West — where the businessman, the farmer and the ordinary citizen dominate the legislatures — has pioneered in the movement to place freedom of information laws on the states' books. Virtually all states in the Far West have laws guaranteeing public inspection of the records of government, and California, Idaho, Washington and Utah have recently adopted statutes guaranteeing open meetings.

In the conservative East and South, the great opponents of open government are (1) the lawyer and (2) common law. Several years ago I made a survey, in behalf of a national journalistic organization, of our legislatures. After long years of battling the political lawyer over his proneness to secret huddles, my findings did not particularly surprise me.

In every case wherein the lawyer dominated the legislature, usually in the East and South, I found always two decided tendencies: (1) a large number of lawyer-inspired bills to handcuff the free press, and (2) at least 10 per cent of the bills finally adopted by the legislature were designed either to help the lawyer in his practice or to collect his fees. In those legislatures dominated by the ordinary citizen, usually in the Far West, I found the opposite tendencies.

When you tell this to a lawyer, you inspire great anguish in his soul simply because of his conscience and his knowledge that the lawyer once was the great leader in the American fight for the individual rights of man. I once told this to the Florida Bar in a meeting in Miami and promptly got into a hassle with the secretary of the Dade County Bar Association. But when I sent this gentleman a nine-page letter that carefully compiled the results of my survey of the Legislatures, I heard no more of the matter.

In the absence of statutes involving the question of secret government, most American courts fall back on the old English common law, and this is particularly true in the East and South. Common law was adopted in the English courts in a society of classes; it therefore is a law of and for the classes; and in many instances it does not fulfill the requirements of the American society of the people in their battle with bulging bureaucracy in our government.

New York State, for instance, does not have a statute guaranteeing its people the right of inspection of government records, and its courts rely largely on common law in those cases. Common law holds that only those persons having an interest in the record have the right of inspection, and New York court decisions, based on this law, time and again have deprived the people of New York of the right to check on the actions of their public servants.

In the case of the People ex rel. Stenstrom v. Hartnett, State Commissioner of Motor Vehicles — which was affirmed by the New York Supreme Court in 1927 and

by the Appellate Court in 1928, and which is widely
quoted and held as legal authority — the court held
against public inspection of automobile accident records.
The judge in this case said:

> "I do not hold that these records are open gen-
> erally for inspection to the public, but only to such
> persons who establish a proper interest therein, and
> the bureau can undoubtedly formulate a procedure
> by which each applicant for inspection will be re-
> quired to prove his interest and right of inspection
> and that permitted to proper cases only under rea-
> sonable regulation and control."

This old common law principle, which holds for the
classes and not the people, also was the basis of the
New York Appellate Court's decision upholding the barring of the press and public from the recent Jelke vice
trial, which caused a national stir. It held that the complaining New York City newspapers failed to prove their
interest in the court trial.

Similarly, the attorney general of West Virginia, in
advising the legislature on the right of one of its committees to inspect the records of the State Tax Commissioner,
said:

> "In Common law, there is no general or public
> right of inspection of public records, and in the ab-
> sence of statute it may be that the public has no right
> of access."

Florida is one of the states that have fine statutes
guaranteeing the right of public inspection of the records
of government and, because of it, newspapers have very
little trouble in advising Florida citizens on such vital
matters as expenditure of taxpayer dollars. The Florida
law reads:

All state, county and municipal records shall be open for a personal inspection of any citizen of Florida, and those in charge of such records shall not refuse this privilege to any citizen.

But Florida does not have a legal safeguard against the secret meetings of its governmental bodies, and this has resulted in a constant running skirmish between the politicians and the press. In 1957, a press-sponsored bill for open meetings in government was defeated in the Florida House of Representatives, 43 to 33. Representative Cliff Herrell of Miami, who led the fight against it, ranted mightily over the risk of ruining teachers' reputations in discussing their employment at open meetings of Florida school boards, and he shook with horror over the possibility of land speculators attending these meetings and running up the price on the purchase of land for public use.

Subsequently, I wrote a letter to Representative Herrell on the matter of his objections to open government, and I developed the following points:

1. Florida already has a statute on its books stipulating that all meetings of city council, commissions, etc., must be open to the public. I do not know of a single case wherein Florida's open municipal government law has not served the best interests of the Florida people. On the other hand, I have in my files a number of cases wherein the best interests of the Florida people have not been served through the abuse of this statute.

2. It is my firm belief that Representative Herrell's stand on the specific matter involving "the character or morals of an individual" discussed at a public meeting would not be in the best interests of the Florida people. Again I refer to my files and tell you of a case wherein the school board of a certain county met in secrecy and fired the principal of a high school for being a sex

pervert; and two weeks later the school board of an adjoining county met in secrecy and hired this character as the principal of one of its schools. Where was the protection for the citizens, not only of the second county but throughout the area where this character might land a job in our educational system through the secret proceedings of government?

3. All elected public officials of the United States must put their personal reputations on public display on the election platform; therefore, all appointed government officials should undergo the same tests for the very great benefit of the American people. I never have understood the tender regard of our elected public officials for the reputations of those whom they would appoint to serve the American people, sometimes in key jobs.

4. Public officials, for their own protection, should demand that all governmental meetings be open to the public. All secret meetings are suspect in the eyes of the public, since the pages of history show plainly that all the great corruptions of history, including those wherein our public officials have gotten rich in speculation involving public lands, always have taken place behind the locked doors of secret government and not out in the open where the restraint of public opinion has perfect play.

Representative Herrell never did answer these four points, and to date, although I have corresponded with hundreds of our public servants from the White House on down, I have never received from a single politician, logical answers to my queries.

15.

Uncovering Federal Abuses of Privilege

OUR FEDERAL GOVERNMENT OFFERS the finest field imaginable for newspaper crusading, yet I can not conscientiously recommend it to you unless you have an iron constitution, nerves of steel, a tough set of personal feelings, a strong streak of stubbornness, and the faculty of sleeping peacefully at night regardless of the stress and strain of the day. This is where you separate the men from the boys.

Over the last 25 years, an arrogant Federal bureaucracy has clamped a tight vise of secrecy over all records of government at Washington. The bureaucrats take your tax dollars from your weekly pay check, but they never account to the taxpayer for the spending of one penny, and you do not actually know whether your tax dollars are wasted, misappropriated or spent wisely.

You can dig your crusading shovel into almost any spot in Federal Government and strike gold. But the headaches are rending and the political pressure trying. I speak from great personal experience, having for many years been pushed around by our better bureaucrats from the White House on down. And I can tell you a bit sadly that we in free America face a newly developed political philosophy: once our public servants are elected or appointed to office, they look upon government as their private domain in which they may do as they wish without the restraint of public opinion, and that they sincerely feel that the free American people should be satisfied with spoon-fed propaganda and the decisions of government *after* they have been made.

Stewart Alsop, writing in the *Saturday Evening Post,* once put this in somewhat plainer words when he said:

> The American government these days is rather frequently cast in the role of the Daddy of us all, telling us that Daddy knows best and not to ask questions. And Daddy's warning is often implied or explicit — "or Daddy spanks."

This philosophy of "Daddy spanks" even prevails down on the local level where the Pentagon maintains military bases. Tampa has MacDill Field, an Air Force bomber base, and once the *Tribune* revealed that MacDill bombers were flying jeeps to the Dakota hunting grounds so that some of our leading generals could hunt pheasants comfortably, all at taxpayer cost. We also reported that subsequently our Chamber of Commerce leaders were entertained at special pheasant dinners, also at considerable cost to the taxpayers. On another occasion, we informed our readers that a certain MacDill colonel was forcing a sergeant and several privates to trim his lawn and move his household furnishings, which was nothing other than military peonage.

On both occasions, key MacDill officers turned up at our Chamber of Commerce and talked long and earnestly of the beauties of the MacDill weekly payroll and what a

shame if Tampa should lose it through poor press relations. All of this, of course, was a lot of hooey since the
Pentagon selects its military bases on conditions other
than relationship with the press. But always some businessmen fall for this, and the newspaper must undergo
the resulting pressure.

When I sent a staff writer to Cape Canaveral in late
1957 to watch the efforts to fire the ill-fated Navy Van-
guard, the Pentagon press agent demanded that my reporter sign an agreement that he would send only that
news which had been approved by the press agent. Otherwise, he could not watch the firing. My staffer telephoned
me and I instructed him to write a full report of this outright censorship on the part of the Pentagon. I sent this
report, along with a strong protest, to Representative John
E. Moss (Dem., Calif.), chairman of the House Subcommittee on Government Information. Moss subsequently
publicly reprimanded the Pentagon for its censorship of
the missile firings, but, of course, that did not stop it. I
am afraid that it will take more than a lone congressional
committee to stop the manipulation of news of government, which is so prevalent in all Federal circles today.

Many newsmen, through their location, do not contact
the Pentagon and its numerous military tentacles and thus
escape these frustrations. But no American newsman can
escape some contact with Federal Government, regardless
of whether he works in Maine or Arizona, simply because
the Federal bureaucracy today reaches down into every
walk of American life and puts a restraining finger upon
the life of every American citizen. It may be in the matter
of welfare, all of which is strictly censored, or it may be
in the routine matter of our weather reports. I was interested to note recently that the Federal Weather Bureau
had decided to censor its new, long-range forecasts because of some errors in a new scientific experimentation
made during the unusual winter of 1957–58. And I can
only observe somewhat sadly that it is a great pity that a
newspaper also cannot censor its mistakes.

Late in the Truman Administration, one of my string of correspondents in Pinellas County reported that a handsome new beach apartment project, built with FHA funds, had landed in the circuit court at Clearwater and was in the process of being wrung out of its financial monkeyshines. I immediately dispatched one of my staffers to the courthouse and he spent several days poring over the hundreds of pages of court records in the case, and finally came up with a story that threw a lot of light on the somewhat nebulous operations of the FHA. This was many months before the national FHA scandal broke in Washington and helped to break the back of the Truman Administration.

This particular beach apartment project had been built under FHA Regulation No. 608, and in adopting it Congress had stipulated that it applied to only those projects to house war veterans and defense workers. Since Florida at that time was no great haven for gigantic defense projects, I naturally wondered just how many such projects had been built in our state with these lush Federal tax dollars.

Therefore, I wired Walter L. Greene — then the deputy commissioner of the FHA, but who later resigned under fire when the investigating committee headed by Senator Homer E. Capehart (Rep., Ind.) disclosed the windfall profits in the FHA — for a list of all Federal projects built in Florida under Regulation No. 608. Greene wired back rather abruptly that these loans — even though they were a matter of taxpayer funds — were private deals between the lender and the lendee, and he declined to give me the information. I wired right back that there could be no privacy in the matter of taxpayer funds and I warned Greene that if he still declined to reveal the loans, I intended to advise every major journalism organization in the country to make the matter a major protest against Federal censorship.

Under this pressure, Greene telephoned me from Washington the next day and grudgingly said he was sending me the official list of FHA loans made in Florida under Regulation No. 608. The reason he telephoned me was very evident. If he had wired his consent, it would have written into the official records the precedent of the FHA making public its loans. But by telephoning me, he was in a position of making the next editor who asked for the loans go through the same sweating and frustrating process. That, of course, is the usual Federal process in the release of records of spending taxpayers' funds.

Anyway, the *Tribune* not only printed the list of FHA loans in Florida under Regulation No. 608, but we also recounted for our readers the difficulties we had in getting this legitimate information from the Federal Government. Furthermore, I promptly sent a staffer on a tour of these FHA projects and he was unable to find a single war veteran or defense worker who ever lived in one of them. Instead, the projects were luxury beach resort apartments, which rented from $100 a week upwards and were patronized largely by our wealthier tourists.

Our investigation revealed that several of these FHA luxury projects had been put through the same financial wringer as the one at Clearwater which had started us on the crusade, and we discovered that in every such case, the dear old RFC had stepped in and bailed out the equally dear old FHA, all with taxpayer funds. I promptly wired the RFC for a list of its loans in Florida but again I had to go through the same frustrating rigmarole, which I previously had gone through with the FHA, to get the list to print in the *Tribune*.

On January 14, 1955, William G. Lodwick, chief of the Department of Agriculture Foreign Service, while being interviewed by the Des Moines *Register* and *Tribune* in its crusade in the Wolf Ladejinsky security case, was asked if government business is not public business. "It is not and you know it," he replied.

On February 5 of the same year, Secretary of Agriculture Ezra Taft Benson passed through Tampa and I had one of my reporters buttonhole him at our airport and ask if Mr. Lodwick's statement reflected the policy of the Department of Agriculture. Mr. Benson replied: "We give public information, but there are times when it is not to the public benefit to make certain announcements concerning governmental functions."

The reason I was interested in this was due to the headaches that the Secretary of Agriculture and his assistants had given me in the release of legitimate Florida information from the Department of Agriculture. On September 15, 1952, I had asked Senator Spessard L. Holland of Florida to obtain from Secretary Charles Brannan's vast bureau a list of the names, locations, duties and salaries of the employees of the Soil Conservation Service. On October 1, Senator Holland sent me a copy of a letter from Acting Chief D. A. Williams of the Soil Conservation Service, which turned down the request and which said:

> "Since The Tampa Tribune is an outside commercial organization, and, since it is contrary to the policy of this department to give out the names, salaries or addresses of our employees, other than those listed in official documents of government, we have supplied the attached information in the hope that it will be sufficient for their needs."

The attachment was nothing more than the number of employees, the general type of work and the civil service rating, listing only the lowest salary paid to that rating. There was no indication whatsoever as to whether there were any communists, bandits, bankers or preachers in the employ of this department of Federal Government, nor was there any hint as to whether the American taxpayers' dollars were being spent wisely or foolishly in salaries.

I immediately wrote a strong letter of protest and then got involved in a correspondence that lasted two months with the Chief of the Soil Conservation Service and the Administrator of the Production and Marketing Administration, in which we discussed many things including freedom of the press, the taxpayers' dollars, Communism and Democracy. It developed that the Department of Agriculture wanted to protect their secret employees from the pressure of loan sharks and the farmers, and cared little for the restraint of an informed public opinion.

In October the Production and Marketing Administration sent me a partial list of its Florida employees. I wrote back that this was insufficient, and what did they have to hide? Again we went round and round through Uncle Sam's mail, and finally in late November G. F. Geisler, the Production and Marketing Administrator, sent me a complete list, which we duly printed in the *Tribune*. But you will note that it required nearly three months of frustrating correspondence to get this simple information relating to the expenditure of the American taxpayers' dollars.

By this time my appetite for information from the Department of Agriculture really was whetted, so I asked the Secretary for a list of soil subsidy payments in Florida. This provoked a new correspondence of another three months, in which we thoroughly thrashed out the matter of privacy involved in the payment of American tax dollars to privileged recipients — in many cases for absolutely nothing. By now Ezra Taft Benson had become Secretary of Agriculture, and again I warned that I fully intended to make this matter a public affair of censorship before the national journalism organizations, and the Department finally grudgingly consented to let the *Tribune* have the lists.

I sent a reporter to the Federal agriculture office at Gainesville and he spent six weeks copying more than 11,000 names of the Florida recipients of soil subsidies. We printed these names in the *Tribune* and they had huge reader interest. For one thing, they revealed that a lot of wealthy Floridians were milking the Federal cow. For another, we were able to put the facts together for the first time in a special Page 1 story that showed the Lykes

Brothers Steamship Company, in south Florida, and the DuPont Banking Interests, in north Florida, as the two biggest owners of Florida real estate. This, of course, revealed why both of these huge business interests wielded so much political power in our legislature, simply because they owned most of the land in several counties and controlled the elections of officials there.

I do not know whether our stories shamed any of the wealthy Floridians into refusing subsequent soil subsidies, but I do know that a year after we printed the lists, the Department of Agriculture announced that Florida, a great agriculture state, had less soil subsidy payments than any other southeastern state.

But all of this was nothing compared to the hassle we got into with the Department of Agriculture over the matter of the Rural Electrification Administration in Sumter County in 1956. A delegation of Sumter County farmers appealed to the *Tribune* for help in a developing scandal involving the REA, and I sent a staffer to cover a special meeting of the Sumter Electric Cooperative at Sumterville. His news story revealed:

1. The Sumter Electric Cooperative was in a deplorable state of confusion.
2. The Department of Agriculture had sent three investigators into the mess the previous year but had declined to reveal the results.
3. That dozens of Sumter farmers had written the Department of Agriculture urging that the results of its investigation be made public so that they could put their government house in order.
4. That there were considerable taxpayer funds unaccounted for, and that the records of this cooperative were in a worse condition than utter confusion.

A Federal official appeared before this meeting, rapped the press and declared that it was not the policy of the Department to give to the public information of REA operations. I, of course, reached for my typewriter, and there sizzled out a letter of protest to Secretary of Agriculture Benson, in which I asked how come, in free America, did a branch of the free government stoop close to the communistic position of conducting a secret investigation. Once again we explored the beauties of privacy in the matter of the American citizen's tax dollars in a correspondence of several weeks. We never did pry the results of that secret investigation out of Secretary Benson, but we did quickly achieve a cleanup in both personnel and records of the cooperative, which put it back on its feet.

The case of the Florida hotel cadging brought down the wrath of the White House upon the *Tribune*. In the middle of the congressional investigation of industrialist Bernard Goldfine's expensive gifts to Presidential Aide Sherman Adams, a friend of mine in Washington, who travels in circles close to the politicians, gave me the tip that James C. Hagerty, press agent for President Eisenhower, had arranged in Washington for a free vacation at swank Ponte Vedra Club near Jacksonville Beach.

I sent a staff writer to the club and the management forthrightly confirmed that Mr. and Mrs. Hagerty had been their guests on a five-day golfing vacation the previous year, had occupied a spanking new cottage, and that their bill of $260.97 had been complimented by the club. It has been my experience over 35 years of newspapering that the average businessman always will answer all questions honestly; that is, he will until his lawyer enters the picture. But perhaps politicians and lawyers have had more experience in the business of clouding facts.

The Associated Press picked up the *Tribune*'s account of this and White House correspondents immediately asked Hagerty about it. Hagerty shrugged it off with the following statement: "I'll stick with what I said before. I tried to pay the bill and they were equally insistent that there was no bill. That's all there is to it. I was a guest."

But the influential Washington *Post* and *Times Herald* did not shrug it off. In an editorial the next day, the newspaper called it "free loading" and said that the net effect of the Hagerty stay was ". . . to use the prestige of The White House for commercial purposes." The newspaper added that Hagerty should have made the following statement to the Ponte Vedra Club officials:

"I can't possibly accept free hotel accommodations without embarrassing him (the President). Consequently, you must accept my check or I shall never be free to set foot in your club again."

I then sent my staffer to Miami to check into Vice President Richard Nixon's vacations at the equally swank Key Biscayne Hotel. He found that Nixon and his family occupied a villa at $150 each time but always paid the bill with personal checks. Also, he learned that the Vice-President was generous with $10 tips. The management informed us that "nobody stays here on the cuff." We duly recorded this in the *Tribune* for posterity.

At this point, there walked into our office an apparently enraged Republican woman, who turned over to us a copy of the stenographic report of a secret Senate Judiciary Committee meeting which considered the qualifications of south Florida's Republican U.S. District Attorney, and suggested that we look into the hotel bill of the Eisenhower campaign party at the swank Miami hotel Roney Plaza in 1952.

This stenographic report of the Senate Committee procedures related testimony of Miami Republican leaders that the Eisenhower campaign party ran up a bill of $4,280, including flowers and food for a big pre-election party, and then left it unpaid. These Miami Republican leaders testified further that they were refused admittance to the Eisenhower party by big hired bouncers but afterwards they were presented the bill by the hotel.

I sent my staffer hot-footing it back to Miami, but the Roney Plaza management, apparently having noted our previous stories on Hagerty and Nixon, greeted his questions with "No comment." We went ahead with our story based largely on the stenographic report of the Senate Committee's hearing, but we mentioned the hearing, itself, only casually. In fact, we played down the story, which always is a wise procedure in crusading newspapering, and we did not say outright that the bill had never been paid. We simply recorded that the Eisenhower party had left it unpaid, which was the absolute truth, and we further did not relate the testimony of the Miami Republican leaders.

Again the Associated Press picked up our story and it really upset the White House. Press agent Hagerty held two conferences with White House newspaper correspondents the next day; angrily declared that the National Republican Party had paid $964.13 of the hotel bill; and admitted that there had been some discussions with the hotel management over what he said was a bill of about $1,500. Then he teed off specifically on *The Tampa Tribune* with the following statement: "It would seem to me that a newspaper before using such a story could have at least checked with either the White House or the Republican National Committee."

Asked by one of the correspondents whether he had any idea as to how the *Tribune* story originated, Hagerty said he had no idea where the $4,000 figure came from and then he said: "I'll let the facts speak for themselves and let you gentlemen draw your own inferences."

The Associated Press asked me for a statement in reply, and I gave out the following paragraph, which was carried over the wire:

> A senatorial investigating committee showed that a bill of more than $4,000, including flowers and food, had been run up at the Roney Plaza Hotel by the Eisenhower campaign party. This was many months later and had not been paid at the time of the investigation. Now Mr. Hagerty has accounted for $964.13.

It would be most interesting for an accounting of the remaining $3,035.87 for which the hotel apparently held the bag.

Then the *Tribune* carried a 2,000-word story, part of which was picked up by the Associated Press, which related word for word the testimony of the Miami Republican leaders over the post-election controversy over the $4,280 bill. This Senate hearing also brought out that the Roney Plaza Hotel threatened to sue for the bill, which action no doubt led to a settlement of part of the bill by the Republican National Party.

But no Washington politician offered satisfactory answers to the moral questions of why highranking Federal officials are entitled to "free loading" in swank Florida resorts or why a Presidential campaign party has the right to walk out on a $4,280 election party bill.

16.

Bureaucratic Strangulation of Government

BUREAUCRACY HAS GROWN MORE SUBTLE as it has matured. The privilege of withholding facts — first granted in the faith that Cabinet members and department heads would consider it a privilege and use it sparingly and with discretion — has been abused and distorted into a monstrous farce.

One of many serious distortions is the practice, common among bureaucrats, of releasing only enough facts to give favorable weight to the propaganda they are pouring out for or against a controversial issue.

For example, on May 19, 1956, the Air Force "leaked" to the New York *Times* a high altitude picture of the Navy's new carrier, the Forrestal. The picture showed the carrier as a sitting duck, an easy prey for aerial bombs, and it was "leaked" at the very moment our military services were debating how much of the defense dollar each would get. The Air Force hoped to show that carriers were obsolete and that the Air Force deserved to get some of the

Navy's defense funds. Incidentally, one week after the picture was printed, *Life Magazine* learned that 100 pictures of the carrier had been taken, and asked for them, but neither the Air Force nor the Pentagon would admit that the pictures were even in existence.

Similarly, the Central Intelligence Agency, all operations of which are super-secret, "leaked" to favored newspapers on November 19, 1956, the fact that it had given the White House 23 hours notice of the British-French-Israeli attack on Egypt. This "leak" came 24 hours before CIA officials were to testify before congressional committees, and was designed to impress both Congress and the taxpayers on the great worth of the CIA and its need for a bigger and better slice of the budget.

In 1957, the Department of State "leaked" to the New York *Times* and Washington *Star* only part of a public opinion poll on foreign policy. This, of course, made the Department and its foreign policy look good. But a congressional investigating committee later proved conclusively that the part of the poll released was slanted and that the whole poll was paid for illegally with taxpayer dollars.

One case several years ago involved the production of B-52 bombers. General Curtis E. LeMay, in testifying before the Symington Senate Committee, declared that he could not give the size of the new B-52 Wings because because this was top-flight, top secret security information. But a day or so later, Secretary of Defense Charles E. Wilson, in his press conference plea for bigger and better defense dollars, said the number of planes in the B-52 Wings had been increased from 30 to 45. When the press jumped the Pentagon about this, military spokesmen said the disclosure was made "reluctantly" after weighing public interest against giving our enemies such vital information.

But had the press dug out this information on its own and printed it, bureaucrats would have raked it fore and aft as traitorous.

Currently this is called "management of the news," and it is indeed a growing menace in daily communication of facts of American Government to the people. Often Washington correspondents who play ball with bureaucrats, are rewarded with these "leaked" news breaks. On the basis of evidence, one and all of the "leaks" are made solely for the benefit of the bureaucrat and sometimes at the actual expense of American security.

At the other extreme are the masses of documents classified as "secret" that could not possibly endanger our security. Here is the key paragraph of a letter written May 13, 1960, by Representative John E. Moss (Dem., Calif.) to Secretary of the Army Wilbur M. Brucker:

> At the request of Congressman Byron Johnson of Colorado, the House Government Information Subcommittee investigated restrictions on a ground water contamination research report prepared by University of Colorado scientists for the Rocky Mountain Arsenal, a chemical warfare installation near Denver, Colorado. The main objective of the research project was to determine the source of chemicals that were poisoning wells north and west of the Rocky Mountain Arsenal. The sum total of the scientists' conclusions was that contaminated water was flowing downhill, underground, from Arsenal waste disposal reservoirs into the ground water supply of nearby farms.

> The reports by the University of Colorado scientists were made public by the Chemical Corps at the insistence of Congressman Johnson last November but the use of a military security stamp to withhold information on the research project was reported only recently and raises a number of questions.

There continues to be growing confusion in the minds of the people giving thoughtful consideration to the use and abuse of the privilege of classifying documents of

Federal Government in the interest of national security. In fact, I doubt that any citizen, be he in or out of government, can safely negotiate the security regulations without putting his foot into the bucket.

Prior to 1953, under the Truman postwar directive, every one of the approximately 7,000 Federal agencies, bureaus, commissions, etc. and every one of the approximately 2,000,000 Federal bureaucrats could censor any and all information of government in the sacred name of security. The wide abuse of this privilege aroused so much protest from the press — which found itself stymied on all sides in the matter of printing legitimate information of government — that President Eisenhower, on November 5, 1953, issued a new directive.

This new directive, entitled Executive Order 10,501, gave 51 Federal agencies and departments and all its employees the blanket privilege of classifying as Top Secret, Secret, or Confidential "official information which requires protection in the interests of national defense." These are listed later in the chapter. And it also listed 17 other Federal agencies and departments in which the authority to classify defense information was limited to the head of the agencies or departments. These 17 agencies were:

CIVIL AERONAUTICS BOARD

DEFENSE TRANSPORT ADMINISTRATION

DEPARTMENT OF AGRICULTURE

DEPARTMENT OF HEALTH, EDUCATION AND WELFARE

DEPARTMENT OF INTERIOR

DEPARTMENT OF LABOR

FEDERAL COMMUNICATIONS COMMISSION

FEDERAL POWER COMMISSION

NATIONAL SCIENCE FOUNDATION

NATIONAL SECURITY TRAINING COMMISSION

PANAMA CANAL COMPANY

POST OFFICE DEPARTMENT

RECONSTRUCTION FINANCE CORPORATION

RENEGOTIATION BOARD

SMALL BUSINESS ADMINISTRATION

SUBVERSIVE ACTIVITIES CONTROL BOARD

TENNESSEE VALLEY AUTHORITY

Under the Eisenhower directive, all other Federal agencies and departments could NOT censor information of government in the name of sacred security, and this, of course, should have resulted in a smoother and bigger flow of information from Washington to the people by way of the newspapers. But it didn't work out this way. The bureaucrats in these agencies and departments quickly concocted a new classification termed "for official use only" and they stamped this upon any and every bit of government information which they chose, at their discretion, to withhold from the people.

This, of course, precipitated a new running debate between the press and the Moss House Subcommittee on Government Information on one side and the bureaucracy on the other. On March 9, 1960, President Eisenhower issued an additional memorandum intended to clarify the authority to classify defense information for agencies established since November 5, 1953. This memorandum listed eight agencies granted blanket authority to classify defense information and stated that all other agencies created since November 5, 1953, were denied such authority.

These eight new agencies given blanket privilege of classifying information were:

COUNCIL ON FOREIGN ECONOMIC POLICY

DEVELOPMENT LOAN FUND

FEDERAL AVIATION AGENCY

FEDERAL RADIATION COUNCIL

NATIONAL AERONAUTICS AND SPACE ADMINISTRATION

NATIONAL AERONAUTICS AND SPACE COUNCIL

OFFICE OF CIVIL AND DEFENSE MOBILIZATION

PRESIDENT'S BOARD OF CONSULTANTS ON FOREIGN INTELLIGENCE ACTIVITIES

In announcing the new Eisenhower memorandum, James C. Hagerty, Presidential press secretary, said that 30 other agencies and departments created after November 5, 1953, had been denied the authority to classify. Representative Moss immediately wrote a letter to President Eisenhower asking for a list of these agencies, and on April 27, 1960, Jack Z. Anderson, administrative assistant to the President, furnished a list to the Moss Committee which contained the names of 33, not 30, agencies:

ADVISORY COMMITTEE ON FEDERAL PUBLIC WORKS

ADVISORY COMMITTEE ON THE ARTS

ALASKA INTERNATIONAL RAIL AND HIGHWAY COMMISSION

CABINET COMMITTEE ON PRICE STABILITY FOR ECONOMIC GROWTH

CABINET COMMITTEE ON SMALL BUSINESS

CANAL ZONE BOARD OF APPEALS

CAREER EXECUTIVE BOARD

CIVIL WAR CENTENNIAL COMMISSION

COMMISSION ON CIVIL RIGHTS

COMMISSION ON INTERNATIONAL RULES OF JUDICIAL PROCEDURE

COMMITTEE FOR RURAL DEVELOPMENT PROGRAM

COMMITTEE ON GOVERNMENT ACTIVITIES AFFECTING PRICES AND COSTS

DISTINGUISHED CIVILIAN SERVICE AWARDS BOARD

FEDERAL COUNCIL FOR SCIENCE AND TECHNOLOGY

FEDERAL HOME LOAN BANK BOARD

FOREIGN CLAIMS SETTLEMENT COMMISSION

FRANKLIN DELANO ROOSEVELT MEMORIAL COMMISSION

INTERDEPARTMENTAL COMMITTEE FOR THE VOLUNTARY PAYROLL SAVINGS PLAN FOR THE PURCHASE OF U.S. SAVINGS BONDS

INTERNATIONAL DEVELOPMENT ADVISORY BOARD

LINCOLN SESQUICENTENNIAL COMMISSION

OUTDOOR RECREATION RESOURCES REVIEW COMMISSION

PERMANENT COMMITTEE FOR THE OLIVER WENDELL HOLMES DEVISE

PRESIDENTIAL ADVISORY COMMITTEE ON ENERGY SUPPLIES AND RESOURCES POLICY

PRESIDENT'S COMMITTEE FOR TRAFFIC SAFETY

PRESIDENT'S COMMITTEE ON EMPLOYMENT OF THE PHYSICALLY HANDICAPPED

PRESIDENT'S COMMITTEE ON FUND RAISING WITHIN THE FEDERAL SERVICE

PRESIDENT'S COMMITTEE ON GOVERNMENT EMPLOYMENT POLICY

PRESIDENT'S COMMITTEE ON MIGRATORY LABOR

PRESIDENT'S COUNCIL ON YOUTH FITNESS

RIVER BASIN STUDY COMMISSION FOR TEXAS

RIVER BASIN STUDY COMMISSION ON SOUTH CAROLINA–GEORGIA–ALABAMA–FLORIDA

SAINT LAWRENCE SEAWAY DEVELOPMENT CORPORATION

TRADE POLICY COMMITTEE

In his covering letter to Representative Moss, Anderson said ". . . work is going forward on a simplified positive listing of the departments and agencies that are to have classification authority."

This prompted Representative Moss to select 30 agencies and departments which seemed least likely to need blanket authority to classify, yet had been included in President Eisenhower's original list of 51 agencies created before 1953. Moss wrote the heads of these agencies, asking this question:

> What type of material is handled by your agency which requires the authority to classify "official" information affecting national security?

Seven of these 30 agencies wrote that they never originated classified documents but occasionally handled them, 23 said they *neither originated nor handled classified information.*

In the following list of the 51 agencies and departments given blanket privilege of classifying, the 23 agencies admitting they *never* originate nor handle classified information are identified with the letter N. The seven agencies answering that they never originate documents, but sometimes handle them are indicated as S.

N   Administrative Committee of the Federal Register

N   Advisory Board on Economic Growth and Stability

N   Advisory Board on National Parks, Historic Sites, Buildings, and Monuments

S   AIR COORDINATING COMMITTEE

ATOMIC ENERGY COMMISSION

S   BOARD OF FOREIGN SCHOLARSHIPS

S   BOARD ON GEOGRAPHIC NAMES

BUREAU OF THE BUDGET

CANAL ZONE GOVERNMENT

CENTRAL INTELLIGENCE AGENCY

CIVIL SERVICE COMMISSION

N   Corregidor Bataan Memorial Commission

COUNCIL OF ECONOMIC ADVISERS

DEPARTMENT OF THE AIR FORCE

DEPARTMENT OF THE ARMY

DEPARTMENT OF COMMERCE

DEPARTMENT OF DEFENSE

DEPARTMENT OF JUSTICE

DEPARTMENT OF THE NAVY

DEPARTMENT OF STATE

DEPARTMENT OF THE TREASURY

N   District of Columbia Board of Commissioners

N   District of Columbia Redevelopment Land Agency

N   Federal Fire Council

N   Federal Records Council

N   Federal Safety Council

N   Foreign Trade Zones Board

GENERAL SERVICES ADMINISTRATION

N   Government Contract Committee

GOVERNMENT PATENTS BOARD

N   Indian Arts and Crafts Board

S   Interdepartmental Committee on Trade Agreements

N   Interdepartmental Savings Bond Committee

N   Marine Corps Memorial Commission

N   Migratory Bird Conservation Commission

NATIONAL ADVISORY COUNCIL ON INTERNATIONAL MONETARY AND FINANCIAL PROBLEMS

N National Agricultural Advisory Commission

N National Archives Trust Fund Board

N National Historical Publications Commission

N National Park Trust Fund Board

NATIONAL SECURITY COUNCIL

OPERATIONS COORDINATING BOARD

S PRESIDENT'S ADVISORY COMMITTEE ON GOVERNMENT ORGANIZATION

N President's Committee on Employment of the Physically Handicapped

S UNITED STATES ADVISORY COMMISSION ON EDUCATIONAL EXCHANGE

S UNITED STATES ADVISORY COMMISSION ON INFORMATION

UNITED STATES INFORMATION AGENCY

UNITED STATES MISSION TO THE UNITED NATIONS

N United States National Committee for UNESCO

N United States Territorial Expansion Memorial Commission

N Virgin Islands Corporation

But on January 10, 1961, just 10 days before moving out of the White House, President Eisenhower issued a new order stripping the blanket classification authority from the 30 bureaus and agencies to which Congressman Moss had written. This deprived such bureaus as the Migratory Bird Conservation Commission from stamping their papers "secret," thus preventing the incoming administration from making early political capital out of the ridiculous secrecy.

In 1956 and 1957, top officials of 19 key Federal agencies testified before Moss' committee that they were accustomed to withhold legitimate information of government from both the public and the press. During the next year, bureaucrats extended this arrogancy to Congress, and in my files are documentations of 15 cases wherein the Executive Branch of Federal Government, mostly appointed officials, declined to yield certain information to committees of Congress. In 1958, Attorney General William P. Rogers defended this withholding of information in testimony before the Senate Subcommittee on Constitutional Rights headed by the late Senator Thomas C. Hennings, Jr. (Dem., Mo.), expounding his new theory of the "Doctrine of Executive Privilege."

At best, the "Doctrine of Executive Privilege" is nothing more than fancy terminology used by Federal bureaucrats as a mandate for doing as they choose, with little regard for the rights and privileges of either the American people or their elected representatives in Congress. Their contention is unsupported either in the courts or in the precedents of past American administrations.

Later in 1958 I testified before Senator Hennings' committee and I dubbed Attorney General Rogers' Doctrine of Executive Privilege a "legal smoke screen" and, at the same time, I presented the "Doctrine of the People's Privilege." In support of my doctrine, I filed in the committee's records a list of 93 cases of direct abridgment of the American people's inherent right to know about their government. These had been carefully compiled during 1957, and I found our Senators most sympathetic and particularly so when I warned them of the dangers, which are pointed up time and again in the pages of man's history, of an autocratic bureaucracy.

I could recite many of these cases of direct abridgment of freedom of information, but I believe the best way for me to present this great problem of modern American Government is to trace the course of a President's budget which, of course, delineates the bureaucratic spending of 70-odd billions of dollars which the Department of Internal Revenue so deftly extracts from American taxpayers each year.

The President's budget always is conceived in secrecy, so secret that late in 1956 President Eisenhower publicly castigated several members of his official family for "leaking" information of the bureaucrats' spending plans to the American people. The offending bureaucrats, of course, had been trying to rally public opinion behind their pet projects, but the President apparently wanted no such information to be released until he presented it in his annual message to Congress.

Before going further with the budget, I want to assure you that this is no political diatribe. I could have used one of President Truman's budgets of 10 years ago or one of President Roosevelt's budgets of 20 years ago, because our public servants have been steadily developing their secret government in Washington for the last 25 years.

When Eisenhower unveiled to Congress in January his budget of 70-odd billions of dollars, it disclosed only so many billions for defense, so many billions for this and that department, etc. This, of course, gave the lowly taxpayer little knowledge and less satisfaction, since it is extremely difficult for a man whose pay check is being tapped for $5 a week in income taxes, to appreciate a billion dollars. He would much rather know whether his $5 a week is going to buy a new plush chair for a Cabinet member or be used for some truly necessary expense.

Actually, the average President's message on the budget consists of about 800 pages, and no man can in one brief speech properly break down the distribution of 70-odd billions of dollars among approximately 7,000 Federal agencies and commissions. Even the 800 pages cannot account for each detail.

Congress listened to this budget with little stir, perhaps because they knew that no definite action would be taken until the President's figures have been whisked into the secret confines of the Congressional Appropriations Committees. There, from January until September, these committees of the people's representatives got their own whack at the people's tax dollars.

Thomas Jefferson, who gave us the principle of open government, probably has turned over in his grave a good many thousand times because of the secret government practiced today by the people's representatives in Congress. A survey shows that more than 1,200 congressional committee meetings are held in secrecy each year, with both press and public barred.

These secret meetings are made possible through a set of rules of procedure which Congress, itself, devised and which utilize the high sounding term of "executive session" to lock out the public. The rule in question reads:

> All hearings conducted by standing committees or their subcommittees shall be open to the public, except executive sessions for making up bills or for voting or where the committee by a majority vote orders an executive session.

Few of these secret executive sessions deal with defense or national security affairs; instead, they deal with virtually every matter of the people's business before Congress. Nearly every one of 200 meetings of the appropriations committee, in which our public servants tinkered with President Eisenhower's budget, was held in secrecy.

Much of this legislation was railroaded through Congress with a minimum of debate and with little opportunity for the restraint of public opinion to be exerted. Actually, some of it did not see the light of public print until after it became law.

President Woodrow Wilson once plaintively remarked:

> "They promise you a particular piece of legislation. As soon as the legislature meets, a bill embodying that legislation is introduced. It is referred to a committee. You never hear of it again. What happened? Nobody ever knows what happened."

You gather from this that in Wilson's time the President was very much in the congressional doghouse, that Congress was the boss of all legislation of that day, and that the people, having elected the members of Congress, perhaps had a little voice in the proceedings.

But today, under the expert direction of the bureaucrats, Federal legislation is railroaded through Congress, and the ordinary American citizen has little to say about his legislation. If there is any doubt about this, consider just one two-hour session during a hot summer afternoon in July a year or so ago. The Senators whooped through no less than 134 laws, an average of better than two a minute, and I doubt seriously that any of them knew even 10 per cent of the details of the legislation.

So, along late in the summer President Eisenhower's budget, expanded to about 1,200 pages in length and weighing about five pounds, was railroaded through Congress; and again I doubt that 10 per cent of our congressmen knew how the money was going to be spent.

It then went quietly into the Executive Branch for actual spending, but if you think you're now going to find out where your $5 weekly take-out is going, you have another think coming.

Bureaucrats guard the records of their expenditure of citizens' tax funds as they would their honor, often abusing old Federal statutes, which provide only for the *custody* of the records, to lock out the public. This is in striking contrast to the lower levels of American Government where the ordinary citizen can go to his City Hall, county courthouse and even state capitol and take a personal look at the records of where his tax dollars have been spent.

If you think a citizen can march up to some Federal bureaucrat and obtain from him the facts of the ultimate disposal of your tax dollars, you should see the scars of my correspondence with the White House; the Attorney

General; the Secretary of Treasury; the Secretary of Commerce; the Secretary of Agriculture; the Department of Defense; the Department of Health, Education and Welfare; the Rural Electrification Administration; the Federal Trade Commission; the FHA; the Federal Civil Service Commission; the U.S. Post Office Department and numerous other assorted bureaus and agencies over this important matter of information of government.

I have even visited the White House, the Attorney General and the Department of Defense in quest of this legitimate information, but, while they didn't say it, their attitude was "What are you doing up here?"

Let me show you just one scar of my sorties into Federal Government. In 1953, I asked Philip Young, then chairman of the Federal Civil Service Commission, to release to the public a list of Federal pensions being paid to former Congressmen. This started a correspondence that lasted three years and wandered through Attorney General Herbert Brownell, Jr.'s, office and into the White House and finally was concluded in a great burst of frustration on my part. And I have not the faintest idea to this day as to whether or not the taxpayers' dollars are being paid out properly to the proper persons in this department of Federal Government.

After some months of deliberation, which is quite usual when you correspond with bureaucrats, Mr. Young finally responded to my original letter and wrote in sanctified horror that he could not violate the privacy of the former Congressmen by disclosing their pensions. At the same time, he sent me a copy of the formula by which the Government is supposed to figure the pensions and he told me that I could do my own figuring.

I wrote right back and asked this distinguished public servant how in the world could there be any privacy in the matter of the people's tax funds. And in the matter of his government formula, I asked him how could I tell whether or not it was being properly figured unless I could see a list of the pensions actually being paid.

Mr. Young did not answer these questions, which

also is not unusual on the part of bureaucrats, so I inquired of Attorney General Brownell what business a Federal public servant had in withholding facts of the people's business from the public. Mr. Brownell did not condescend to respond to my letter but a few months later he appeared before a national meeting of newspaper editors at Chicago and assured us that the Federal Government was a great friend of the press and stood for freedom of information.

The chairman of this meeting asked if there were any questions from the floor and I promptly arose, complimented Mr. Brownell on his speech, but, I asked, what about Mr. Young's refusal to make public those pensions of former Congressmen? Mr. Brownell assured me that I would hear from him and then fled from the platform, simply because my question really had opened him up to a very probable raking-over by the editors on the general question of Federal secrecy.

I waited a reasonable time, then reminded Mr. Brownell of his promise, which is routine today in dealing with bureaucracy. Finally I received a brief note from an assistant Attorney General that the entire matter had been turned over to Bernard M. Shanley, special counsel to the President.

I didn't want to hurry the White House, so I waited weeks before I sent a reminder to Mr. Shanley. He did not answer my letter at the time, but some weeks later he did issue a public statement to the press, which upheld Mr. Young's argument in behalf of privacy. Here is Mr. Shanley's public statement, which he upheld in two subsequent letters to me:

> "I think individuals are entitled to keep such information private if they want to. It's sort of like the privacy covering a person's income tax returns."

Right in the middle of this correspondence, Senator John J. Williams (Rep., Del.) rose on the floor of the Senate on June 28, 1955, and charged that, through "manipulation": (1) a former Congressman, by paying only an additional $10.22, was able to get a second pension of $444 a year on top of the $2,626 a year pension he already was drawing as a former Congressman; (2) another former Government employee, by paying an additional $64.04, was able to hike his Federal pension from $1,400 to $2,612 a year; and (3) a third former employee of the Government who, by paying only $37.19 and working only one month for a congressional committee, was able to get a $720 pension.

In his speech, Senator Williams said:

> "These manipulations could not have been possible without the full knowledge and cooperation of the top officials of the agencies, Congressional Committees and members of Congress involved."

I promptly wrote a new letter to Mr. Young in which I quoted liberally from Senator Williams' speech and again asked him to release a list of pensions paid to former Congressmen. One year later he replied to my letter and stated that the Civil Service Commission had now changed its policy and that he would release the pensions provided the former Congressmen gave their permission. But whoever heard of a free people having to beg permission from their public servants before they can find out how their tax monies are being spent? I asked Mr. Young this question in my reply, but he did not respond, and there the matter rests today.

17.

The White House Run-Around

THE IRONY OF THIS WHOLE QUESTION of Federal secrecy, wherein no records of the expenditure of your tax dollars are open to inspection and no audited reports of this spending are made public, is that on January 30, 1957, in answer to a question at a White House press conference from Pat Munroe, correspondent for the Albuquerque, New Mexico, *Journal,* concerning the release of information on expenditure of public funds by junketing Congressmen, President Eisenhower said:

> "As far as I am concerned, I stand on this general truth, there is no expenditure of public moneys except only that involving that where public security itself is involved, that should not face the light of day any time any citizen inquires for it."

On April 4, 1957, the Associated Press, reporting on a Republican Women's Conference at Washington, said:

President Eisenhower invited the American people to be "watchful" of their government leaders to make sure there is "no looseness, no squandering, no racketeering, no lining of the pockets" in the "big spending for peace."

But how can the American people be watchful for the "big spending for peace" when the bureaucrat classifies virtually every record pertaining to the Federal expenditure of tax funds in the sacred name of security? This question has bothered the press over recent years, and it eventually developed into a running debate between newsmen, including the author, and the White House.

On May 17, 1954, in a letter to Secretary of Defense Wilson, President Eisenhower wrote:

Because it is essential to efficient and effective administration that employees of the executive branch be in a position to be completely candid in advising with each other on official matters, and because it is not in the public interest that any of their conversations and communications, or any documents or reproductions, concerning such advice be disclosed, you will instruct employees of your Department that in all of their appearances before the Subcommittee of the Senate Committee on Government Operations regarding the inquiry now before it they are not to testify to any such conversations or communications or to produce any such documents or reproductions. This principle must be maintained regardless of who would be benefited by such disclosures.

The President's letter, of course, was prompted by the political struggle between the Executive and Legislative Branches of Federal Government at that time. Many officials have admitted publicly that they use the

President's letter as a precedent not only to withhold legitimate information of government from the Congress but also from the American people.

In a White House conference, held on September 6, 1957, with Mr. Gerald D. Morgan, special assistant to the President on legal matters, I brought up the matter of these conflicting statements from the White House.

Mr. Morgan replied that Mr. Eisenhower's letter to Secretary Wilson had been misunderstood, that it meant private communications among agencies which under ordinary circumstances would not interest the public.

I countered with a question concerning a current case wherein the Secretary of Agriculture had declined to make available to a newspaper in Mississippi some requested lists of soil subsidy payments.

"Those soil subsidy payments should be made public," declared Mr. Morgan.

Then I asked about a recent case at Fieldale, Virginia, wherein the Post Office Department had declined to reveal the terms of a new lease.

"Why, carbons of that lease should have been given the press," said Mr. Morgan.

"That is why I am sitting in your office," I replied.

Mr. Morgan observed that perhaps the President should issue a positive statement on what news of government should be available to the press.

"That would be very helpful," I replied.

Clark Mollenhoff, Washington correspondent for the Des Moines *Register* and *Tribune,* twice engaged the White House in a continuation of the running controversy in 1959, and both incidents involved the Foreign Aid Bill then before Congress.

On July 15, 1959, at the President's press conference, Mollenhoff stated that committees of Congress had accused the administration of using secrecy "to hide imprudence, mismanagement, fraud and in some cases material that has later resulted in indictments." Then he asked:

> "I wonder if you have taken any steps to correct this, or how you reconcile this withholding with the Budgeting and Accounting Act which says it must be put forth to the Comptroller General, and your own constitutional requirement that you faithfully execute the laws?"

News accounts reported that this question visibly angered President Eisenhower, who replied as follows:

> "I think you had better put that question in written form and let me take a look at it, because you start right off the bat, with the premise or implication that someone is guilty of fraud. And I don't believe it."

Mollenhoff started again: "Mr. President . . ." but President Eisenhower cut him off with:

> "I will see your letter, if you would like to submit it."

In his subsequent letter, Mollenhoff pointed out that Congress had complained that Federal Agencies were using the "doctrine of executive privilege" to withhold information from it, and that Comptroller General Joseph Campbell had complained that the International Cooperation Administration and the Department of Defense both had violated the law by withholding several reports from his office. Then Mollenhoff asked:

> "Do you feel you have an executive responsibility to carry out the law in line with the Comptroller General's views?"

The White House did not answer this question. In his reply, Gerald D. Morgan, deputy assistant to the President, wrote that the Eisenhower position has not changed since the President wrote on the same subject last year to Representative Clare Hoffman (Rep., Mich.). Morgan quoted the President as saying then:

"I believe, of course, that the public, the Congress and such auditing units as the General Accounting Office should have all the information departments and agencies can properly make available.

"However, the public interest also demands order and efficiency in the operation of these departments and agencies. And in my judgment the public interest is not necessarily served by divulging the advice, suggestions or recommendations which subordinate employees periodically make to their superiors.

"In this connection, recommendations of inspectors general have been a most useful advisory tool in administering the military departments; and historically, recommendations and other advisory matter in such reports have not been released. I think this practice is a correct one, and is in the best interest of the nation."

Such statements, coming directly from the President and sounding as reasonable as they do, have furnished the umbrella under which the Federal bureaucrats have effectively hidden while they withhold legitimate information from both the public and Congress, as has been brought out time and again by the hearings of the Hennings and Moss Congressional Committees.

The $3,186,500,000 Foreign Aid Bill before Congress included a section that would cut off all foreign aid funds except military assistance if the administration held back from Congress reports evaluating the aid program. The White House had publicly opposed this provision.

On July 29, 1959, Mollenhoff rose at the President's press conference and asked if the President regarded the ". . . 'freedom of information' provision of the Foreign Aid Bill as a criticism of the administration's 'secrecy policies.' " The President, again apparently angered, said sternly:

> "You start your question with an implied fact that is not a fact. You say the administration's secrecy policies. There has been no administration . . ."

At this point, Mollenhoff again rose to amplify his question.

"Please sit down," President Eisenhower said sharply. Mollenhoff sat down, and the President continued:

> "There has been no administration since my memory, and I have been in this city since 1926, who has gone to such lengths to make information available as long as the national security and the national interest of this country is not involved."

I promptly wrote the following public letter to President Eisenhower:

> "The official reports of the Moss Subcommittee on Governmental Information in the House of Representatives and the Hennings Subcommittee on Constitutional Rights in the Senate, covering their investigative hearings of the last three years, show clearly that there is more unnecessary secrecy in the Federal Government today than at any time in our history.

> "These reports, totaling millions of words, carry the testimony of scores of leading Federal officials, who stated for the record that they were accustomed to withholding information of government, which had nothing to do with either the security or the interests of our country, from both the press and the people.

These reports are easily available to the White House.

"Mr. Mollenhoff's question at the press conference about your administration's 'secrecy policies' had to do with the House of Representatives' provision in the Foreign Aid Bill that would force the bureaucracy to give information of this foreign aid to the Congress. I would like to state relative to this that since the end of World War II some $75,000,000,000 of the American people's tax funds have been expended on foreign aid, yet the American people have not been given an accounting of a single penny of these expenditures by the Federal bureaucrats.

"This secrecy, of course, explains the great confusion in the public mind over the expenditure of our tax funds in foreign aid, and the same secrecy in other departments of our Federal Government also explains the great confusion over other leading issues of our day in the public mind. Both the Congress, which votes the expenditure, and the American people, who pay the tax funds, are entitled to full information.

"The mere declaration by the bureaucrat that publication of news of government would affect the public interest is not sufficient safeguard for the interests and the future well-being of the American people. Congressional hearings during the last three years have revealed time and again that such declarations simply are not justified and that they are being freely used by the bureaucrat to eliminate the proper restraint of public opinion, which is so necessary to the functioning of the free, American society.

"I am enclosing copies of the 1957 and 1958 reports of the Freedom of Information Committee of Sigma Delta Chi, the professional journalistic fraternity, of which I am chairman. These reports will show clearly the following trends in Federal Government today, which are carefully documented:

1. Virtually all of the records of the expenditure of the American citizen's tax funds by the Federal Government are closed to both the press and and the public, and most of the meetings of Federal Government dealing with these expenditures of tax funds are closed.

   I would like to point out that in the last seven years, while the Federal Government has been increasing its secrecy, the Legislatures of 19 states have adopted laws against secrecy in both governmental records and meetings. Today 32 states have laws guaranteeing their citizens open records of government and 23 states have laws stipulating that governing bodies must meet in the public for all to see and hear.

2. I have in my files 15 documented cases in the last two years wherein the bureaucrat has denied proper information of government to the Congress, and this, of course, points up definitely the usurpation of the functions of our Legislative Branch of Federal Government by the bureaucracy, a most dangerous trend for the future well-being of the free American people.

3. It would take a super-Houdini to navigate the mushrooming maze of the Federal bureaucracy which places a restraining finger upon every phase of living of every American citizen.

4. There is an unhealthy 'hostility of attitude' among the Federal bureaucrats toward the free press and its obligation to report all the facts of free American government to the free people.

"Let me stress to you that the free press of our country is just as interested in preserving the national security as you, and that this letter deals solely with the legitimate information of American government and not with the revelation of security secrets. And I point out that the record shows clearly, despite the numerous charges of the bureaucrats, that not one case has been documented wherein the press revealed a security secret that harmed the interests of our country.

"Therefore, this is to call upon you, both humbly and respectfully, for a change of attitude in your administration toward freedom of information and the American people's right to know about their government, which is so necessary to the retention of American freedom in a most trying era."

The White House did not even acknowledge this letter. In January, 1958, a copy of my Sigma Delta Chi Freedom of Information Committee's 1957 Freedom of Information Report, documenting 93 cases of outright abridgment of the American people's right to know, also was sent to Mr. Eisenhower. All of which leads me to the belief that those around the President carefully kept from him the true state of affairs in our national problem of freedom of information within the Federal Government. Subsequent developments supported my belief.

On November 4, 1959, the Associated Press carried the following news story on President Eisenhower's press conference:

> President Eisenhower today disputed claims that secrecy in government has grown during his administration.

> The President said: "Frankly, I don't believe it" when told by a reporter at his news conference that many people contend executive secrecy increased as a result of his 1954 order on the release of government information.

> "I have done my very best to make certain that every department and agency of the United States Government makes available all information that is obviously not detrimental to the national interest if it is disclosed at that time," he said.

This prompted me to send the following letter of November 5, 1959 to James C. Hagerty, Press Secretary to President Eisenhower:

"I note from the Associated Press that President Eisenhower told his press conference of November 4, 1959, that 'Frankly, I don't believe it,' when a reporter informed him that many people believe that the executive secrecy in our Federal Government has increased during his administration.

"Frankly, I do not believe that the President would make such a statement had he been given the facts.

"I am chairman of the national Freedom of Information Committee of Sigma Delta Chi, the professional journalistic fraternity, and our annual reports of 1957 and 1958, which contained documentary evidence of growing secrecy in the executive branch of the Federal Government, were sent to President Eisenhower. I doubt that he ever personally received these reports.

"The 1957 Sigma Delta Chi Freedom of Information Report contained 93 cases of direct abridgment of freedom of information, which I compiled at the direct suggestion of Mr. Gerald D. Morgan, executive assistant of President Eisenhower, after a personal conference with him in the White House on September 6, 1957.

"On July 30, 1959, after President Eisenhower had made a similar statement about freedom of information in another of his press conferences, I wrote him a letter of protest, again enclosing copies of these Sigma Delta Chi Freedom of Information Reports, and I referred him to the millions of words of testimony during the last three years before the Hennings Senate Subcommittee on Constitutional Rights and the Moss House Subcommittee on Government Information. I doubt that the President ever saw my letter, the Sigma Delta Chi reports or was referred to the Hennings and Moss documentary reports of growing secrecy in the Executive Branch of our Federal Government.

"This is to urge most sincerely that you, as the President's press attache, personally submit to him the tremendous volume of evidence that secrecy has been widely expanded in the Executive Branch of Federal Government during the last seven years.

"This, I believe, is a most reasonable request, and I will appreciate word from you."

On December 3 Hagerty replied, as follows:

"In your letter of November fifth, you urge that there be personally submitted to the President such reports as those of the Freedom of Information Committee of Sigma Delta Chi on the subject of the withholding of information by executive departments and agencies during this Administration.

"The gist of the reports has been brought to his attention. His statements on this subject of several press conferences disclose his lack of belief in the claim that during this Administration there has been increased withholding of information. In his most recent statement on Nov. 4, 1959, the President recognized, as I assume you do, that the sheer size of the Government makes it doubtful that every judgment which must be made as to whether the disclosure of particular information is in the public interest will be free of error."

Meanwhile, on December 2, 1959, there was a new freedom of information explosion at the President's press conference. This time it was originated by William McGaffin, Washington correspondent for the *Chicago Daily News*. Here is the exchange, taken from a stenographic report of the news conference:

McGAFFIN: "Mr. President, could you tell us whether you have received the Sigma Delta Chi Freedom of Information Reports and, if so, what was your reaction to them, sir?"

THE PRESIDENT: "You will have to describe them. There are too many reports for me to remember them by title."

McGAFFIN: "Well, sir, the reason I asked is that Mr. V. M. Newton, Jr., the chairman of the committee that prepared the reports, says that he sent them to you twice, but he feels that you have not personally seen them, or you would not continue in the belief that you have repeatedly expressed about secrecy in Government during your Administration."

THE PRESIDENT: "Well, I think I'll have to see the report and give you an answer, because I simply can't answer on something that I can't recall the contents of."

On December 3, 1959, I hastened to write a new letter to President Eisenhower, as follows:

"I note from the Associated Press of December 2 that you told Mr. William McGaffin of the Chicago Daily News that you could not recall having seen the Sigma Delta Chi Freedom of Information Reports of the last two years.

"For the record, I have sent two sets of these reports for you to the White House, and I am enclosing a new set, which includes our reports of 1957, 1958 and 1959.

"Believe me, we in the American press will be greatly appreciative if you will read these reports, which show an alarming increase in secrecy in the Federal Government during recent years.

"I particularly call your attention to the 1957 report, which contains 93 cases of direct abridgment of freedom of information, which I prepared and sent to you after a direct suggestion from Mr. Gerald Morgan during our conference in the White House on September 6, 1957."

On the same day, I also wrote the following letter to Gerald D. Morgan, Deputy Assistant to the President:

"This is to call your attention to the enclosed clipping of an Associated Press story of December 2, 1959.

"I have mailed new copies of Sigma Delta Chi's 1957, 1958 and 1959 Freedom of Information Reports to President Eisenhower.

"We in Sigma Delta Chi will be most appreciative if you will personally call these reports to his attention."

I received the following letter, dated December 5, 1959, from Morgan:

"This is to acknowledge receipt of your letter of December third with the enclosed clipping regarding Sigma Delta Chi's Freedom of Information Reports to the President. I understand that Mr. James Hagerty wrote to you on December third regarding this matter."

On December 7, 1959, I replied to the Morgan letter as follows:

"Mr. Hagerty's letter of December 3 was most unsatisfactory in that it in no way shed light on a most grave problem in our Federal Government. I am enclosing a copy of my reply to him.

"We in the free press still will be most grateful if somebody in the White House will bring the Sigma Delta Chi Freedom of Information Reports to the President's attention.

"It begins to appear as if the press is being denied the Constitutional privilege of petitioning the government for a redress of grievances."

On December 8, 1959, I wrote a new letter to Press Secretary Hagerty, as follows:

"Thank you for your letter of December 3.

"I cannot understand the statement in your letter which reads as follows:

'The gist of the (Sigma Delta Chi Freedom of Information) reports has been brought to his (The President's) attention. His statements on this subject at several press conferences disclose his lack of belief in the claim that during this Administration there has been increased withholding of information. . . .'

"On December 2, President Eisenhower told his press conference that he had not received the Sigma Delta Chi Freedom of Information Reports, even though several copies had been sent to the White House, and that he could not discuss them until he knew their contents.

"I agree with you that the sheer size of the Government 'makes it doubtful that every judgment which must be made as to whether the disclosure of particular information is in the public interest will be free of error.'

"But I would like to point out that the Sigma Delta Chi Freedom of Information Committee, of which I am chairman, is not making an issue of any single case, wherein there was possible error. We are protesting the growing secrecy in Federal Government on the basis of the general picture, as illustrated by (1) our research reports of 1957, 1958 and 1959, as well as by (2) the voluminous reports of the Hennings' Senate Subcommittee on Constitutional Rights and the Moss House Subcommittee on Government Information during the last three years.

"As the result of the President's statement at his December 2 press conference, I have sent new copies of our 1957, 1958 and 1959 Freedom of Information Reports to him at the White House and we in Sigma Delta Chi will be most appreciative if this research information is called to his personal attention.

"Please believe that we are most sincere in our approach to this very grave problem in Federal Government."

The last minute acts of Eisenhower in January, 1961, could be hoped to prompt the new administration to lift more of the absurd cloak. Despite repeated statements that there is no withholding of legitimate information of government from the American people, the evidence is overwhelming that a general policy of secrecy dominates virtually all business of the Federal Government.

Almost every day new cases are brought to light illustrating this general policy of secrecy in Washington, much of it needless and some of it ridiculous. As a good example, on September 21, 1960, the Wage and Hour Division of the Department of Labor informed *The Tampa Tribune* that "government rules of secrecy" forbid it from even admitting that it had made a wage investigation among 1,400 employees of a Tampa cigar factory.

Meanwhile, the owner of this factory gave the *Tribune* reporter complete details not only of the investigation but also of the settlement.

This case, wherein a business man believed in giving more information to the public than does the Federal Government, was so ridiculous that I turned the matter over to the Moss House Subcommittee on Government Information. Representative Moss promptly sent to me copies of a year-long running debate between his Committee and the Department of Labor which went far beyond the ridiculous.

On May 20, 1960, Representative Moss wrote Secretary of Labor James F. Mitchell as follows:

> "The concern of Congress about the administration of wage-hour laws stems from the expanding volume of adminstrative adjudications. More and more, decisions that affect millions of persons are being made through administrative hearings and investigations instead of through the judicial and legislative processes.

> "Reflecting its concern, Congress provided in the Administrative Procedure Act that administrative justice must be dispensed under the same safeguards guaranteed by our open judicial system. Information about findings, decisions, penalties and appeals is made available to the public with a double purpose in mind. First, the right of the public to fair and impartial enforcement of the laws is protected by disclosure of decisions on law violations. Second, the rights of individuals to fair and equal treatment under the law is protected by disclosure of the findings and punishment meted out to law violators.

> "Neither of these safeguards is available under the system which the Department of Labor has established for administrative enforcement of provisions of the Wage-Hour Act. When a member of Congress asked for the names of violators of the law and the amounts of back wage settlements, he was rebuffed. Instead, a cloak of secrecy was drawn around the facts. The Department announced only that during 1959 investigators turned up nearly $22.5 million in lost wages. And during that same period, less than $13 million of those wages were returned to employees.

> "Without the facts, the people cannot determine the propriety of the $10 million discrepancy be-

tween wage losses discovered, and wage settlements made. They cannot determine whether the $10 million represents legitimate compromises of violations, or whether there is one kind of settlement for certain employers, and another kind for other employers.

"In addition to an outright refusal to provide a Member of Congress with needed information, your Department compounded the issue by arrogantly censoring information sought by the House Government Information Subcommittee in the discharge of its legislative duties.

"The Subcommittee's request for copies of rules and regulations governing the release of information about Wage-Hour Act violations was rejected. Instead, the Subcommittee was 'informally' handed a censored photostat of several paragraphs apparently lifted from the rules and regulations governing enforcement of the Wage-Hour Act. Even the paragraph numbers were censored.

"Not only does the Department enforce the Wage-Hour Act in secret, but it is attempting to censor the very regulations which set up this secrecy."

In a letter dated August 23, 1960, Secretary Mitchell wrote Representative Moss as follows:

"As stated in our June 23 letter, we are firmly of the opinion that to disseminate publicly the names of employers who have voluntarily made restitution after they have been investigated, and the amounts paid purely of their own volition, would severely impede future enforcement of the Act.

"These voluntary payments play an important part in the FLSA enforcement program. They help us secure maximum compliance with the law. Publishing the names of these payors would largely destroy the incentive which leads them to follow this procedure and would soon vitiate the effectiveness of this part of the program. The interests of neither the Government nor the public would be served by such a result."

Further illustrating the general policy of Federal secrecy was the case in December, 1960, of the 29-page pamphlet entitled "The Freedom Academy" mailed to most newspaper editors by Senator Thomas Dodd (Dem., Conn.). A reprint of the Senator's speech in support of a school for training cold war leaders, the pamphlet was printed at the government printing office but carried a note stating it was published "not at government expense." It, of course, was mailed under the Senator's frank at taxpayer expense.

This intrigued Reporter David Kraslow of the Chicago *Daily News* and he inquired about it at the Senator's office. An employee told the reporter that the cost of printing 50,000 of the pamphlets was $1,000 but he could not or would not supply the names of the private individuals who were paying the bill.

Reporter Kraslow then took up the matter with Raymond Blattenberger, head of the government printing office.

"I know all about it," he told Reporter Kraslow. "But Congress can get me fired. I can't give you any information on work we do for clients."

"Is there any law which says you can withhold this kind of information?" Reporter Kraslow asked.

"I can't cite any law. I'm just saying what the policy is," Blattenberger replied.

On December 7, 1960, the Des Moines *Register* related the above details in a lead editorial, then asked the following questions:

> Who are the persons who are so interested in establishing a school of political war that they are willing to spend a thousand dollars for the pamphlets? Why are they interested? Why should there be any hesitancy about making their names public?
>
> Are the charges made by the government printing office sufficient to cover the costs of the paper, ink and manpower that went into it? If not, was the publication of the pamphlet subsidized by the taxpayers? If so, how much did this pamphlet cost them?
>
> Are members of Congress making proper use of their free mailing and printing-at-cost privileges? Or are they allowing those privileges to be used for propaganda and lobbying purposes by special interest groups and private citizens for promoting pet bills and projects?
>
> Can you think of any good reason why these questions should not be answered frankly, fully and honestly?
>
> We can't.

How can the White House justify such cases as these with its pretense that there is no bureaucratic withholding of legitimate information from the American people?

18.

Bureaucracy Cows Congress

During the dire days of the depression and the exciting days of the war years, the American press was gravely preoccupied with those tragic affairs. And, at the same time, it became accustomed to accepting in good faith the proclamations, reports, and propaganda issued in an ever-growing stream by Washington's new Federal press agents.

So, ignored by the press and left largely on his own in Federal office, the fledgling American bureaucrat developed the new American philosophy that our government belongs to him as his private domain; that he feels he has the privilege to give out or to withhold information as he sees fit; and that he sincerely thinks the American people should be satisfied with the decisions of government after he has made them.

When did secret government get its start in Washington and will it last in the face of growing opposition from the American press?

The paper curtain of censorship began to descend on the Federal Government in the Roosevelt Administration. It covered just about all the records of the expenditure of the citizens' tax funds and most of the actions of our public servants in relationship to those tax funds during the Truman and Eisenhower Administrations.

The fate of this secret government will depend largely upon the outcome of a struggle begun in 1958 between the appointed bureaucracy of the Executive Branch and the elected lawmakers of the Legislative Branch. Hardly noticed by the American people, it gathered considerable momentum in 1959 and 1960. The questions that it brought out must be answered eventually if free American Government, as we know it, is to survive in the troublesome years ahead.

Reviewing briefly: American bureaucracy, with its accompanying secret government, got its start in the thirties when the Roosevelt Administration, in coping with the great depression, moved New Deal welfare into all phases of the citizen's private life. It became entrenched at Washington during the forties and early fifties when the Roosevelt and Truman Administrations put more and more power into central government in coping first with World War II and then with the Korean War and the Cold War.

After the Korean War, when the press finally turned its attention back to the domestic affairs of our nation, it found itself confronted with a tight secret government in Washington. Under the Truman Administration, by White House Executive order, every Federal bureaucrat had the right of censoring information of government under the stamp of security, regardless of whether the information actually affected our national security.

The press so protested this blanket security censorship that President Eisenhower eased somewhat our security regulations upon his arrival in the White House in 1953. But not even this Presidential action stopped our bureaucrats. They simply pulled out an old dust-covered Federal

Statute pertaining solely to the safekeeping of governmental records as their excuse for censorship, and then blandly went right on doing the people's business in secrecy as they chose, with little restraint from anyone.

By this time, and under pressure from the press, Congress became aroused over the problem. The American bureaucrat, in his new-found arrogancy, had begun to deny essential information of government to our Federal lawmakers, even though this information was necessary in the making of proper laws for the people's benefit.

So Congress created the Hennings Subcommittee on Constitutional Rights in the Senate and the Moss Subcommittee on Government Information in the House to investigate the matter of the free flow of information of Federal Government to the American people. During more than 50 public hearings in 1956 and 1957, the heads of no less than 19 major Federal bureaus testified before these two Committees that they had frequently used the old Federal record-custody statute to withhold legitimate information from the people, the Congress and the press.

Supported by the press, Congress early in 1958 amended this old record-custody statute with a sentence stipulating that it cannot be used to withhold information of government from the people. This should have put the bureaucrat in his place and assured the American people of information on the expenditure of their tax funds.

But by this time, the American bureaucrat really was flexing his muscles. Deprived by the President of his blanket right to censor any and all information under security stamps and deprived by Congress of the old record-custody statute as his excuse for censorship, he simply reached into the bureaucratic grab bag and pulled out a new dodge to avoid exposing his daily activities to the inspection of the people who furnished the tax funds and paid his salary.

On March 6, 1958, Attorney General William F. Rogers appeared before the Hennings Committee and sanctimoniously gave the country his "doctrine of executive privilege" in a 38-page statement.

In brief, the Attorney General argued that this doctrine, based on the separation of powers in our Federal Government, gave the bureaucrat all the legal right he needed to withhold information of government from the people, the Congress and the press.

Actually, as I have pointed out previously, this ridiculous "doctrine of executive privilege" is nothing more than the bureaucrats' fanciful theory of doing as they please in the domain of the people's business. In subsequent testimony before the Hennings Committee, I pointed out that there was not a single judicial decision upholding it and I called upon the Senators for a return to the original American "doctrine of the people's privilege."

I also wrote Attorney General Rogers a three-page letter in which I included the following paragraphs:

> Cloaked in the high-sounding language of the legal technicality which always appears to be designed deliberately to confuse the layman, your statement simply re-states the ancient doctrine of "executive privilege" wherein the government bureaucrat can do as he wishes with no restraint whatsoever from the people who pay his salary.

> It further insinuates strongly that the press, in its demands for open government, has been reckless and thoughtless in its stand for freedom of information.

> That is far from the truth. The press recognizes the necessity for guarding security secrets. The press recognizes the American doctrine of the separation of powers of the three branches of Federal Government. The press recognizes also the President's discretion to withhold documents of his office, even though there are times when this seems ill-advised, but not the discretion of his underlings, who are appointed and are not answerable to the people.

> But the press cannot, under its obligation to the people which bestowed freedom upon it, condone the

wide abuse of these principles so prevalent in Federal Government today.

In the months that followed, the "doctrine of executive privilege" kicked up considerable dust in the halls of Congress and in our law journals, wherein a number of eminent lawyers wrote that it had no standing whatsoever in the law. Representative George Meader (Rep., Mich.) in particular lambasted the doctrine in a 60-minute speech in the House of Representatives, in which he said:

> "The net effect of the Attorney General's statement is that the Executive branch of the Government will give to the Congress or its committees such information as the Executive branch chooses to give and no more.

> "I wonder if the American people and their elected representatives in Congress appreciate the significance of this latest pronouncement of the Executive branch of the Government. If this is sound constitutional doctrine, then it is permissible, without amending the Constitution, for the huge Executive bureaucracy we have built up over the years to become the master, not the servant, of the people. It places within the sole and unfettered discretion of an organization of well over 2 million persons in the Executive branch of the Government the power either wholly to deny Congress access to facts about the public business, or to make known, only on such terms, at such times and under such conditions as the Executive sees fit, those portions of the total picture which the Executive wants the public or the Congress to know. The latter course makes possible a rigged, distorted, slanted factual foundation for the formulation of public opinion and thus grants the Executive greater power over policymaking than is healthy under a system of self-government by the people."

In subsequent correspondence with Attorney General Rogers, Representative Meader put his finger squarely on the key questions facing free American Government in the sixties when he asked the following questions:

1. "Is the 'executive privilege' one which may be exercised solely by the President personally with respect to each congressional request for information, limited only to the request?

2. "May the President validly issue a blanket order to all officials and employes in the Executive branch of the government instructing them to deny Congress: (a) all requests for information; (b) all requests for a certain type of document or testimony, (c) all information in certain areas of governmental activities?

3. "May this Presidential 'executive privilege' and the power to exercise it be delegated to inferior officials in the Executive branch of the government? If so to (a) Cabinet members? (b) division heads? (c) economists and clerks? (d) any and all of the personnel in the executive branch of the government?

4. "Is the decision to withhold information from the Congress on the basis of 'executive privilege' subject to any review whatever?

5. "With respect to information properly classified, can the 'executive privilege' be invoked where satisfactory arrangements are made to preserve the classified character of the information?"

Attorney General Rogers did not answer these questions, and the "doctrine of executive privilege" is still with us today.

Withholding of information on its ballistic missile program by the Air Force prompted Representative Moss to place the following statement in the report of his Subcommittee on Government Information:

> The Air Force refusal to the Comptroller General is based solely on a naked claim of "executive privilege." The Constitution grants no such authority nor has the mythical doctrine of privilege been supported by the courts. The refusal not only violates the duly enacted law of the land but also is contrary to a specific constitutional requirement (Art. II, Sec. 3) that the President "shall take care that the laws be faithfully executed."
>
> No executive act can modify, amend, or contravene a statute. Laws can be amended only in the way they were enacted. Any attempt by the Executive to alter or supersede the law does violence to the Constitution.
>
> When the Executive can select which laws shall and shall not be enforced; when this selective power is applied to laws providing information necessary for the legislative branch to carry out its constitutional duties; when the "executive privilege" to control information for the Congress flows down from the President throughout the executive bureaucracy, then the Government of the Nation ceases to be a representative democracy. Sweeping claims of an unrestrained "executive privilege" to control the facts of Government are a step toward despotism.

But it was the refusal of the International Cooperation Administration to furnish Congress information on the Foreign Aid program that provided the big Congressional fireworks over the "doctrine of executive privilege."

Representative Hardy had been denied requested information on the foreign aid to Formosa, Laos, Brazil, India, Guatemala, Pakistan and Bolivia, and on June 15, 1959, he issued a report of his Foreign Operations Subcommittee which documented waste, mismanagement and bribery in foreign aid to Laos, based on outside reports and information.

On May 15, Acting Director Saccio of ICA testified before the Senate Subcommittee on Constitutional Rights on his refusal to give information to Congress on foreign aid. He made it emphatically clear that he believed he had the "privilege" to refuse the General Accounting Office any document in his agency. He told the Senate Subcommittee:

> "I am not falling back on principle here. I am saying in effect that if the ICA wanted to apply the 'executive privilege,' the General Accounting Office would not see one thing because practically every document in our agency has an opinion or a piece of advice."

Thus, Acting Director Saccio put into the record the belief of our American bureaucracy that its opinions and advice are beyond the restraint of the people's representatives, even though those opinions and advice are a key factor in the people's business.

Representative Hardy then offered the following amendment to the foreign aid authorization bill and the House unanimously adopted it on June 18:

> All documents, papers, communications, audits, reviews, findings, recommendations, reports, and other material which relate to the operation or activities of the International Cooperation Administration shall be furnished to the General Accounting Office and to any committee of the Congress, or any duly authorized subcommittee thereof, charged with considering legislation or appropriation for, or

expenditures of, such Administration upon request of the General Accounting Office or such committee or subcommittee as the case may be.

The Senate subsequently approved this amendment, but President Eisenhower, in signing the bill on July 24, issued a statement upholding the "doctrine of executive privilege." He said:

> "I have signed this bill on the express premise that the amendment relating to disclosure is not intended to alter and cannot alter the recognized constitutional duty and power of the Executive with respect to the disclosure of information, documents, and other materials. Indeed, any other construction of these amendments would raise grave constitutional questions under the historic Separation of Powers Doctrine."

On the same day, Representative Hardy requested and was refused information on foreign aid operations in Laos and Vietnam by Director James W. Riddleberger, of the ICA. This prompted him to offer an amendment to the Mutual Security (Foreign Aid) Appropriations Bill of 1960 that would cut off funds to the bureaucrats in the event that they refused information to Congress. The House quickly adopted this amendment, which said:

> None of the funds herein appropriated shall be used to carry out any provision of Chapter II, III or IV of the Mutual Security Act of 1954, as amended, during any period when more than twenty days have elapsed between the request for, and the furnishing of, any document, paper, communication, audit, review, finding, recommendation, report, or other material relating to the administration of such provision by the International Cooperation Administration to the General Accounting Office or any

committee of the Congress, or any duly authorized subcommittee thereof, charged with considering legislation or appropriation for or expenditures of the International Cooperation Administration and the Department of State.

On July 29, President Eisenhower told his press conference that he doubted that the Hardy amendment to the appropriations bill ". . . will ever get to my desk."

The Senate apparently heeded these words, for the Senate Appropriations Committee hastily substituted a watered-down version by Senator A. Willis Robertson (Dem., Va.), which would not cut off the funds in the event of a refusal if the President certified that it was his decision in each case to withhold the information.

This, of course, put the burden of proof on the President in the matter of the withholding of information of government, but it did not answer general questions arising from the "doctrine of executive privilege" which Representative Meader originally laid on the line to Congress.

But again it was foreign aid which spawned the big Congressional debate. On August 31, 1960, Representative Hardy issued a report to Congress from his House Subcommittee on Foreign Operations which said the foreign aid program had ". . . been plagued with roadblocks, delays and denials of information imposed by the Executive Branch," and he called on Congress to make more use of its powers over Federal purse strings to assure Congress access to government documents and files.

In support of the report, Representative Hardy again proposed his amendment to the appropriations bill for foreign aid which would cut off funds for the agency if information were refused "relating to the expenditure of funds." He carefully explained to Congress that his amendment was not an attempt to get ". . . every small piece of administrative information but affected only information about expenditures."

"Surely," he said, "none could seriously contend that the Executive Branch has the privilege of denying to the Congress, information necessary to determine whether appropriated funds have been spent with economy and efficiency."

The House quickly approved Representative Hardy's amendment but once again the Senate emasculated it in conference with the same old 1959 compromise that put the burden of proof on the President in each and every case.

The fight over foreign aid secrecy flared up again on December 9, long after Congress had concluded its 1960 session. The House Subcommittee on Foreign Operations, in pursuing its investigations, asked the bureaucrats for the facts and figures on foreign aid to Brazil, Uruguay, Argentine, Chile, Bolivia, Peru and Colombia.

The Department of State withheld the information on the grounds of "executive privilege" and the General Accounting Office promptly notified Secretary of State Christian A. Herter that ". . . program funds will no longer be available for expenses unless the documents are furnished."

Representative Moss immediately issued the following statement:

> "Comptroller General Joseph Campbell is to be commended for his courageous action, for I know he has been under great pressure from Executive Branch officials who want him to ignore the law as they do."

But this was only a temporary tempest in a boiling teapot inasmuch as the actual power to withhold funds from the bureaucracy is vested in Congress, as a whole, and not in one of its branch arms such as the General Accounting Office.

On December 23, President Eisenhower intervened in this particular case, upheld the Department of State's withholding of information from Congress, and ordered the General Accounting Office to release the funds for the foreign aid program in Latin-America. The Associated Press reported as follows:

> Eisenhower said in a statement that while it is the established policy to provide Congress and the public with fullest information, the executive also has a recognized constitutional duty and power to refuse to disclose documents that might adversely affect national interests.

But it also was revealed that the President, himself, had advised the Department of State to withhold the information, and the Associated Press carried the following explanation:

> The President said it was vital for administration officials and employees to be in a position to be completely frank in advising each other and in informal exchanges with foreign officials.

> He said the forced disclosure of certain conversations, communications or documents "can tend to impair or inhibit essential investigative, reporting or decision-making processes or the proper conduct of our foreign relations.

> "Such disclosure must therefore be forbidden as contrary to the national interest, where that is deemed necessary for the protection of the orderly and effective operation of the executive branch," he said.

Thus the White House — spearhead of America's gigantic bureaucracy — tossed the glove of challenge at the feet of Congress, the American people's elected representatives, on the whole matter of our secret government.

On December 20 I wrote Representative Wilbur D. Mills (Dem., Ark.), Chairman of the House Ways and Means Committee, as follows:

> As the freedom of information representative of 16,000 publishers, editors, newsmen and newscasters, I respectfully wrote in good faith on Nov. 30, to you, an elected representative of the American people, in protest of the secrecy provisions in the 1960 Federal Social Security Amendments pertaining to the new Federal medical care program. I also asked your views.
>
> In reply to my letter to you, I received a letter dated Dec. 20, from Mr. Leo H. Irwin, chief counsel for the House of Representatives Committee on Ways and Means which enclosed a copy of a letter from Mr. W. L. Mitchell, commissioner of the Department of Health, Education and Welfare.
>
> Mr. Mitchell's letter discloses the fact that the new Federal medical care program is barred to the inspection of the American citizens, whose taxes will pay for the program, through the general policy of bureaucratic secrecy at Washington. His letter also gives a defense of this policy of secrecy.
>
> Frankly speaking, I am not interested in the bureaucratic defense of the policy of secrecy which encompasses just about every record of the Federal expenditure of the American citizens' tax funds today. The record is plain that this Federal bureaucratic policy of secrecy is neither good for the American taxpayers nor free American government.
>
> During the last five years, key representatives of 19 major Federal agencies and bureaus callously testified before Rep. John E. Moss' House Subcommittee

on Government Information that they were accustomed to withholding vital information from the American people.

But the record for the last two years is even more conclusive since it shows that our appointed Federal bureaucracy has extended its arrogancy to Congress, composed of the American people's elected representatives. Let me recite this record for 1959:

January 22 — Comptroller General Joseph Campbell formally protested the Navy's refusal of access to report on procurement activities of the Military Sea Transportation Service.

February 17 — Representative Richard E. Lankford (Dem., Md.) complained that the Navy had refused his request for a report on the Naval gun factory at Washington.

March 19 — The House Subcommittee on Government Information protested the refusal of the Air Force to furnish the General Accounting Office with a report on the billion-dollar-a-year ballistic missile program.

April 2 — Acting Director Leonard J. Saccio of the International Cooperation Administration refused a request from Representative Porter Hardy (Dem., Va.), chairman of the House Foreign Operations Subcommittee, for facts and figures on the foreign aid program.

April 15 — Comptroller General Campbell protested to the House Appropriations Subcommittee that refusals by the ICA and the Department of Defense to give information had severely handicapped the General Accounting Office in the performance of

its statutory duties and may prove fatal to its effectiveness.

Let me recite further the record for 1960:

1. The National Aeronautics and Space Administra-
    tion withheld information on its contracts to
    spend millions of dollars in the manufacture of
    manned satellite capsules.

2. The International Cooperation Administration
    withheld information on foreign aid programs in
    Iran and Thailand.

3. The Navy withheld information from the Gen-
    eral Accounting Office on the management of
    the Military Petroleum Supply Agency and on
    construction activities at the Philippines naval
    bases.

This brings up the natural question of why Congress
continues to aid and abet appointed Federal bureaucracy in its general policy of secret government when
bureaucracy now has applied that policy of secrecy
to Congress.

I also feel impelled to point out from the record that
the American people, who pay all expenses and salaries of their government with hard-earned tax dollars,
do not approve of the secret government of their public servants. No less than 33 States have laws on
their books stipulating all records of city, county and
state government must be open to inspection by the
people. And no less than 25 state legislatures have
gone beyond that by adopting laws stipulating all
meetings of city, county and state governing bodies
must be open to the people.

Therefore, again solely in the interests of the American people's inherent right to know about their gov-

ernment, I respectfully protest to you the secrecy provisions of the new Federal medical care program and I call upon you for your views on this growing danger of bureaucratic secrecy in free American government.

On December 29, 1960, I replied to Chief Counsel Irwin, pointing out:

. . . you will note from the enclosed copy of my new letter to Representative Mills that all of this so far has been most unsatisfactory to me.

In addition, I would like to take issue with Mr. Mitchell's statement in his letter taking issue with the statements of Mr. Stanford Smith, executive director of the American Newspaper Publishers Association. Mr. Mitchell states:

"We arc interested in Mr. Smith's statement that the passage of the 1951 modification when implemented by States resulted in the exclusion of chiselers and served as a check on maladministration. From reports kept by States, we have not had evidence that it resulted in reducing assistance rolls. In general, we have understood that few people came to look at the records. Those that came were largely creditors such as land lords, relatives, the recipients who wished to see the amount of other recipients' payments, and newsmen."

I don't believe Mr. Mitchell has gone deeply enough into these records at the state level. In Florida, for instance, we have had a most difficult time in getting the welfare administrative people to prosecute the chiselers and to correct the maladministration. It begins to appear as if our welfare bureaucrats have installed themselves as chosen autocrats beyond restraint of anyone, much less American people who pay all welfare, all expenses and all salaries.

There the matter of freedom of information and the American people's inherent right to know about their government rested as a new administration took over in the turbulent and fateful sixties. The bureaucrats' "doctrine of executive privilege," ridiculous as it may be in free democratic government, is still with us and it must be eliminated from the American political scene once and for all if we are to avoid the great dangers of a bureaucratic dictatorship in the years ahead.

In the debates over our foreign aid program, Congress clearly brought out that it has the power, if it chooses to use it, to control bureaucracy through the withholding of its appropriations of the people's tax funds. But Congress has not yet elected to utilize this power, even though it well knows that American government is the servant, not the master, of the American people; that man's freedom always has been extinguished by secret government; and that only an informed public opinion can preserve the processes of free government.

After 10 years of wrestling with this problem, as the chairman of a national journalistic freedom of information committee, I am not overly optimistic of immediate solution simply because Congress, the people's representatives, as yet has shown no strong inclination to take away the American Government from the bureaucrats and restore it to the American people. Reasons for my general pessimism, particularly in relation to Congress' responsibility, are as follows:

First: In recent years, Congress has yielded more and more of its power to the bureaucracy. Too much of our major legislation is railroaded through Congress with little debate and less awareness of it by the people, who are paying all the bills of government with their hard-earned tax dollars. The fact that the Senate twice yielded to Presidential persuasion in the matter of full disclosure of foreign aid expenditures points this up most emphatically.

Second: Unlimited expenses and unchecked expense funds on both foreign and domestic junkets are easily available behind the locked doors of governmental secrecy. There have been many revelations in recent years of Congress' utilization of such political privileges. Need I remind that in early 1959, Vance H. Trimble, Washington correspondent for the Scripps-Howard newspapers, wrote a widely-printed series of stories on congressional nepotism, which revealed that many senators and representatives had wives, children and political kin on secret congressional payrolls and which bared much secret political privilege in the rental of congressional office space.

Third: Congress has its own brand of secrecy in which more than 30 per cent of its committee meetings, or 1,200 a year, are held in so-called "executive session" behind locked doors, with both the people and the press barred. None can tell exactly what political privileges are being enjoyed by whom today behind these locked Congressional doors, but there have been many "leaks" and rumbles of this which have not enhanced the reputation of the world's greatest free legislature.

Fourth: After five years in operation, the Hennings Committee in the Senate and the Moss Committee in the House can boast of just one minor law in behalf of freedom of information — that preventing the bureaucrats from using the old Federal statute on record custody to withhold information. On the basis of this, it will take perhaps a half century for Congress to achieve anything that even approaches reasonable legislation guaranteeing the American people their rightful information of government.

On the optimistic side, in my opinion, is the fact that hundreds of sincere editors of the free American Press are alerted to the problem today and are doing something about it on their news and editorial pages. They alone will be responsible if Congress ever makes up its mind to put the bureaucrat in his place and restore the government to the people. A free press simply cannot exist in a secret government.

19.

The Dubious Role of the Press Agent

THE IDEAL WAY for an American citizen to get his news of government is to go, himself, to the records, look them over and then personally demand his public servant to explain the expenditure of his tax funds. But, with America's mushrooming population, bulging bureaucracy and soaring suburbia, this has become an impossibility.

There now are approximately 180,000,000 citizens in the United States and it goes without saying that not even an appreciable percentage of them could inspect government buildings to check on unnecessary extravagance in construction or furnishings.

American newspapers, in response to the very human curiosity of the public, frequently send reporters to look over the records of government and interview politicians. The reporters' stories, based on records, statements of the politician and what the reporter, himself, witnessed, have given the American taxpayer a secondhand account of his government and the expenditure of his tax funds, and was a fairly good substitute for firsthand information.

But this did not please the politician simply because he could not control the press. Having gotten rid of taxpayers breathing down his neck, he set out to rid himself of reporters, who poked around in his business and occasionally dug out a story that was extremely embrassing to him.

This was finally achieved in Washington with the device of the government press agent, although this new governmental bureaucrat usually was cloaked under some such high-sounding title as "Director of Public Information." Under this system, the politician decides what news should be released, turns it over to his press agent who pretties it up, then releases it to the newspapers, and finally it reaches the taxpayer fourth hand.

Several years ago I made a survey of all Washington news carried on the nation's news wires and discovered that 75 per cent of it was based on press agents' handouts and therefore reached the public fourth hand. And perhaps this explains why there is so much confusion in public life today and so little understanding of national and international affairs by the citizen who pays the bills.

The press agent not only has firm control of the release of news of government, but he also effectively protects the politician from both the public and the press with their sometimes embarrassing questions. This is borne out by cold figures of the Federal record.

When I began my newspaper career in 1923, there were few governmental press agents on the horizon and, regardless of present claims of the politician and his director of public relations, newspapers did a pretty good job of supplying the taxpayers with news of their government. But with the entrance of Franklin Delano Roosevelt and his bureaucracy upon the American political scene, the governmental press agent really came into his own. And a report of a U.S. Senate Subcommittee on Appropriations in 1946, one year after Mr. Roosevelt's death, revealed 23,009 full-time press agents on the Federal payroll at a total taxpayer cost of $74,829,467.

During those hectic New Deal and war years, the Federal public servant had not yet learned the niceties of separating himself from the embarrassing questions of the press. Mr. Roosevelt held 998 press conferences during his 12 years in the White House, an average of about 83 a year. Secretary of State Cordell Hull went him better by exposing himself to the questions of the press on an average of five times a week, and every one of the other members of the Cabinet held one or more press conferences a week.

But compare all of these figures with the record of Federal Government 10 years later, when the press agent really came to rule the Washington roost. During the Truman Administration, the number of Federal press agents jumped to 50,000 and the government was spending $100,000,000 for them and $200,000,000 a year for printing their handout releases.

This provoked criticism from the Hoover Commission on Government and in 1952 Congress voted reductions in appropriations for "public relations specialists" of from 10 to 25 per cent in certain bureaus. But this apparently was only window dressing, for the bureaucrats simply changed the titles of their "public relations specialists," kept them on the Federal payrolls, and went right ahead with their business of grinding out governmental propaganda.

In the summer of 1958, Stewart Alsop wrote rather cynically in *The Saturday Evening Post* that Vice President Richard M. Nixon was the only politician of any consequence in Washington who did not have his own personal press agent.

Presidential press conferences differ as much as the men who hold the office differ. Regular press conferences were established first by Theodore Roosevelt, who answered any and all questions, but prohibited direct quotations. Woodrow Wilson continued this policy until World War

I, when the need for secrecy was readily apparent. President Harding again permitted reporters to ask questions directly from the floor but, following an embarrassing error in interpretation, he required questions to be submitted in advance. This method was continued by both Presidents Coolidge and Hoover.

Franklin D. Roosevelt inaugurated the wide-open, dish-it-out-and-hand-it-back press conference, but he required that no one could quote him without obtaining special permission. In many instances, this put an even tighter rein on facts of government that people were entitled to know. President Truman continued this policy.

President Eisenhower permitted radio and television recordings to be made of his press conferences, and direct quotations from stenographic reports. He, too, permitted direct questioning from the floor, but insisted that regular White House meetings with the press be taped for showing after the text of presidential remarks had been rechecked. In this way the public enjoyed for the first time the feeling that they were actually "sitting in on" a press conference. This had a tremendous psychological value, but did little to increase the amount of factual news of government to reach the people because the conferences were held so infrequently. Many times serious developments at home and abroad arose and were settled without the public "airing" they should have had.

President-elect Kennedy promised to try "live" press conferences, apparently willing to risk the presidential boo-boos his predecessors didn't want to take a chance on.

While no President is required by law to hold a press conference, it definitely is desirable that he do so with a certain amount of regularity. Each new President taking office can learn from the errors made by the man who preceded him. Each new President conscientiously intends to improve the conduct of the Nation's business. But the weight and complexity of demands, both domestic and international, upon the time and the energy of the President soon force him to relinquish more and more authority to trusted members of the "official family." Which responsibilities and decisions he delegates to others will depend upon the nature, talents and stamina of the particular man. It is in the selection of these subordinates that a President may do grave damage to the freedom of American citizens.

While the presidential press secretary does not have Cabinet status, he wields far more power than any Cabinet member. He has the authority to screen all information that reaches the President as well as to control the information given out by the President in all instances except the open press conference.

The use of press agents by heads of bureaus and lesser agencies has increased the distance between each Federal public servant and the public he serves. By dealing with the public and press only through a press agent, he can always deny a statement, a policy and even a fact, on the sanctimonious grounds that he, himself, did not give it out. He can heap all the blame on his press agent while he sails on his angel's wings in the outer space of faceless government, far above the ordinary taxpayer.

But sometimes he has embarrassing moments. Prof. Marian D. Irish, of Florida State University, in an address before the Southern Political Science Association at Gatlinburg, Tennessee, on November 22, 1957, revealed one of these, as follows:

> "It is, in fact, almost impossible to ascertain who is responsible in Eisenhower staff decisions. For example, early in 1955, the President made the news headlines when he reversed a unanimous recommendation of the Civil Aeronautics Board. The Chairman of the CAB immediately made certain facts public. Whereupon, the President hastily compromised. His only explanation for the double reversal was that he had accepted a White House brief without sufficient questioning. In the spirit of teamsmanship, The White House refused to say who goofed."

In 1951 an editor of the Cleveland *Plain Dealer* and I debated the Director of the Office of Publications, Department of Commerce, and the Director of the News Branch of the ECA, before the American Society of Newspaper Editors. We editors laid on the table, for all to see, the sins of Federal press agents including their absence when their bosses are on the grill, their glorification of their bosses and their propaganda. The two press agents gave us a lot of pleasant platitudes on how they were God's gift to both the press and the public in the way of information of government. They denied our charge of propaganda but they did admit that they went in a large way for educating the public.

This really intrigued us and we immediately inquired of the two press agents if, by educating the public, they meant the following pamphlets, released to the press in recent weeks, which the Federal press agents had prepared at great taxpayer expense:

How to eliminate bats from buildings — Federal advice was to close the openings, a conclusion doubtless requiring great research.

Fleas of North America — 142 pages, dealing with classification, identification and geographical distribution.

The Cuban frog leg industry

The Venezuelan salt fish industry — 81 pages, with pictures.

Mist netting for birds in Japan — 40 pages with pictures.

How to tell the sex of a watermelon

Recipes for cooking muskrat meat — This told how to prepare fried muskrat, smothered muskrat, broiled muskrat, shreded muskrat, muskrat with tomato sauce, muskrat salad, stewed muskrat liver with onions, pickled muskrat, and muskrat pie.

In my rebuttal in this debate, I concluded by quoting a paragraph from a speech Representative Forest A. Har-

ness (Rep., Ind.) delivered to Congress in 1948. Mr.
Harness said:

> "The first instinct of bureaucracy is self-preserva-
> tion. The second is expansion. Just like any living
> organism, an administrative agency, once launched,
> seeks constantly to justify its existence, to perpetu-
> ate itself and to expand. In the salubrious climate
> of governmental paternalism which has prevailed
> under this and the preceding administration, bu-
> reaucracy has luxuriated into a tropical jungle. It has
> grown to the alarming extent that it touches and
> shadows the daily life and daily thinking of every
> citizen."

I have no great dislike of governmental press agents,
I only wish they would live up to their platitudes of public
service. I am not alone in being confused by the polished
"run around" that exists in Washington. Confirmation of
this emerged following my personal conference in the
Pentagon at Washington on September 6, 1957, with Murray Snyder, Deputy Secretary of Defense for Public Affairs, who is the No. 1 press agent for American defense
affairs.

I had obtained the engagement with Mr. Snyder to
present to him formally the protest of a national journalistic organization that an air-tight curtain of secrecy had
been draped over all news in the Pentagon, that President
Eisenhower's 1953 Order No. 10501 in behalf of security
was being badly abused, and that the free editors of
America were deeply concerned over this.

Mr. Snyder smiled deprecatingly and declared that he
couldn't agree with me; that all legitimate news of the
Pentagon was available to the press; and that I could
have any news of the Pentagon that I wanted.

I said that, as an example, how about the records of
the expenditure of the taxpayers' funds for the furniture
in "this office." I knowingly had stepped upon Mr. Snyder's pet corn, for his face turned red and he spoke long
and earnestly upon how secondhand furniture had been

obtained for his office at little cost to the taxpayers. It developed that some member of the press corps had made a public issue of Mr. Snyder's office furnishings and that this had wounded him deeply.

Mr. Snyder assured me over and over during our hour's conference that life in the Pentagon indeed was an open book, we discussed a number of incidents of direct Pentagon censorship with very little satisfaction on my part, and he never did pull out the records of the expenditure of our tax funds on his secondhand office furnishings.

An hour later I sat down in another room in the Pentagon with a dozen Washington correspondents who covered defense affairs; included also were representatives of all the wire services and several news magazines.

"Well, gentlemen," I greeted the correspondents, "it appears that I have wasted my time in coming to Washington. Mr. Murray Snyder has just informed me that all facts of Pentagon business are available to the press and that I can have any news that I want."

This really broke the ice, for the correspondents responded with a long, loud and unanimous hoot of derision. And for the next hour and a quarter, I listened to indignant stories from every one of them on how the curtain of press agent secrecy over the Pentagon blocks them from all legitimate news even down to the ridiculous. Typical statements from these correspondents follow:

"We are buried under a mass of directives."

"The No. 1 brains of the government draw the directives; the No. 8 brains abuse them."

"A million people wield the stamp of secrecy; 500,000 do the stamping; the other 500,000 check on the stampers."

"The real stumbling block is at the civilian level." This, of course, referred to press agents.

"Every item of news, regardless, must go through the red tape of policy clearance. Somewhere along the line somebody always stamps 'for official use only' upon it. Even the most trivial news takes days, weeks and months to negotiate these roadblocks into the light of day."

"It's all due to fear — fear of reprimand and loss of job — and to just plain stupidity."

"The most important problem is the attitude at the top — at the White House and in the Department of State. Until that is changed, the guys at the pick-and-shovel level will be afraid to put out information."

Despite this coyness practiced by leading governmental press agents in releasing true facts of government, they are not coy in the least in production of their handout releases. In fact, studies by congressional appropriations committees show that the Federal Government is operating 61 printing plants in Washington, 23 in San Francisco, 25 in Philadelphia, 16 in New York, 16 in Chicago, 6 in Kansas City and single units elsewhere, most of which are engaged in the processing of these press agent handouts, largely governmental propaganda.

Perhaps the greatest Federal propaganda splurge was the bureaucrats' 10-year fight to foist socialized medicine upon the American public. In 1945, President Harry S. Truman sent a message to Congress calling for his national health program, which was nothing more than socialized medicine couched in press agent verbiage. Shortly afterwards, Thomas Parran, Surgeon General of the United States Public Health Service, sent a letter of instructions to all employees of that governmental agency which said:

> Every officer of the Public Health Service will wish to familiarize himself with the President's message and will be guided by its provisions when making any public statement likely to be interpreted as representing the official views of the Public Health Service.

Later an official of the Public Health Service was called as a witness before a House committee investigating government propaganda and quizzed as to why the propaganda issued by his agency supported socialized medicine as embodied in the pending Wagner-Murray-Dingell bill. This government official replied:

> "We would naturally give emphasis to that, because that is why we are in the government. Otherwise, we should get out of government."

The government campaign to promote the Wagner-Murray-Dingell bill was spark plugged by the press agents of the Social Security Board but it also received a large helping hand in the press agent releases of the Public Health Service, the Children's Bureau, the U. S. Office of Education, the U. S. Employment Service and the Department of Agriculture.

Over the years, hundreds and hundreds of press agent pamphlets, booklets and handout releases were issued by these six Federal agencies in behalf of the benefits of socialized medicine operated by the government. *Not one* pamphlet or press release was issued pointing up the evils of state medicine as practiced by the German government under Hitler or socialized government as practiced in Great Britain.

One pamphlet issued by the Public Health Service even went so far as to advise its recipients as follows:

> You can write a letter to the readers' column of your local newspaper and tell your editor why the readers of the paper should back the Wagner-Murray-Dingell bill.

One Federal Security Agency official was asked by a congressional committee: "Did you give both sides of the question of compulsory national health insurance?"

The government official replied: "I don't know what you mean by both sides."

The public uproar over this outright propaganda campaign on the part of our Federal Government, paid for by taxpayer funds, has somewhat dampened the enthusiasm of our Washington governmental press agents for the blatant brand of propaganda. Today they are more restrained in content, but not in output.

All of the foregoing, and particularly my statement that 75 per cent of our Washington news is based on press agents' handouts, no doubt has aroused your curiosity as to what in the world are our approximately 1,500 regular newspaper correspondents doing in Washington today.

The best way for me to answer this question is to quote to you one sentence from William Whyte's book, *Man and Organization,* (Richard D. Irwin, Inc.), which says: "The whole tendency of modern organization life is to muffle the importance of individual leadership."

Political life in Washington, from the White House on down, revolves around "the team" and cooperation with it. Our Washington correspondents, it is sad to report, apparently have joined "the team." They are part and passel of the Washington cocktail circuit, of the great Washington political games of "you scratch my back and I'll scratch yours" and "footsie;" and of the great, happy bureaucratic family of Washington. Should a correspondent pass up these games, he would be termed a "Fancy Dan" or an "outlander." Those that play them always stand the chance of being rewarded by the bureaucrats in the form of an exclusive "leak" of an important story.

William L. White, Washington news columnist, wraps all of this up neatly in his sad commentary on Washington news reporting in the August, 1957, issue of *Harper's Magazine* as follows:

It is thus not surprising that the notion of "the team" has an enduring vitality — in spite of the fact that it is demonstrably and absurdly inapplicable to the Presidency. The office by definition is magisterial; its obvious Constitutional burden is upon one, never upon many. But when a large part of the nation takes up a dogma of living such as this, the press is bound to do the same — if only because it is a part of that common body.

I have dwelt at length on the governmental press agent, simply because his is the public's business paid for by taxpayer funds and thereby is the newspaper's business. I have ignored the press agent of business simply because that is a private affair and actually involves the matter of whether or not a newspaper wishes to give its valuable space for private propaganda. The *Nieman Reports* (a publication for journalists) of September, 1954, gave the following summary of the press agent releases received by a New Hampshire weekly newspaper over a 10-day period:

Type of Release	No. of Words	No. of Pages
Business	133,000	532
Philanthropic	60,000	210
Government	21,000	83
Pressure groups	18,000	71
Educational institutions	10,000	41
Political	3,000	13

That weekly undoubtedly receives double this amount now, for all groups have increased their volume of handouts. *The Tampa Tribune* receives many times this quantity of press agent releases because space in a big daily is much more valuable than that in a small country weekly.

One enterprising citizen recently opened an office in Washington and circularized newspapers offering to provide them with the press agent handouts of the leading Federal bureaus — this for the modest sum of $25 a month. Curious, I subscribed to the service for one week at a cost of $6.25 and I received a seven-inch stack of 1,100 pages of press releases from about 25 major Federal agencies. After carefully thumbing through these 1,100 pages, I can report:

1. If these 1,100 pages had not seen the light of day, the American taxpayer would not have been deprived of one iota of knowledge about the expenditure of his tax funds, which is a carefully preserved Federal secret.

2. Some of our Federal press agents apparently have their eyes on the taxpayer dollar because they are now writing their releases on both sides of the paper.

All of this priceless prose is carefully filed in *Tribune* waste baskets simply because we prefer to give our readers secondhand accounts of the news, whether it concern the government or business, and not fourth-hand accounts.

20.

Press Agents
in Political Campaigns

SHOULD A MADISON AVENUE PRESS AGENT in his gray flannel suit so glorify a can of beans with his priceless prose that you invest 15 cents in it and then, upon opening it, discover that it is indeed a sorry collection of beans, there is no great loss. You can dump the beans into your garbage pail, change brands and check the 15 cents off to experience.

But when the same Madison Avenue press agent in the same gray flannel suit so glorifies a politician with the same priceless prose that the citizen invests his vote in him and then discovers, upon his election, that he is indeed a sorry politician, where is the public responsibility? You cannot brush a politician into your garbage pail; you cannot change brands; and deteriorating government indeed is a bitter, costly and dangerous experience for the free citizen.

Gray-flanneled Madison Avenue has entered the American political arena in a big way and has sought, through dynamic phrases, to reduce all things in government — from the lowliest voter to the highest principle of free democracy — to a salable commodity, as a can of beans.

Jon M. Jonkel, the Chicago press agent who was hired as the campaign manager of John Marshall Butler in the 1950 Maryland Senatorial race, later testified before a Senate investigating committee that he regarded his political client as "an unknown commodity," much as a crack advertising executive would have described a new soap or breakfast cereal.

Vance Packard, in his book, *The Hidden Persuaders* (David McKay Co.), quotes the strategy of an advertising executive in politics: "I think of a man in a voting booth who hesitates between two levers as if he were pausing between competing tubes of tooth paste in a drugstore. The brand that has made the highest penetration on his brain will win his choice."

This "commodity" approach to the political campaign is, of course, not good for free government, which should be fought out in the realm of principle on the platform. But it is as nothing when compared to the danger that the citizen undergoes when Madison Avenue enters government, itself.

The Air Force propaganda program, which lists specific campaigns "lasting through mid-1958," is a good example. Written in the language of Madison Avenue, its very wording states that it is for management of the news that will be favorable to the Air Force rather than for the release of strictly factual information to the people. It states:

> Flooding the public with facts is very helpful. But facts, facts and more facts are quite useless unless they implant logical conclusions. Facts must be convincing, demonstrated living salesmen of practical benefits. These are the only kind of facts that mold opinion and channel the vibrant tensions of public thinking.

It was the "convincing, demonstrated living salesmen" kind of facts from the government that lulled the "vibrant tensions of public thinking" into our false assurance that America was far ahead of communistic Russia in the business of death-dealing missiles. The Russian Sputniks shattered this American assurance of defense security, and they also wrote in outer space a huge question mark over the Madison Avenue press agent's responsibility to the public.

The press agentry propaganda policy for management of the news of not only the Air Force but of the entire Department of Defense went blithely on its way after 1958. This was clearly shown by the report of the House Subcommittee on Government Information report for 1959, which listed the following cases:

1. The Defense Department established an elaborate "hold for release" system to control nonsecurity information about missile and satellite projects and create a favorable public reaction.

2. The Defense Department shrouded the Atlas-Score talking satellite project in deep secrecy and, when the event was publicized, created the false impression that the satellite was more than twice as big as the largest comparable Russian satellite.

3. The Defense Department refused to release pictures of the outside of the Titan missile even though the outside configuration had been declassified and the missile stood in full public view but pictures were released of the President viewing the completed missile just before the November 1958 elections.

4. The Defense Department reorganized information activities to give the Department's public relations office greater control over the release of information by the military experts.

The Pentagon's campaign against Admiral Hyman G. Rickover, the great Jewish scientist who has revolutionized the world's naval warfare with the nuclear energy submarine, wrote an equal question mark under the oceans. *Newsweek Magazine* reported on August 25, 1958, that while the Nautilus was under construction, Navy public information officers planted stories calling the ship an expensive failure. But in voyaging under the Arctic ice cap at the North Pole, the Nautilus beamed the light of public responsibility squarely on these irresponsible military press agents.

In our Tampa political race of the summer of 1958, both the incumbent, state Senator Paul Kickliter, and his challenger, former Representative Sam Gibbons, hired Tampa public relations concerns. The race started out in beautiful Madison Avenue style with fancy billboards decorating our city, but the first time the two Democrats faced each other on the speaking platform, there promptly erupted an old-fashioned name-calling, mud-slinging explosion that no doubt would curl the crease in a pair of gray flannel trousers, but actually warmed the hearts of the listeners.

And so it was in Florida's U.S. Senate race of 1958. Senator Spessard L. Holland hired a Jacksonville public relations concern for the six-weeks campaign, and then hired an additional Tampa press agent. Whereupon, the good Senator promptly ignored all of this talent, teed off on his opponent, former Senator Claude Pepper, as a Communist sympathizer, and the cat was in the dog kennel.

Former Senator Pepper hired a Miami public relations concern and for a few days he would say nothing unless it had his press agent's stamp of approval. But the executive of the public relations concern who traveled with him suffered a heart attack after the first week, and the Holland old-fashioned name calling soon got under his skin. The result, of course, was just one more rip-roaring Florida Democratic melee.

But such was not the case in the Maryland senatorial campaign of 1950. America, a land of politics, has seen many a strange stunt on the part of candidates seeking public office. But nothing in the past ever equalled the slick, big-time press agentry that was employed in plucking John Marshall Butler, an unknown Republican lawyer, out of anonymity and elevating him into the U.S. Senate over the political corpse of Democratic Senator Millard Tydings, one of President Harry S. Truman's nationally known key leaders. And that supersuccessful Madison Avenue campaign in Maryland had a profound influence on the future of political campaigns.

Jonkel, the Chicago press agent, later testified before a Senate investigating committee that he was employed by the late Senator Joseph McCarthy (Rep., Wis.) and the late Col. Robert R. McCormick, publisher of *The Chicago Tribune*, to manage Butler's campaign at $1,250 a month. He further testified that he had never before met his candidate, that he knew no one in Maryland, and that on his arrival in Baltimore, he was indeed surprised to learn that less than 1,000 voters in Maryland had ever heard of Butler. Then Jonkel testified:

> "We used little jingles, something like they use for Bromo-Seltzer, 'Be for Butler, Be for Butler, Be for Butler.' And then ended up with 'Be for John Marshall Butler, United States candidate for United States Senate, Republican candidate for United States Senate.'
>
> "That is the kind of thing we were doing. We had machine-gun fire, we had mortar shells, we had a ricochet sound, 'Bowie,' and things like that, and something to the effect of, 'That is the way the war in Korea sounds.'
>
> "Our Bromo-Seltzer jingles were worked out by a very competent advertising agency. We played them before and after each of Tydings' radio appearances in the last days of the campaign."

As for Butler's personal campaign, Jonkel told the Senators:

"We would have to dictate part of his releases and part of his statements over the telephone to him. He followed that day in and day out across the state.

"We, in the office, coordinated that caravan. We, in the office, did the releases on what he was going to say on the caravan. We had contacts with the politicians, one, two or three days ahead of him. We had contacts with fraternal groups and everybody we could get to listen to him."

Thus, the people of Maryland were sold a political "commodity" just as the American housewives are sold a new washing powder.

In the testimony before the Senate investigating committee, there was this exchange between Ralph F. Becker, assistant counsel for the committee, and Jonkel:

MR. BECKER: Did you spend funds for anything illegal or immoral?

MR. JONKEL: We didn't do anything illegal or immoral.

Less than a month after this, Jonkel was indicted by a Maryland grand jury and on June 4, 1951, he pleaded guilty to six charges of violating Maryland's election laws and paid a $5,000 fine, which indeed was cheap civil redress for the great crime of demolishing democracy. These charges involved his failure to register as an outsider engaged in a Maryland election campaign, his refusal to file a "full, true and detailed account" of campaign expenses, and his failure to keep financial accounts. Nothing illegal or immoral? Court procedure took care of the illegalities, but had no jurisdiction over the immorality of a press agent irresponsibly foisting on the public a "product" about which he knew nothing; nor could there be any way of measuring the honesty of the picture he was presenting.

There were other press agent experiments in politics as the fifties hove upon the American scene. William Benton, erstwhile partner in the Madison Avenue advertising agency of Benton and Bowles, bombarded Connecticut voters with one-minute radio spots, comic strip ads, pictures of pretty girls in street-corner booths, five minute movies, and got himself elected to the U.S. Senate. "The problem is to project yourself as a person," Benton said.

Meanwhile, in California, the man-wife press agent team of Clem Whitaker and Leone Baxter were busily employing the same flashy tactics in winning 70 out of 75 election campaigns for their political clients. *Time Magazine* reported on them: "They taught Earl Warren how to smile in public and were the first to recognize the publicity value of his handsome family. They brought the ebullient Goodie Knight before the public with a grueling speech-making campaign and have tried to keep check on him ever since." In *The Hidden Persuaders*, Vance Packard reports that Miss Baxter, replying to a question from a reporter as to what would have happened had they represented the other side in the 70 winning elections said, "I think we would have won almost every one of them."

Stanley Kelley, Jr., of the Brookings Institute, made a study of the 1952 campaign and in his book, *Professional Public Relations and Political Power* (Johns Hopkins Press), he concludes: "The campaign . . . reveals some interesting differences in the place occupied by professional publicists in the councils of the opposing parties. The strategy, treatment of issues, use of media, budgeting, and pacing of the Eisenhower campaign showed the pervasive influence of professional propagandists. The Democrats used fewer professionals, were less apt to draw upon commercial and industrial public relations experience in their thinking, and their publicity men apparently had less of a voice in the policy decisions of the campaign."

After the campaign, ex-Governor Howard Pyle of Arizona, a former Phoenix advertising executive who was installed as the No. 2 executive assistant in the White House, said of the advertising concern, Batten, Barton, Durstine and Osborne: "The Republican Party has long been identified with B.B.D.&O. They represent us at campaign time and all the time in between on a retainer. We're a regular account, and when you get to kicking around the appropriations, it's a valuable account. We have underlying obligations to B.B.D.&O."

Vernon Duff, president of B.B.D.&O., summed up his victorious Republican campaign as "merchandizing Eisenhower's frankness, honesty, and integrity, his sincere and wholesome approach." But Vance Packard was considerably more cynical when he devoted several pages of *The Hidden Persuaders* to dwell at length on what he called "the father image" which the press agents implanted in the minds of the American people and particularly women.

Political press agentry did not fare so well in the hurley-burley of the congressional investigation of the Bernard Goldfine case. When it was first revealed that Goldfine had bestowed gifts of vicuna coats, rugs and hotel bills on Adams and that the wealthy New England industrialist was getting deeper into the sordid water of the political pay-off, a Madison Avenue press agent hustled down to Washington and set up all the public relations trimmings, including special TV shows. Joseph Alsop, the syndicated newspaper columnist, reported:

> The plan was to present Bernard Goldfine as none other than good Mr. Pickwick. And the same happy end was hoped for — the final proof to all the world that Goldfine, like Pickwick, was guilty of nothing but genial, natural warmth.

For two days, the Goldfine eyes beamed benevolently upon our country from the TV screen and he uttered carefully couched phrases, written by his press agent, which sought to convey innocent bewilderment and righteous outrage. But the Charles Dickens characterization went sailing up the well-known creek when Goldfine got into an old-fashioned row with members of the House investigating committee over the question of whether or not he had paid the proper income taxes in recent years. This, of course, restored Goldfine and his paid-for political privilege to the proper perspective in our Washington picture; his press agent was sent hustling back to Madison Avenue; and Goldfine, himself, went on to an overwhelming indictment by the House of Representatives for contempt, even though he sent personal letters to all members and their secretaries, too.

Press agentry fared even worse in Pennsylvania in a public quarrel between railroads and truck lines between 1953 and 1958 in which most everybody suffered. The Federal judge, in ruling for the truck lines, held both the railroads and their Madison Avenue press agent guilty and ordered both to share in paying the $852,074 damages and legal fees. In his decree, which did not deal gently with press agentry, the judge issued restraining orders for:

1. "Seeking to create resentment or hostility to plaintiffs in the minds" of the public, customers, legislators, law enforcement officers or other public officials.

2. Publishing or disseminating "false, defamatory or derogatory materials with regard to plaintiffs or their business." This included the preparation or subsidizing of information relating to the truckers "without disclosing to the reader or viewer that it has been instigated, prepared, composed, published, disseminated, produced, paid for or subsidized" on behalf of the rails.

3. "Seeking out or creating organizations apparently independent of defendants to carry out any activity prohibited by this final injunction without publicly disclosing the relationship between defendants and such organizations."

In all of these cases, the press agent professed to tell the truth. The Madison Avenue public relations expert for Bernard Goldfine in the Congressional investigation of his sordid attempts at political payoff, even boasted of this when he said: "You have nothing to fear if you tell the whole truth to the press, because the press is ultimately fair: as professionals, we tried to tell the truth directly to the press, the public and the committee, in that order." Yet the cold fact remains that Goldfine, in his political dealings, was anything but a kindly Mr. Pickwick. Otherwise, Congress would not have indicted him.

The California press agents also professed to tell the truth in behalf of their winning political candidates. Yet if a candidate is not a smiling man in public, a phony smile painted on his face by a press agent does not change him. This, of course, is a small matter but it illustrates perfectly how the press agent regards the politician as a commodity and how he'll dress him up in glowing, if phony colors, as he would a can of ordinary beans.

By 1960 the role of press agents in political campaigns had increased enormously in power, if not in prestige. Candidates of both major political parties made extensive use of press agents — openly as well as behind the scenes. Caught in a fantastic deluge of propaganda, the voter was bombarded every waking hour with conflicting press agentry, cleverly planned to delude and confuse him. Human emotions were assailed with every trick of demagoguery known to the marketers of mass media.

Totally saturated with the volume of propaganda, the sentiment of the average voter was best expressed by the fictitious "Senator Soaper" who said on election eve, "All the average American expects of the president-elect is that he balance the budget, keep the peace, and *stay off TV for two months!*"

Of all forms of mass media, television had by far the greatest impact on the public mind. Conditioned as Americans are to this blatant intruder of livingrooms, they somehow were unprepared for the distortion of facts cunningly contrived as "hidden persuaders" (to borrow Vance Packard's term). It still is a matter of conjecture whether the public was seriously deceived by a studio makeup-man's deft application of the powder puff to present one presidential candidate as young and self-assured, the other as gaunt and worried. The simple placing of studio lights could easily flatter or disfigure a candidate, and millions of viewers may accept this as a true picture of the man. Should so much power be entrusted to studio personnel?

It is too soon to analyze with any certainty the influence of the "mechanical brain machines" used election eve on nationally televised news programs to forecast voting trends. Here are the facts: Two hours before voting booths closed in western states, news analysts were announcing presumably infallible trends in national voting that proved with finality that certain states were safely in the columns of one political party or the other, even though in many instances *less than 20 per cent of the precincts had reported.* Only one analyst had the foresight to caution viewers that such scattered returns were inconclusive — the others were confidently predicting a landslide in popular vote and a phenomenal majority in electoral votes for one candidate.

In following days the cold light of truth disclosed a popular vote so nearly even that the winning candidate had a margin of one tenth of one per cent, and a slim majority of electoral votes.

Who can measure or judge without prejudice the psychological influence such distortion of truth would have on the minds of citizens who had not as yet cast their votes? Surely television networks and their news analysts should accept moral responsibility for keeping news programs of election returns on the high level of political impartiality until the last voting booth has closed.

Publishers and editorial writers must share some of the blame for another form of press agentry: the brainwashing practiced by syndicated columnists. Many newspapermen have drifted into shilly-shally fence-riding on political issues, preferring to buy the opinions of syndicated writers, thus avoiding responsibility for the thinking expressed.

The press agent is here to stay. All of modern life has become most complex and both the big businessman and the politician has learned that it is much easier to place a press agent between him and the newspaper reporter with his notebook. There are, for instance, more press agents in Tampa than there are professional newsmen. And you will find this true throughout our country, particularly so in such big news centers as Washington, New York and Los Angeles. *Editor & Publisher* proudly hailed in March, 1957, the fact that there were more than 100,000 press agents in operation.

Their number has increased steadily and today they control news in every phase of American life.

Some months ago a Tampa *Tribune* reporter sat in the office of the chairman of the Pensacola Port Authority and sought to interview him for a series of stories comparing Florida's ports. The authority's press agent was present simply because the chairman declined to be interviewed unless he was there. My reporter asked for the Pensacola tonnage figures. The press agent frowned. The chairman promptly declined to give them to the reporter. The press agent then talked long and loudly about the beauties of an increase in the number of ships calling at the port of Pensacola. My reporter replied that it was the tonnage of cargo flowing through a port, not empty ships, that indicated the true picture of a port's business.

This, of course, resulted in a stalemate, and my reporter left the office minus the tonnage figures, although he saw them on the chairman's desk. But a day later he obtained the official Pensacola figures from the port authority of another Florida city and his eventual story showed that tonnage handled at the port of Pensacola between 1950 and 1956 had dropped in national ranking from 74th to 96th.

These are no isolated incidents of press agentry sin-
ning and I cite them merely to show that they are among
the day-to-day problems confronted by the journalist in
his quest for the truth. The press agent is hired to do
a job in exchange for dollars, and be it in politics or private business, he displays his employer in the best possible light. For his own protection, he sticks to the record
whenever possible, but there are times when the record
does not cast a glowing aura and, as a veteran newsman,
I can only warn the young journalist to be ever-question-
ing.

Knowing where the average press agent stands, I have
no great personal objection. But I would like to point out
the very great difference between the press agent and
the professional newsman in the matter of restraint.

The press agent is governed largely by his success in
selling his goods, whatever it may be. If he sells his prod-
uct, good or bad, he goes on to greater fields, with very
little restraint other than than his conscience. In the case
of the Maryland Senatorial election of 1950, the press
agent was successful and, in this day of million-dollar
political campaigns, his $5,000 fine was not a great sum
to pay for a seat in America's most exclusive club.

On the other hand, the free American press acquires
all its rights and privileges from the people and it retains
custody of those rights and privileges only so long as it
exercises proper professional ethics, vigilant judgment
and public spirit. In short, the press is the servant of the
people and it must bear all responsibilities thereof and
command respect of the people, who can control it overnight by the simple refusal to pay the subscription price.

Through all of the turbulence of modern life, the
newspaper, by necessity, must remain close to the people
who bestowed the rights and privileges of freedom upon
it. The people, by the simple expedient of refusing to
pay the subscription, hold a constant check upon the
newspaper editor. And the history of our profession is

strewn with the relics of those newspapers which failed in their responsibility to the people and crumbled under the force of that simple check. The people destroyed the sensational penny press of a half century ago. The people ruled out the love-nest journalism of the twenties. And the people today will put a relentless finger upon the irresponsibility of journalism.

But there is no such day-to-day restraint upon the press agent in politics, and the increasing power of his influence, used deceptiously on the American citizen, gravely threatens our right to have the truth in our news.

21.

Analysis

of a Politician

POLITICIANS HAVE RAKED ME OVER THE COALS of ire, both publicly and privately, throughout my 35 years of newspapering, so it is only fair that I finally sum up my thoughts on the typical politician.

From the first day when he chases an ambulance or a fire truck as a young police reporter until his final day when he pounds out on his typewriter the last word for public print, the newspaperman is confronted with the political mind.

Sometimes it is complex; sometimes it is simple. Sometimes it rises to great (oratorical, only) heights; sometimes it sinks to low levels. But always, it is fixed on the next election, for the average politician will make almost any compromise that will assure his reelection.

I have been associated, in one way or another over the years, with thousands of politicians in American Government, and I have yet to find among them a notable statesman. Yet each one, in all his mediocrity, fancies himself as God's answer to the people's prayers.

American people, themselves apathetic toward their government, perhaps are to blame, simply because they permit the politician to pick his job and do not pick the politician for the job, and also because they condone, if they do not expect, political privilege on the part of the politician.

It seems a great tragedy in this day when man's advance into science has catapulted the world's greatest problems, that a citizen can look over the United States Senate, the world's greatest legislative body, and see not a Webster, a Clay or a Calhoun.

Instead, he sees the sorry spectacle of legislators who might have become statesmen had they not been caught in the mesh of obligations to campaign contributors — and now serve more as errand boys to their masters. If you doubt this, just listen in on any congressional political race and you'll hear little other from the incumbent than the boasts of what he has done for his constituents, and equal boasts from his opponent as to what he would do, if elected.

In Florida, we spend upwards of a millon dollars on any Governor or U. S. Senate political race and a large proportion of it goes for political privilege. If a newspaper exposes that the State Road Department built a special road to the country home of a citizen who contributed $1,000 to the Governor's campaign, it creates little stir among the people simply because we are permitting political privilege to become the key to the modern American way of life. Similarly, in Washington nothing is too good for the citizen who contributes heavily to a Senator's campaign.

In the summer of 1958, various county departments presented to the Hillsborough County (Fla.) Commission, unusual budget increases which would call for proportionate increases in taxes. The Commission did little about paring down these requests in the interests of the taxpayer, so I inquired of one of them the reason why. He said:

"You just don't understand. Two of the commissioners are up for reelection. If they cut the budget requests, then those departments will see that they will have opposition, and that will cost them money and perhaps their reelection."

This very small incident of local government perhaps will give you a sneaking idea of why American taxes have mounted so today and why bureaucracy has mushroomed on all levels of American Government.

The Tampa Tribune revealed back in the forties that a citrus grower, a gambler and an industrialist each had contributed $165,000 to the successful campaign of a Florida Governor. The exact political privilege never was pin-pointed, and particularly in the case of the industrialist. But the Governor pushed Florida's no-fence law through the legislature. Most citizens favored the no-fence law, since it was a good piece of legislation for a booming state in that it forced Florida's cattle barons to take their grazing cows off the highways and fence them in their own pastures. But even in the face of being tagged as cynical, I cannot refrain from pointing out that this law required millions of miles of new fences; it takes steel to make fences; and the industrialist was in the steel business.

When I graduated from the University of Florida, I had a friend whom I was sure would eventually become Florida's Governor, simply because he had all the attributes of a Governor. I even pledged him my personal support in my callow, naive days. He got into politics and was successful, but to win his first election, he made a few minor concessions to the underworld in exchange for votes. As the years rolled by, he made bigger concessions for reelection, and soon he was the underworld's errand boy. And his career, of course, eventually went up into political smoke, yet I am positive that he never personally accepted a dime of the tainted money.

Most politicians start out in life deeply inspired by

the obligations of representing the people and of developing good government. But something always happens, perhaps because of public apathy, and they make these concessions in principle, usually for reelection. But there are elements other than political self-preservation, and among them are security and power.

Back in the sordid era of Tampa's political alliance with the underworld, a minor judge made the following callous statement to one of my reporters:

> "I don't take graft," he said. "Power is all I want. With power, I can get legitimate advantages that bring me far more money, anyway. So why take graft?"

After 35 years of newspaper crusading, I am not certain that I am competent to judge the modern American politician. And I will be the first to admit that perhaps I am prejudiced and cynical when I observe that the politician is the most honest man in all the world — on the election platform. Perhaps I am equally prejudiced and cynical when I observe further that, based purely on my own experience, the average politician is solely interested in: (1) the development of his personal fortunes and those of his political friends, and (2) his preservation as a politician.

I presume there are some politicians who live up to their election platform promises, hew to all the principles of honest democratic government, and give their all solely for the benefit of their fellow citizens who elected them — but I've seen few of these. On the other hand I have spent a newspaper career printing the derelictions in political principle practiced by the high and the low from the White House down to the school board.

In view of my prejudice and cynicism, I asked the six veteran members of my news staff, whose aggregate career of dealing firsthand with the politician totals more than 150 years, to give me their experience with political honesty. My veteran research reporter, who has dealt with the politician over 40 years, said:

> "Don't ask me that question. I cannot forget that early in my career, a group of five so-called respectable City Hall politicians offered to take me into their syndicate, which grabbed up land which the city foreclosed from citizens who got into financial difficulties. Now they're all rich and sanctimonious, while I am poor and am getting ready to retire on my little pension. But I do sleep at night."

My day-side City Editor, with 27 years newspapering experience including the coverage of Georgia and Michigan legislatures, said:

> "Politicians are a self-seeking lot. They'll do anything that (1) gets votes or (2) is profitable to himself or a friend, even when it is at the expense of the public. I have seen highways rerouted to serve a politician's pique or his friends. I have seen faithful state employees ruthlessly fired to make way for the politician's friends. I have seen a state university become a political pawn to serve the political interests of a governor. I have seen the politician vote for laws to punish his enemies, to reap hidden profits for himself, to make his friends rich."

My night City Editor, who has spent more than 25 years newspapering in Mississippi and Florida, said:

> "The politicians seem to think they own the government and, if it were not for watchdog newspapers, they soon would — literally. I keep feeling them insulting my intelligence. And it burns me up to see them actually doing exactly that to the taxpayers."

A veteran reporter of over 25 years in Florida news-papering said:

> "Such a thing as moral honesty is virtually an unknown standard among the politicians I have known. Legal hair-splitting seems their only guide for conduct. That hair-splitting can be described by the paraphrased saying: 'A politician's conscience is that small, still voice that tells him when somebody's looking.' "

My City Hall reporter, who the previous day had been warmly shellacked by the Mayor for reporting the truth on a secret deal with the Board of Representatives, said:

> "The majority of politicians are honest and sincere — when they announce for office. Then a chain reaction of compromises sets in, which the record clearly shows; compromises designed to cater to his own particular weaknesses, to his friend's profit, and to the back-scratching of his fellow politician."

Another veteran, with more than 25 years experience in Canada, St. Louis and Florida, said:

> "The evil gets worse as it goes upward. A tip on a future highway construction can turn a real estate profit. A 'leak' on an agency ruling can produce a killing in the stock market. A vote in the legislature can make or break a grateful corporation. From this, it is only a step for the politician to decide that, if he can't do much for his country, certainly he can nobly assist the security of his children."

I might have proposed a "Be Kind to the Politician Week" among newspapermen, had it not been for the seriousness of thinking expressed by these men, and the great tragedy of the people paying for the weaknesses of human nature. But this is far from a laughing matter — it is an ominous threat to the American way of life.

When the *Tribune,* reporting solely from the records of the State Comptroller's Office, informed Florida taxpayers of the waste and corruption in its state government in 1948, 1949 and 1950, a member of the Florida Supreme Court took to the public speaking circuit and bitterly charged that newspapers were destroying the faith of the Florida people in their government.

But what about the stories of moral dishonesty in government which the *Tribune* did not report, simply because they were not written in the privileged records? It is difficult for a newspaper to find moral dishonesty in the records. For one thing, the politician has custody of the records. For another, most moral dishonesty in politics is the compromising of principle — not the dipping into the public till.

Actually, the public record often hides a multitude of sins and the mere printing of it simply is not sufficient for safeguarding public interests. As an example, the public record of one Florida police court showed that a certain Negro truck driver had been sentenced to 120 days in jail on the charge of petty robbery involving the theft of two tires. That public record should have satisfied everybody, particularly the police who could righteously boast of one more solved crime, and feel secure that no one would worry about one Negro truck driver.

Yet a *Tribune* investigation revealed that this Negro was held four days in jail without charge, contrary to the Constitution. He was not permitted legal counsel, contrary to the Constitution. One story on our Page 1 forced a red-faced city judge, much to the chagrin of the police, to order a new trial. In this new trial, it was brought to light that the accused Negro was the victim of vengeance from his accuser, another Negro, and in no way guilty of the crime.

But why get excited over one Negro truck driver? The answer is written in the pages of history. Permit any police to get away with the railroading of even a Negro truck driver into jail and the next victim would be any man of equal economic standard, then political enemies, finally leading to tyranny over all.

It was comparatively easy for the *Tribune* to go behind this deceptive public record, but what about the case wherein a minor public official sent a check for $10,000 to a United States Senator (now dead), in "gratitude, not graft" for getting the donor's son an appointment to Annapolis? And what about the case of the public servant, scrupulous in the fine legal technicalities of his office, who became extremely wealthy through purchase of tax-distressed property he learned about through political friendship in an adjoining county office?

Those were infractions of political morality hidden behind the public record and it would be interesting indeed, if the Supreme Court Justice, who severely criticized newspapers for printing the public record, would come out from retirement to discuss the moral and legal principles of these particular cases.

What about the case of the highly respected public servant who, through his legal firm, became extremely wealthy in the refunding of Florida's boom-time governmental debts? What about the highly respected public servant, who appeared far above the tumult of everyday politics, whose law firm represented big corporations, which could profit from his vote and influence?

What about the public servant who reaped a nice personal profit by trimming the meals of prisoners? What about the public servant who used political privilege to build up huge insurance businesses? What about the public servant who saw no harm in accepting campaign contributions from racketeers? What about the public servant who righteously and indignantly protested that his personal note, found in a slain gangster's safe, was nothing more than a respectable business loan?

What about the public servant, extremely honest personally, who publicly announced he saw no wrong in privately advising his business friends of the location of a new state highway? What about the public servant who collected campaign contributions from Florida concerns in a certain business line and then never used for his election a cent that he collected? What about the public servant, personally honest by his own declaration, who thought it was all right to sell to a big corporation a piece of property for a huge profit and then vote for that corporation's interests?

These are but a few of countless cases which you won't find written in the public records but which you encounter constantly in a career of newspapering. I believe that Senator J. William Fulbright (Dem., Ark.) summed up the current American political philosophy most aptly in a brilliant speech to the U.S. Senate when he said:

> "One of the most disturbing aspects of this prob
> lem of moral conduct is the revelation that among so
> many influential people, morality has become identi-
> cal with legality. We are certainly in a tragic plight
> if the accepted standard by which we measure the
> integrity of a man in public life is that he keep
> within the letter of the law."

Senator Fulbright was chairman of the Senate Committee which unearthed scandal in the RFC and at the time the Truman Administration was in the middle of its mink coat and freezer scandals. The succeeding Eisenhower Administration coasted right into similar scandals, and no doubt some members of the Kennedy administration will be unable to resist temptation.

In July, 1958, the U.S. Senate adopted a code of ethics for its members, which prohibits such gifts. Not only was this an ironic gesture on the part of the world's greatest legislative body, but it is interesting to note that this code had lain on a dust-covered shelf for 11 months after the House adopted it, then was hastily pulled out and adopted on the day after a House investigative committee revealed that Bernard Goldfine had paid hotel bills for three Senators.

Seven years after Senator Fulbright's perspicacious lament, with no evidence that the nation had taken his words seriously, FBI Chief J. Edgar Hoover warned the American Bar Association that ". . . the moral fibre of the nation is growing weaker, not stronger, at this most crucial period of world history."

Another *Tribune* reporter, a veteran observer of 20 years petting and pampering of politicians, said:

> "Once a man is elected to high office, he appears to withdraw into another world, where he places himself alongside God. He regards it as worse than rank heresy for such a lowly creature as a newspaperman to question his conduct in any way."

This actually is putting it gently. The higher the office, the bigger the angel's wings the politician visualizes as his and the louder his squawk when a newspaperman ruffles those wings. Political pomposity, when punctured by a Page 1 newspaper story, spills all over the premises in sanctified adjectives and adverbs.

Senator Spessard L. Holland, former Governor of Florida, has not to this day forgiven the *Tribune* reporter who wrote from facts the Holland Administration's handling of off-shore oil leases. Governor Millard Caldwell came to Tampa on our annual Governor's Day and mightily blasted the *Tribune* for its stories of the sweatbox torture in Florida prison camps.

Governor Fuller Warren, one of the greatest exponents of the alliterative adjective in all the world, belabored the *Tribune* throughout his four-year administration and during six years thereafter for our stories of the political peccadilloes of his administration. Governor Charlie Johns campaigned against me personally in Tampa. And Governor LeRoy Collins, who delicately affixed the biggest and most virtuous wings of all to his shoulder blades, came very close to apoplexy over the *Tribune* reporter who dared to report the monkeyshines at the women's prison at Ocala, and personally read his title clean. And the *Tribune* printed every word of these political criticisms.

So I speak with authority on political pomposity of our day. But I would not have you think that Florida has a monopoly on this touchy human quality. In July 1958, Drew Pearson, the columnist, reported that Senator Robert S. Kerr (Dem., Okla.) opposed a freedom of information bill in a secret meeting of the Democratic Policy Committee and he quoted this public servant as saying:

> "The newspapers want it changed, but I can get along without the newspapers. Why should we act just to please the newspapers?"

I wrote Senator Kerr and asked him for an explanation of this statement. He wrote me a steaming two-page letter in which he called Pearson "a bald-faced liar" and wound up by stating that I was a "bald-faced liar," too, because I repeated Pearson's words in my letter. It was not my letter of inquiry, itself, nor was it Pearson's words that stirred the good Senator's wrath. The thing that turned him livid with rage was the fact that I sent carbons of my letter to the 12 key editors in Oklahoma.

I had the same experience with Senator Paul H. Douglas (Dem., Ill.). I wrote him asking his views on secret congressional committee meetings and sent carbons of my letters to 10 Illinois editors. This so infuriated the good Senator, who once was a professor, that he sent carbons of his acrimonious reply to all Florida editors. I thanked him for this and told him that if I had the stenographic help I would have sent carbons of our exchange to every editor in our land.

In July, 1956, Senator Pat McNamara (Dem., Mich.) issued a public blast at the secrecy which he said was wrapped around President Eisenhower's illness. I wrote the good Senator, congratulated him for his stand against the Presidential secrecy, but, I asked, what about the secrecy which the U.S. Senate has wrapped around its committee meetings, the expenses of its offices and the junketing at public expense by its members?

This, of course, stirred immediate senatorial wrath and it developed into a public controversy. Senator Mc-Namara told me in no uncertain words that he did not like the tone of my letter. Then he informed me that the press did not have sufficient representatives in Washington to cover secret meetings should they be opened; that the expenses of a Senator's office involved a confidential relationship between employer and employee and that he was certain this did not interest the people of Michigan; and finally, that he did not feel it his duty to report to the people on the expenditures of junketing Senators.

I am telling you all this, not as a matter of disillusionment, but as a lesson in human nature and what a newspaperman encounters from day to day. Modern politicians are mere humans, regardless of their craving for angel's wings, and they differ little from the horde of humans who are engaged in the world's other endeavors today or the horde of humans who have marched down the pages of history.

Newspapermen, too, are human, and their reaction to the reactions of other humans also is human. But there is one point that I would like to make here: Although they are in a position to accept bribes and gain wealth in one way or another, most newspapermen die poor. On the other hand, many politicians die rich, even though their sole publicly acknowledged earnings were the scanty pay of the office-holder.

It is not my intention to destroy your faith in free democracy of the American Government. I can tell you honestly and sincerely that the American way of life is the greatest government yet devised by man. Of course, we have erring politicians. But a free crusading newspaper can expose them and the people can kick them out of office and we can try again. Meanwhile, the individual

American can enjoy the greatest fruits of individual freedom.

I am reminded of my exchange of letters with Senator Irving M. Ives (Rep., N.Y.) over the matter of secret Senate committee meetings. The good Senator wrote me that such secret meetings were far more efficient than public meetings, wherein political oratory had full sway. In reply, I asked this question:

> "Which is better for the people, the efficient harmony of the secret communistic government in Russia or the turbulence of free open government in democratic America?"

I think the answer to this question would also answer all questions involving political manipulations in free American Government. Don't you ever forget that communistic Russia has just as many erring politicians as free America, but it has neither free newspapers to expose them nor a free public opinion to kick them out of office. We in free America cannot afford to sacrifice the basic freedom of our country because another way is speedier, easier or more efficient. The world's history shows that once freedom is sacrificed, it is regained only through bloodshed.

22.

The Challenge
of a Newspaper Career

THE AMERICAN NEWSPAPER became an integral part of
the American way of life through its crusading for and
against the English Government in our Revolutionary
War of Independence and it has remained so down
through the intervening 185 years.

The newspaper editor duly records the American's
birth; he hovers backstage as the American graduates
from school; he ushers the American down to the altar of
matrimony; he listens in as the American pleads his
cause in divorce court; and he serves as pallbearer at the
American's funeral. And in between, he scribbles madly
recording the American's triumphs and tragedies in this
material life of ours.

In short, the newspaper is a faithful member of the
American family. Other members of the family, including
in-laws, may come and go, but the newspaper is an honored guest in the American home every single day of the
year. It is with the American at breakfast, lunch and
dinner, and sometimes even accompanies him to bed.

You may disagree violently with its editorial policy on some political candidate, but you read avidly the news accounts of your neighbor, be he living next door or in Afghanistan. And you believe these news accounts simply because down through the history of the free American press, those newspapers who courageously printed the truth have established themselves in a position of honor, while those who have been false to this principle have perished.

You may be feeling optimistic after a great sale in your store, but if your newspaper the next morning informs you that General Motors and other business leaders are slipping in the stock market, you immediately wonder about business retrenchment. You may not like the way your daughter's bridal gown was snipped off on the women's page, but that doesn't stop you from trying the recipe in the adjoining food column.

You may not like the color of your editor's ties, but you always ask, get and depend on his help in getting new roads, bridges and public buildings in your community. And the editor's help for these community projects is always forthcoming simply because if you prosper, then he and his newspaper will proper. And likewise, though you may be a trifle hard-up, you will, as a good citizen, respond to your newspaper's plea in behalf of community drives, church drives and even to help a single family which has run astray of fortune.

You may be a man of peace, but your newspaper, in bringing you accounts of the abridgment of your fellow man's rights and dignity, can turn you into a man of war and you will send your sons into bloody battle. You may swear by that man in the White House, but your newspaper's stories of corruption in Federal Government can cause you to send him into private life to write his memoirs.

You may prefer four-in-hand ties, but if your wife notes from newspaper advertisements that the well-dressed man is wearing bow ties, then you'll turn up in bow ties, even if she has to tie them. And you'll even forget to take it off until after you have sneaked a look at the sports pages to check the home-run record of your favorite baseball star.

There is no substitute for this very close daily relationship between the American citizen and his newspaper. It is valuable to him for the little notices of local meetings as well as for the great trends of man's march into the future. The American citizen may listen in and watch those great entertainment media of radio and television with their capsule condensation of the news, but he still wants the privilege of digesting in leisure the details and facts that make the news important, and to make his own analyses. These he can do only by studying the printed pages of his newspaper.

But even more important, he depends upon his newspaper as the sentinel and guardian of his freedom. I am afraid that too many of us take our freedom for granted. Too many of us have forgotten that American freedom was bequeathed to us from a thousand bloody battlefields of yesteryear. Too many of us, weighed down by our daily circumstances and by the pressures of life, are inclined to overlook the stark fact that the fight for freedom is still going on; that American freedom could become only a brief flash of light in the long-dark history of man's enslavement; and that we could lose our most precious inheritance far quicker and easier than we won it.

If the free press is derelict in these great responsibilities and obligations, God help the free people. The pages of history tell us over and over that wherever and whenever the people are barred from knowledge of their government and deprived of the opportunity of exerting upon the politician the restraint of public opinion, man's liberty always descends into the tragic limbo of forgotten privileges.

Basil L. Walters, the executive editor of the *Chicago Daily News*, has described the American press of today as the "watchdog of government." He said:

"No longer does the reporter merely report what some official tells him. He examines the record himself and keeps the eye eternally on the official."

That is the way it must be if American freedom is to survive in the troublesome days ahead. Government has grown so complex in our day that reliance on the politician's carefully edited report of his own regulation of the people's business is not sufficient protection of the people's freedom.

By one stroke of the pen, government today can authorize spending billions of the people's tax monies, sums too vast for the average citizen to comprehend. By another stroke of the pen, government spills the blood of our young men on foreign battlefields in a maze of conflicting political propaganda that would perplex even an Einstein. As the government takes on additional responsibilities, it intervenes in all phases of the citizen's private life, and it has done this through a veritable army of political press agents who pour out millions of words of propaganda designed to make the citizen receptive to this intervention; to prolong the future political life of the current office holder; and to promote political privileges.

And therein rests the great conflict between the political mind and the journalistic mind. Most politicians seek to lull the people with the pleasantries of government. The journalist seeks the cold, hard facts of government, and lets the chips fall where they may. Often these don't jibe; whereupon, the politician reaches for the nearest microphone and assures the people that the journalist is the worst sort of a skunk.

Need I remind that President Truman, in a public statement from the White House, once called Drew Pearson, the columnist, an S.O.B.?

All of which explains why the newspaper editor rises up in indignation whenever the politician attempts to conduct the people's business behind the locked doors of secret government; why the journalist casts a cynical eye upon political privilege so prevalent today; and why he questions the motive behind some congressional "reviewing" of the Constitution.

Exactly 37 words in the American Constitution spell out the difference between freedom and tyranny. Modern American politicans have attempted some tinkering with our Constitution and, if permitted to get away with this, sooner or later will get around to tinkering with these 37 words.

Twenty-six of these words protect you from secret and arbitrary arrest and guarantee you a public hearing before the bar of public opinion of your fellow citizen. They are found in Paragraph 2 of Section 9 of Article 1 of the Constitution:

> The privilege of the Writ of Habeas Corpus shall not be suspended, unless when in cases of rebellion or invasion the public safety may require it.

Eleven more words give the free American press the right, and impose upon it the responsibility, to alert the free people any time the politican violates the right of habeas corpus. These are found in the First Amendment of the Constitution which states in part:

> Congress shall make no law . . . abridging the freedom . . . of the press.

Together, these 37 words distinguish free American citizens from citizens of Soviet Russia and all the slave states in man's history. And they actually serve as a guarantee for all the other freedoms so carefully spelled out in our Constitution.

What good are these other freedoms if the politician can, at his will, throw the citizen into jail without benefit of a public hearing? And what good is this great freedom from secret arrest if the press is deprived of the right and opportunity to alert the public in the event of its abridgment?

I ask these questions to show how vital is this purely American principle of freedom of the press. The Russian politician throws his political opponent into jail and keeps him hidden there because the Soviet press, shackled by tyranny, has become the tool of dictators and cannot alert the Russian public to the horrors of the Siberian concentration camp. With this condition existing less than 24 hours flying time from America, need I remind you that this very great danger hangs constantly over the free world today and, sad as it may be, it will face our young men and women for many years to come, and possibly throughout their lifetimes?

It can easily be seen that American newspapering goes considerably deeper than ripping the world's news off the AP and UPI printers, putting headlines on it and printing it in the newspaper. There is a good deal more to it than putting out a smartly edited editorial page, the most complete financial pages, sports pages that contain the results of the smallest tiddly-wink contest, and women's pages that carry pictures of these horrible styles actually adopted by few women.

It goes deeper even than a fair news policy, and I can assure you that *The Tampa Tribune* has such a policy. We print our news policy in a pamphlet and distribute it to our representatives and at times to our politicians. It is based on two simple rules. (1) accuracy, and (2) impartiality.

We prefer to be scooped on a story rather than print a hasty, inaccurate version. One glaring inaccuracy can tear down in a day the public confidence built by painstaking labor of years.

No matter how vigorously the *Tribune* may champion one side of an issue on its editorial page, both sides get a full hearing in our news columns. No matter whom the *Tribune* may support for Governor on its editorial page, it makes a genuine effort to give all candidates an equal and impartial report in its news columns. We make a practice of staffing all candidates in major Florida political races and the accounts of their daily speeches are carried side by side on Page 1.

Any person accused or attacked in proceedings printed by the *Tribune* has the privilege always of offering his defense in our columns. And we have no "sacred cows" in our news room. We do not make the news; we only print it.

Yet, I tell you with great personal conviction that such a news policy, as accurate and impartial as it may be, and as important as it is, still does not offer the complete answer to the problem of newspapering today. Many newspapers have had such a policy in the past, along with sharp editing and the world's finest features, and yet have expired. Their columns were smartly polished and they printed all the routine news, much of it political handouts from governmental boards, the police court and the political platform. And when you completed reading them, you had the exact feeling that you had when you looked into the eyes of a slicked up man and suddenly discovered that he had no soul.

It is exceedingly difficult to place a finger definitely upon the qualities that make up the soul of a pulsating, free newspaper that is an integral part of a free American community. There are many such qualities; they are of varying importance; and yet the aggregate will reach out from the printed page and strike home as nothing else will in our profession.

And I tell you with great sadness that too many American newspapers today are paying only lip service to this principle of freedom which our founding forefathers bestowed upon them, and they are failing to accept the great obligations and responsibilities that accompany this heritage.

I tell you also with great sincerity that democracy and the American way of life can thrive and prosper only so long as the people are alert to dangers from within as well as from without our gates. And I tell you without equivocation that the American people have an inherent right to expect their newspapers to report conditions which endanger good government or threaten welfare of the public, and that newspapers which fail to do this are false to a sacred trust. They have no soul.

A newspaper cannot live up to this obligation by contenting itself with official handouts and the records on the police docket. It cannot close its eyes to corruptions and to political privilege, hidden though it may be. It cannot stop with just printing the facts of corruption and political privilege — it must go all the way and root out the cause of the evil for the benefit of the people because, under the precepts of free government, the free press is the sole guardian of the people's freedom. This imposes not only great personal responsibility upon the publisher and the editor, but also great sacrifice. You cannot expect to be pals with a mayor whose shortcomings you have just exposed. You cannot expect a Governor or a Senator to come into your office and fawn upon you after you have raked him fore and aft for his political misdeeds. You cannot be a big shot in political circles; sometimes you must undergo scathing political attacks; and often you live a lonely life.

A newspaper must lend a constant and willing ear to pleas of the unfortunate, as well as those in difficulty of one kind or another, and it must heed such pleas just as it must heed the pleas of churchmen who protest the breakdown of law and order in a community. It must heed such pleas because, after all is said and done, a newspaper is just as much a public servant as is the elected official, and helping the unfortunate is an integral part of the soul of a newspaper.

A newspaper must always be ahead of its readers.

It must lead with initiative and enterprise all projects and drives that will benefit the community or mankind as a whole. The printing of handouts from these community services is not sufficient, simply because the newspaper should possess the know-how and practice the art of tugging at the people's hearts.

It must lead in the development of the community as much as in the fight against governmental corruption. It must look into the crystal ball and, whether the news is good or bad, it must lead the way into the future.

In recent months, the *Tribune* looked into the crystal ball and we printed on our Page 1 the bad news that the people of Florida must fork up a good deal more taxes in the next few years. We looked over our birth rate and the gain in population and told our readers that, whereas Florida today has more than 600,000 school pupils, the state will have one million in a few more years. That will be a gain of over 400,000 pupils and it will mean hundreds of new school buildings and millions more in annual taxes. The public may not like what it reads, but it needs to be informed.

Last but not least, a newspaper with a soul must be an integral part of the community. It must share all the fortunes, the sadnesses and joys, and all the adventures, big and little, of its readers. It must share them as a part of understanding the great human family.

Some months ago our mayor and our City Board of Representatives were at logger-heads over the matter of financing some $20,000,000 of new municipal projects. At the same time, there was a small wedding in a downtown church in which one of the *Tribune* staffers was THE honored guest. Some time before, as a practical joke, a Tampa woman had sent a Christmas card, bearing the name of another Tampa woman, to a lonely Navy man in Alaska. The Navy man wrote a letter of appreciation to the woman whose name appeared on the card. She wrote back that she knew nothing of the card. So both parties appealed to the *Tribune* staffer, who went to work unraveling the joke, and the romance developed.

Twenty-million dollars of municipal projects, to be

paid for with taxpayer funds, are a huge matter. And one more marriage is a rather small matter in a large city. Yet both belonged to life in Tampa and *The Tampa Tribune* was in the middle of both.

Sevellon Brown, late editor and publisher of the Providence, Rhode Island, *Journal,* put all of this in words much better than mine when he wrote:

> It is a matter of religious faith with me that we newspaper people will find some special provision for us on Judgment Day to excuse a thousand errors if we can only say, "I meant my newspaper, with all its faults, to do good for my community."

I have told a thousand young men, who were considering entering the profession of journalism, that they cannot hope to accumulate great wealth and particularly so if they are honest. I have pointed out that I know hundreds of newspaper editors by first name from coast to coast and that I know not a rich one among them, although most of them earn a decent living.

Then what does the profession of journalism hold for the young man? This, of course, is a superb question in this day of material things, in this era of worshiping the almighty dollar.

There is, of course, the satisfaction that a man reaps from the very act of creating. When you sit down and peck out on your typewriter your words describing some incident of human behavior and see it printed in the newspaper for the benefit of your fellow man's knowledge, your inner being is flooded with that sense of satisfaction of having created something that is your very own. And I believe that this sense of satisfaction goes far deeper than the satisfaction which a mechanic reaps from helping produce one part of an air-conditioning unit.

There is also the very great satisfaction in your soul for having performed a service for your fellow man. Our ministerial colleges are crowded today with young men,

many of whom have elected to give up the almighty
dollar and dedicate their lives to the service of God. There
can be no question about the satisfaction of the soul
that these young men will reap from their service. But
I hold, after 35 years of newspapering, that the true
journalist reaps a similar satisfaction of the soul because, in serving his fellow men, he too is serving God.
He serves mankind from birth to death, in a thousand
ways, big and little, simply because he is concerned with
life itself. He is concerned with man; with what man
does and does not do; with what man says and thinks;
and, more important, he spends his life in the service
of man.

No one is ever bored with man because, in all his
peculiarities, he is the most interesting creature on this
globe of ours. Men in many other lines of human en-
deavor become bored, but I know not a single bored
editor.

This is the final and perhaps most satisfying fruit
of a journalistic career, and is the choice gift we have
to offer the newspapermen of the future. What more
could a young person ask of life!

Where To Find What